GREEN WORLD
ORACLE

...Nuts are female vulva-symbols birthing an entire universe of lore and wisdom, rich, meaty, nutritious....It is a female realm – yet one in which the male is not only welcomed, but embraced as the beloved. Gender boundaries, both intra-personal and interpersonal, should remain unblurred and clear here, each honored for itself, each half of a whole, co-creators of the universe...

GREEN WORLD
ORACLE

Kathleen Jenks
Art by Sandra Stanton

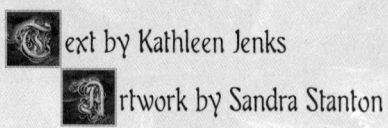

Text by Kathleen Jenks
Artwork by Sandra Stanton

Copyright © 2013 by Kathleen Jenks and Sandra Stanton
Library of Congress Control Number: 2013930420

All rights reserved. No part of this work may be reproduced or used in any form or by any means—graphic, electronic, or mechanical, including photocopying or information storage and retrieval systems—without written permission from the publisher.

The scanning, uploading and distribution of this book or any part thereof via the Internet or via any other means without the permission of the publisher is illegal and punishable by law. Please purchase only authorized editions and do not participate in or encourage the electronic piracy of copyrighted materials.

"Schiffer," "Schiffer Publishing, Ltd. & Design," and the "Design of pen and inkwell" are registered trademarks of Schiffer Publishing, Ltd.

Type set in Alcibiades/Usherwood Book
ISBN: 978-0-7643-4321-6
Printed in China

Schiffer Books are available at special discounts for bulk purchases for sales promotions or premiums. Special editions, including personalized covers, corporate imprints, and excerpts can be created in large quantities for special needs. For more information contact the publisher:

Published by Schiffer Publishing, Ltd.
4880 Lower Valley Road
Atglen, PA 19310
Phone: (610) 593-1777; Fax: (610) 593-2002
E-mail: Info@schifferbooks.com

For the largest selection of fine reference books on this and related subjects, please visit our website at **www.schifferbooks.com**.

We are always looking for people to write books on new and related subjects. If you have an idea for a book, please contact us at **proposals@schifferbooks.com**.

This book may be purchased from the publisher.
Please try your bookstore first.
You may write for a free catalog.

In Europe, Schiffer books are distributed by
Bushwood Books
6 Marksbury Ave.
Kew Gardens
Surrey TW9 4JF England
Phone: 44 (0) 20 8392 8585; Fax: 44 (0) 20 8392 9876
E-mail: info@bushwoodbooks.co.uk
Website: www.bushwoodbooks.co.uk

DEDICATION

For Earth's trees and plants,
and the humans who seek their wisdom.

ACKNOWLEDGMENTS

Deep gratitude is given to the
many authors worldwide whose
research and insights have
enriched this work.

CONTENTS

8
INTRODUCTION

15
HOW TO USE THE ORACLE

1 ACACIA 21	12 EUCALYPTUS 96	23 OLIVE 172
2 AMRITA 27	13 HAWTHORN 102	24 PAPYRUS 178
3 ANCIENT GIANTS 35	14 HOLLY 108	25 PEONY 184
4 APPLE 43	15 LARCH 114	26 PINE 191
5 ASH 51	16 LAUREL 120	27 PIPAL FIG 200
6 BEECH 58	17 LINDEN 127	28 RAIN FORESTS 206
7 BIJA 63	18 LOST FORESTS 134	29 ROWAN 218
8 BIRCH 68	19 LOTUS 141	30 SANDALWOOD 226
9 CORN 79	20 MYRRH 147	31 SEAWEED 232
10 ELDER 85	21 NUT TREES 153	32 SYCAMORE FIG 241
11 ELM 91	22 OAK 164	33 WILLOW 246

252
CONCLUSION

253
BIBLIOGRAPHY

INTRODUCTION

> The image of the tree that speaks, prophesies or warns seems to express a recurrent need of the soul – something that we can all experience.
>
> ~ William Anderson[1]

Trees and plants are ancient symbols of life. They have been with us from the beginning. In mythology, we are created in gardens; trees give us oracles; humans are transformed into flowers; women suffering abuse are rescued by being turned into trees; children are born from trees; gods like Osiris are entombed in them; sacred fire is struck from them. We speak of our "roots," the "fruits" of our labor, trees of wisdom or of good and evil. We use trees and plants to celebrate special holy days, a wedding, a child's birth, and to mourn a loved one's death.

The word "tree" is thought to come from an Indo-European base, *derew-*: in Greek, this becomes *drys* ("tree" or "oak"), and a cognate is *dryad*, a tree or wood spirit. This intimate relationship between *drys* and *dryad*, tree and spirit, shows that from the beginning, humankind sensed the presence of such spirits, or "otherness," around earth's plants and trees. Some spirits were deemed friendly, wise, easily accessible. Others were aloof, majestic, best left alone unless the need be urgent. Some were worshipped, a few feared, most loved.

In some schools of Buddhist thought, trees are already enlightened beings, already in full possession of pure Buddha-nature by virtue of their total alignment with their mode of existence; thus, closeness to trees furthers one's own journey into enlightenment.[2] Trees are called *vanaspati,* "Lords of the Forests," and the reverence shown them reflects the belief that many are actually "Bodhi" trees under which earlier Buddhas reached enlightenment. All trees are illumined, glowing, but certain trees, especially large, old ones, are believed to have a special ability to facilitate deep spiritual growth in humans; among these trees are ironwood, sala, and *ficus religiosa* (see *Pipal*).[3]

When I first started working on this oracle, I kept remembering how J. R. R. Tolkien described an encounter with an ancient tree-being called an Ent:

> ...These deep eyes were now surveying them, slow and solemn, but very penetrating. They were brown, shot with a green light.... One felt as if there were an enormous well behind them, filled up with ages of memory and long, slow, steady thinking; but their surface was sparkling with the present: like sun shimmering on the outer leaves of a vast tree, or on the ripples of a very deep lake.... It felt as if something that grew in the ground – asleep, you might say, or

just feeling itself as something between root-tip and leaf-tip, between deep earth and sky – had suddenly waked up, and was considering you with the same slow care that it had given to its own inside affairs for endless years.[4]

This was Treebeard, one of the "awakened" trees who tended other trees – for all trees have wise Ents of their own kind among them. In Tolkien's world, it is with the help of Ents that the tide is turned towards hope and sanity. When I first conceived of *The Green World Oracle*, I knew that it would be that deeply "awake" stratum of tree-wisdom into which the Oracle would tap.

Each tree in this oracle has its own voice and many long, unfolding "names," or stories. These do not always provide easy answers. There is rarely a simple "yes," or a resounding "no." Their stories need to be lived with, as a Zen koan is lived with. Trees deal with time in centuries, as well as days and minutes. They sense cycles – they often leave it to us to work out the specifics, but with a deepened awareness of where we are heading.

A friend of mine, a psychic healer from Denmark, told me that she had seen her husband, a computer expert, walk up to a tree, hug it, and vanish into thin air. I asked him what the experience was like from his perspective. "She's wrong," he laughed, "I don't vanish at all. It's much simpler than that: trees have longer cycles and a completely different sense of time. They let me merge into their time frame and I become part of it. To someone still in human time, it might look as if I vanish, but I don't."

Such stories remind us of many mysteries connected with the natural world. Nature mystics have always found ways of communicating with the Green World, which seems so alien and yet is so much a part of us, for we breathe the air it transmutes and eat the food it alchemizes out of soil, air, sunlight, minerals, and water. Psychics speak of a rich green color radiating out of those whose hearts are open and loving. The medieval mystic, Hildegard of Bingen, used the word *viriditas*, "greenness," or "greening power," to describe the manifestation of cosmic energies flowing into our lives.[5] The Spanish poet, Federico Garcia Lorca, expresses the passion and wonder inherent in such greenness in a repeated refrain: *Verde que te quiero verde. Verde viento. Verdes ramas* ("Green, I want you green. Green wind. Green Boughs").[6]

Dorothy Maclean, one of the founders of the Findhorn Community, writes of her communication with *devas* (angels or nature spirits) of the natural world. Like Ents, these are not limited to an individual tree or plant. *Devas* oversee an entire species, holding the pattern for that species within their own energy-field. She writes:

> To them, the formative field for manifestation is abounding joy, so it is not surprising that joy is ever present when one becomes aware of [them]. They

express their joy in praise of life, as well as in the creation of it, and this is the truth behind medieval paintings of angels singing praises....[7]

The Willow Deva tells her:

Here is concentrated stillness and from here radiate plans and patterns. From here I reach out a long arm to each willow in the world, containing it in the stillness and bathing it with radiance. It becomes a distinct entity on its own, but is nevertheless part of the invisible consciousness which I am. From my point of stillness great ripples of energy go forth.[8]

Another nature mystic, Jeffrey Goelitz, tunes into the energies and vibrations from a complementary perspective, that of individual trees. He speaks with a 2,000-year-old redwood called the Mother of the Forest. She tells him:

I am an essence spirit that is very old. I hold the standing wave for the entire surrounding forest. Trees are gravity centers for light and water. We pull in with tremendous force energies that influence the entire earth. Great forests of the world are linked by networks of energy that help sustain and balance the earth's ecosphere. Forests have a special rhythm of existence.... There are powerful energies that pour through me as I am a conduit for heavenly light. Its flow varies with climatic and environmental conditions."[9]

Goelitz learns that what makes some trees more "awake" is their age. The nearby Father of the Forest tells him:

...The purest essence comes from the oldest trees who have peaked developmentally in their beingness. Older trees communicate to younger trees a vibrancy which supports and encourages their growth....[10] (See *Ancient Giants of the Pacific Northwest* for more of this passage.)

Goelitz offers a fascinating description of how energy fields differ:

The energy that trees give off...has to do with white light, sent from the other worlds or the etheric worlds, that is not normally seen by the human eye. Redwoods...are excellent transmitters of white light. A pine tree has a pattern of diagonal lines with curves of different light colors, while a palm tree has

INTRODUCTION

vertical lines with sprays of golden light. Each of these different patterns gives off a different energy band.[11]

Not all trees give out energy in the same way. An apple tree gives back energy into its fruit. The energy of the tree spirals back into the apple and a human who eats the apple would get a certain energy band from it. A redwood tree would transmit light more directly to the planet.[12]

There is also what Goelitz calls a wisdom band, which:

> ...puts out a higher, cleaner vibration which enables people to receive more clarity.[13]

In this oracle, these forces converge. Trees hold a "standing wave" for us as well as themselves. They are "green wind" speaking, *viriditas*, spiraling movements, and ancient wisdom-bands. As devas send forth ripples of energy, there is joy in the patterns. There is also seriousness in their desire to help humans evolve to their fullest potential.

Carl Jung, who made excellent diagnostic use of the *I Ching* in working with patients, wrote a Foreword to Richard Wilhelm's translation of the *I Ching*, which remains a pivotal explanation of the "synchronicity principle" operating in oracular systems. Jung writes of the importance of the moment, and of the lasting traces it leaves:

> ...whatever happens in a given moment possesses inevitably the quality peculiar to that moment. This is not an abstract argument but a very practical one. There are certain connoisseurs who can tell you merely from the appearance, taste, and behavior of a wine the site of its vineyard and the year of its origin....And there are even astrologers who can tell you, without any previous knowledge of your nativity, what the position of sun and moon was and what zodiacal sign rose above the horizon in the moment of your birth. In the face of such facts, it must be admitted that moments can leave long-lasting traces.[14]

In working with oracles, to follow Jung's line of thought, a question arises out of a situation unique to the moment in which it is asked. Ten minutes later, something else might surge to the forefront, but in *this* moment, *this* is the question the querent finds most pressing. According to Jung, hidden within that moment lies an answer – but it must be teased out of dense, many-layered windings of time. An oracle serves to untangle those windings, freeing an answer because it is, as Jung writes, "understood to be an indicator of the essential situation prevailing in the moment of its [the question's] origin."[15] The process works through synchronicity, which Jung explains as the following:

> ...synchronicity takes the coincidence of events in space and time as meaning something more than mere chance, namely, a peculiar interdependence of objective events among themselves as well as with the subjective (psychic) states of the observer or observers.[16]

Thus, in consulting an oracle, whatever emerges:

> ...is what it necessarily must be in a given "situation," inasmuch as anything happening in that moment belongs to it as an indispensable part of the picture.[17]

But could there not be more than one answer hidden in the same moment? Jung wonders about this and replies:

> ...I certainly cannot assert that another answer would not have been equally significant. However, the answer received was the first and only one; we know nothing of other possible answers. It pleased and satisfied me. To ask the same question a second time would have been tactless and so I did not do it: "the master speaks but once."[18]

Without the wise counsel and deep "insight" of oracles, Jung writes:

> [We]...no longer find our way through the mazes of fate and the obscurities of our own natures.[19]

I never set out to create a new oracle. I was content with the *I Ching*, Tarot decks, and the Runes, each with roots in ancient sacred traditions. Why would I create something new when I could consult these older, well-tested sources? But several things changed my mind. When I started my doctoral studies in the mid-1980s, I began focusing on cross-cultural mythology and interdisciplinary approaches to the sacred. The *I Ching*, for all my love of its Chinese roots, no longer spoke to me as it once had: it came from one limited tradition and only gave me images and poetic language. The same was true of Runes from the Nordic world. I wanted more.

I wanted stories, myths, folktales – those nourished my soul in a way nothing else could. Women naturally tend towards narrative, as do many men. Yet I often heard my male professors dismissing contributions, specifically, of women by labeling them "anecdotal." The tone implied that such work was not well-reasoned, cogent, professional. Nevertheless, I could remember stories long after I had forgotten intricate philosophical arguments. So I valued them – they came from the realm of "mother tongue," not "father tongue." This is not to denigrate the logic or linear approach used in academic circles, but neither is it to condone its often inflated status as a means of conveying knowledge and the deeper rhythms of thought.

Tarot decks at that time were beginning to offer more in the way of lore from various cultures and time periods, but there were too many Minor Arcana cards for me to handle and much of the Major Arcana felt unrelated to my own life. I wanted an oracle with more than archetypes identified as Lovers, Emperor, High Priestess. I also wanted more than inorganic symbols like Tower or Wheel of Fortune.

I bought an oracle based on trees revered by ancient Celts and again found a limited focus and no stories. But I could really resonate with the *trees* – they were organic, rich in myth, and also possessed of a different consciousness, one forming a counterpoint to humanness. So I reached out to trees and plants that were sacred to spiritual traditions from all over the world. I wanted a text that would be lengthy, multi-layered, and rich. That meant researching the myths but also exploring levels of insight from the trees' own lives – data from botany, history, linguistics, and pharmacology. Working with all these levels was like working with dreams or past lives (areas in which I have guided hundreds of people since the early seventies). I would layer in one detail, or question, after another, allowing for free associations, new ideas, unexpected perspectives. Slowly, an interpretive alchemy occurred with roots as ancient as any other divinatory tradition.

In the Green World, in addition to trees and plants, there are also active deities – whether known as spirits, devas, dryads, goddesses, or gods. It is likely, in fact, that those beings we call "god" and "goddess" were originally perceived by our ancestors to be powerful nature spirits of mountains, streams, animals, trees, storms, fire, earth, and sky. Shifting vagaries of psycho-social dynamics elevated some spirits to "divine" status and demoted others to nymphs, fairies, demons, and other generic spirits, but all probably began as nature spirits, tending to the specific natural forces in their care. Thus, their myths speak with strong voices in this oracle.

Some years ago I asked the oracle how it sees itself. It responded with Nut Trees, which reads in part:

> ...Nuts are female vulva-symbols birthing an entire universe of lore and wisdom, rich, meaty, nutritious....It is a female realm – yet one in which the male is not only welcomed, but embraced as the beloved. Gender boundaries, both intra-personal and interpersonal, should remain unblurred and clear here, each honored for itself, each half of a whole, co-creators of the universe....

This oracle, then, sees itself as having the power to guide, to catalyze joy, to restrain rage, to transform grief. Even if everything else fails, it sees itself fostering that indestructible "almond-bone," or kernel of hope, around which new life may be constellated.

With all this in mind, I offer *The Green World Oracle*. I have used it over the years for many clients as well as for myself. I have found it to be trustworthy and wise.

Endnotes

[1] Anderson:33.
[2] Lafleur:190-195 and in passim.
[3] Lily de Silva:24.
[4] The Two Towers:83.
[5] Anderson:163.
[6] From "Romance Sonambulo" by Federico Garcia Lorca.
[7] Maclean:80.
[8] Maclean:78.
[9] Goelitz:71; 72.
[10] Goelitz:75-76.
[11] Goelitz:84.
[12] Goelitz:91.
[13] Goelitz:84.
[14] Jung, in Wilhelm/Baynes:iii-iv.
[15] Jung, op.cit.:iv.
[16] Jung, ibid.
[17] Jung, ibid.:v.
[18] Jung, ibid.:ix.
[19] Jung, ibid.:viii.

HOW TO USE THE ORACLE

ny divination system designed to give you more than simple *yes/no* answers is going to be working with symbols, archetypes, and metaphors because they are useful keys to regions of the heart and mind where genuine transformations occur.

Myths and stories, however, which are abundant in *The Green World Oracle*, provide access to many more significant "gates" from which insights may be drawn. These "gates" also invite valuable interactions between your conscious and not-yet-conscious realms.

It takes time to absorb these levels, however, time to allow one's intuition to say, "Yes, this feels exactly right!" Thus, layouts involving many cards may not work well here because the amount of data would be too overwhelming. Five-card or pentacle spreads will probably work well if you are already experienced with them. My own preference is to work with only one card at a time – or, for complex issues, no more than three or four.

In using oracular cards, you might prefer to shuffle the deck, cut it from right to left, and select the card lying on top of the stack to your right. Another way is to fan out the cards or scatter them face down before you. The selection is done by closing your eyes and, with your question clearly in your mind, reaching out with one hand and letting it hover, or circle, until you get a "sense" that it is time to stop.

In ancient times, the left little finger was the "auricular" finger, the one used to stop-up the ear so that you could "hear" the secret whisperings of inner inspiration. If you are right-handed, you have the least amount of conscious control over this finger, which makes it a good channel for oracular insights. If you are left-handed, use the opposite hand. Then, leading with the little finger, lower the hand. The first card that your little finger touches is the one with which you work. If you pick a card lying sideways, you might wish to work with both upright and reversed positions or else follow your intuition and rotate the card a quarter of a turn to the right or left. Whatever your decision, be consistent whenever you do a reading – the oracle will adapt.

Reading Upright and Reversed Positions

Do not force a meaning where you feel none. Just keep reading until a phrase or image gives you a sense of "Aha!" You may not like the insight, but if your body feels that spark of recognition, you are on the right track. Even if the card is upright, many people prefer to read everything, including reversed positions, in case something resonates with them. Interpreting reversed positions can be complicated because they do not always simply reverse the upright position. Their "aha" may be more subtle. They might affirm the upright reading but caution you not to fall prey to a tendency to get stuck in reversed conditions. They might imply a delay in the arrival of upright conditions, or ask you to re-focus on a nuance of the upright. With experience, this gets easier.

One-Card Higher Self's Message

This is a way of contacting the wisdom of your Higher Self by using only one card. The deity, tree, or plant on the card you draw might answer a question you did not know you had or else indicate what you most need in terms of healing or nurturing. Sometimes it is useful to "triangulate" with two other oracles – the *I Ching* and Runes, for example. Additional voices confirm or improvise upon what the *Green World* says, revealing the synergy at work in oracular realms. I have found that oracles used in triangulations continually shift their roles along a practicality/spirituality grid, opening up complementary dimensions.

You might also write down what card you draw at the beginning of a particular period in your life. At the end of that time, whether days, weeks, or months later, look back at what actually happened. You might then wish to make notes on the wider implications possible with a particular card. If you get one card more than others over a long period, you might wish to explore that card in greater depth. You could meditate on it, write a story or song about it, paint a picture, or make a mask inspired by it, put its name or a token from it (e.g., a leaf, nut, seed) under your pillow and see if it induces a clarifying dream. If it is safe to do so, brew a tea from the tree's bark, root, leaves, or fruit. If the tree grows in your area, seek it out, sit under it, or simply stare at it. Pay attention to the thoughts or memories that arise. Free-associate.

The more you use the oracle, the more certain cards may develop a private language with you. Each tree, plant, and deity in the *Green World* is unique and some may be more willing than others to enter upon a deeper relationship with you. When one does, things change. Long companionship may modify the general interpretive "DNA" or energy-field until finally a card whose message you might once have dreaded will be a trusted old friend.

One-Card Question

This is for a specific question, but is otherwise the same as mentioned in the One-Card Higher Self Message. If one question leads to another, ask a series of questions, selecting one card each time, instead of doing a more elaborate lay-out.

The "Adopt a Human for a Day" Program

Sometimes, you might either be feeling playful – or exhausted. You do not have a specific question, nor do you feel up to inviting a message from your Higher Self lest it be too heavy. For such times, the trees, plants, and deities offer you their *"Adopt a Human for a Day* [week, month, season] *Program."*

Shuffle the deck and draw a card in the usual way. This will be the plant or *deva* (deity, angel, nature spirit) who wishes to adopt you, to "parent" you for the time selected. Reversed positions do not count here, although you might wish to read everything, just in case you feel a resonance. In general, however, just as no adoptive human parent would lay heavy burdens on their chosen child, still less would the plants and *devas*. This is also an excellent way to get to know the nuances of the various cards.

Four-Card Karmic "Primal Seed" Layout

- #2 = Good Weather
- #3 = Bad Weather
- #4 = New Weather Front
- #1 = Primal Seed Self

This lay-out is designed to help you discover karmic blocks. Before you start, decide which card will represent your "Primal Seed." It could be one of your favorites; you might prefer to draw one at random from the deck; or you might simply use the *Bija* card, since "primal seed" is its meaning. This first card represents your unsullied potential, your soul-seed. Place it at the base of your lay-out. Then shuffle the deck and draw three more cards.

INTRODUCTION

The second card represents the nature of the strengths you have developed over many lifetimes. This is the karmic "good weather" which is trying to nurture your unfolding. This goes at the top of your lay-out.

The third card is "bad weather." This represents weak areas that block, hinder, or try to shrivel you. Place this one directly below "good weather" – for it functions as an interruption or distortion of that weather.

The fourth and last card is a "new weather front." This is what you must activate to dispel or neutralize "bad weather," while at the same time strengthening the influence of "good weather." Once you do this, "good weather" is free to act on your behalf. It germinates the seed, draws the emerging stem upwards, and enables it to gather strength and flower into its fullest potential.

Ritual of the Sacred Grove

If you have a group of friends who celebrate rituals together, this one could either be done as a single ritual or as an element in another. First, arrange for everyone to meet beforehand for discussion and card-drawing. Although no specific focus is necessary, some groups may prefer to discuss their general celebratory intent – i.e., rejoicing, asking for guidance, seeking protection during difficult times. No general consensus is necessary – the discussion itself serves to stir up and enkindle the group's energies.

Each person then shuffles the deck, selects a card, makes note of what it is, and returns it to the deck. The group could decide as a whole whether or not reversed positions should be used; alternately, this could be left up to each participant.

When you have chosen a card, accept that it wishes to be given ritual "voice" through you. The resonance may be obvious because your life already manifests its qualities. On the other hand, the resonance may puzzle you and feel very alien – in this case, allow the card to activate qualities in you that have heretofore lain secret, hidden, perhaps even deliberately resisted or denied (**Caution**: this does not mean that you should make such qualities a permanent part of your life – they may only be valid for the purposes of *this* ritual in the company of *these* people).

At home, after this preliminary group-meeting, let yourself gradually "become," or "merge with," your card's realm in whatever way feels appropriate. (See One-Card Higher Self's Message for suggestions on deepening your connections to a specific tree or plant.)

When it is time for the actual ritual, either form a circle or else let each person find a place where s/he feels comfortable. Then s/he invokes what the card represents, thereby "becoming" that realm and gifting the others with its insights and abundance. Re-tell portions of the myths to which you feel most drawn. Speak in "first person" as the tree or plant. If you speak about yourself, try to do it from the tree's perspective – if you are Hawthorn, for example, you might admit your struggles:

> I like this human even though she was disappointed to get me because I frequently come with so many limitations. She doesn't like me because she's currently having problems accepting delays. Over the weeks that she's been getting to know me, I've helped her to realize that her heart is good and her path is right. She feels more peaceful now – and it's that sense of peace that she and I wish to share with you.

If appropriate, let each tree-spirit bring a gift for the others. Oak, for example, might bring acorn necklaces; Beech, handfuls of beechnuts; Corn, some cornbread, a painting, or chant. Any tree-spirit might wish to share a reading, dream, song, insight, dance, food, or simply a hug. The sharings should be as simple or as elaborate and dramatic as each person wishes.

Afterwards, each one ritually releases "tree/plant-ness," reclaiming her/his human-self once more, but with a special sense of respect for the tree/plant s/he was allowed to be. Finally, the group should discuss their reactions to the guest-list of tree/plants who appeared in the group's sacred grove. Sometimes the presence of one tree/plant or another might be quite unexpected...and lead to important insights.

An additional possibility: if one member of the group is going through a painful or confused period, the group might make her/him their focus, placing that person in the center of the sacred grove, as each "tree/plant" gives whatever gifts or insights seem appropriate. Always remember to dissolve your "tree/plant-ness" at the end, returning to human form.

There are many other possible layouts, rituals, and meditations involving the *Green World Oracle*, limited only by your willingness to experiment and explore. The oracle welcomes your personal style and needs – be as creative, wild, conservative, fanciful, or practical as you wish.

1
ACACIA

Acacia

...they work, in their flickering ways, to free words of praise, and the joyous white fire that flares from the buried Root of this thorn-bush world.
~ Lawrence Russ[1]

...They shall make an ark of acacia wood....And you shall overlay it with pure gold, within and without shall you overlay it.
Exodus 25.10-11

The Mythic World

Moses' Burning Bush was an acacia, a tree considered sacred by countless generations of desert nomads. Acacia was the Mother-tree – its gum-arabic symbolizing her menstrual blood, its long thorns symbolizing her fierce power to repel harm. Even for Moses and his people, acacia would retain its intimate connection with the Divine Feminine, which is why the Ark of the Covenant, within which the *Shekhinah*, or Divine Feminine, would reside, was constructed of acacia (*shittim*).[2]

Although acacia was believed to be her primary residence, the *Shekhinah* actually vibrates within all matter. This concept of her in-dwelling presence is connected to blessings, or *berakoth*. From sunrise to sunset, star-rise to the lighting of lamps, the world of the ancient Jew unfolded within a climate of *berakoth*, for life was intended to be lived as a single prayer of thanksgiving, a celebration of life and light, an uninterrupted sequence of praise. *Berakoth* spoken over one's food, the ground under one's feet, the clothing one wore, the sound of a cock's crow at dawn, the roof over one's head, released the inner holiness of each of these, activating the coiled power of the feminine polarity of the Godhead. To use without speaking such blessings was considered stealing from God.

Recognizing the all-pervading presence of the *Shekhinah*, the medieval Church honored her as the Blessed Virgin Mary, Mother of God, even though Christian theologians saw her as mortal and refused to accept a female pole of divinity. Yet among the common people as well as poets and artists, the cosmic imagery associated with her clearly links her to the realm of the divine: she is Queen of Heaven, Morning Star, Tower of David, Throne of Ivory, Mystical Rose, Ark of the Covenant, and even Burning Bush. In the Russian Orthodox Church, for example, there are ikons depicting her as the Burning Bush. In these, she appears at the circular heart of petalled fire-blossoms, burning but not burned, consuming, but not consumed, speaking to Moses with the voice of the wind. From the viewpoint of Russian Orthodoxy, just as the first Burning Bush birthed divine words, so the Virgin Mary birthed the Divine *Word*.

As medieval Christians were expressing their mystical beliefs concerning the Virgin, so too were mystical Jewish thinkers exploring and deepening their own beliefs concerning the *Shekhinah*. For them, a joyful spirit was the essential pre-condition for humans to experience this aspect of God. In one legend, for example, the archangel Michael brings a heavenly wine to Isaac:

> ...that an exalted mood might descend upon him, for only when a man is joyously excited the Shekinah rests upon him.[3]

On the other hand, overindulgence in despair appears to drive her away, which is not to say that she ever leaves, but a depressed spirit is too burdened to experience her:

> ...[Moses'] dejected spirit was the cause of his not receiving divine revelations during this period, since the Shekinah dwells only on those whose spirit is joyful.[4]

In addition to joy, it is consoling to learn that sickness also brings the *Shekhinah* to human awareness:

> ...Jacob, noticing the Shekinah over the bed's head, where she always rests in a sick room, bowed....[5]

There are many beautiful stories about the *Shekinah*. She resides at the root of the tree of life.[6] She lives in pure light, a great bright light more intense than that of the sun. When Moses' face shone with radiance on Mount Sinai, it was because he had gone to this place of light, where she is brighter than jewels and pearls.[7] When she speaks, it is with "a sweet, pleasant and lovely voice," ringing out towards those who hear her. Frequently, music, especially that of wind instruments (for her Burning Bush voice was like the wind), accompanies her appearances.[8] The Archangels Michael and Gabriel often announce her presence, going before her.[9] Those whom she protects, she surrounds with her great wings; thus when Moses dies, it is she who bears him aloft into the light.[10] Nothing can exist without her presence.[11]

Moses appears repeatedly in medieval legends as the one with the most intimate relationship with the *Shekinah*. His first encounter was with her Burning Bush manifestation. The thorn-bush was burning, yet unharmed, even erupting into new blossoms, for these flames are from a celestial fire:

> ...the celestial fire has three peculiar qualities: it produces blossoms, it does not consume the object around which it plays, and it is black of color.[12]

Black: the mysterious union of all colors in one, hidden, numinous, the fertile womb of nature, the genesis of all light.

Years later, after Moses had led his people out of Egypt, he is instructed to build an ark from acacia wood. According to legend, Adam took the wood from Paradise – from him it passed into Abraham's hands, then his son Isaac's, then his grandson Jacob's, who took it to Egypt where it remained until the Exodus, when the Hebrews took it out with them. It is from this Paradise wood that the ark was to be constructed.[13] God told Moses that the *Shekinah*-fire would burn forever upon the altar, but Moses worried that such fire would melt the metal overlay and destroy the wood:

> ...God replied: "Moses, thou judgest by the laws that apply to men, but will these also apply to Me?...For, 'I am the Lord who maketh peace between these elements in My high places.'"[14]

The elements: earth, air, fire, and water, form oppositions on earth – earth and water quenching fire; fire exhausting air; air (wind), fire, and water eroding earth. Within the *Shekinah*, however, just as all colors merge into a shimmering darkness, so too do all elements find peace.

This harmony of the elements reappears in medieval alchemy, where the acacia's gum-arabic plays a crucial role. In alchemical literature, Moses' older sister Miriam appears as a prophetess, Maria Prophetissa. Gum-arabic is her "special concern."[15] She tells adepts, "Marry gum-arabic with gum-arabic in true marriage," a confusing request unless this alchemical marriage is understood as a state of total union and peace, like the black fire, the peace made among the elements, or the cosmic serpent (*Ouroboros*) circling around to hold its tail in its mouth. Gum-arabic as a symbol of the *Shekhinah* was a transforming substance, the life force:

> ...[it is] the "glue of the world" (*glutinum mundi*), which is the medium between mind and body and the union of both....So the union of the two is a kind of self-fertilization, a characteristic always ascribed to the mercurial dragon.[16]

The acacia, chosen abode of the *Shekhinah*, produces this gum-arabic, a red-gold substance viewed mystically and alchemically as that adhesive power that holds the world together at every level, from heavenly bodies circling through the cosmos to subatomic particles circling through the nucleus of a cell. This life-energy, deserving of care and respect, is in everything. Thus, acacia gives us a profound example of what it is to live imbued with a sense of the adhesive, holy interconnectedness of all life, even in difficult, painful situations.

Botany/History

Acacia is a shrubby, scrawny, low branching, often multi-trunked and flat-topped tree, usually with delicate feathery leaves, ivory or bright yellow flower-clusters, seedpods, and long thorns. There are approximately 500 kinds of acacia growing worldwide in warm climates, where they blossom even in severe drought. Gum-arabic oozes from an African species, whose limbs also provide space for young, napping lions. Africa's Masai warriors make an acacia bark-brew which serves as an excitant; an acacia species called *cutch* in India provides khaki dye; the Australian trees are called wattles and their bright flowers are the country's national emblem.[17]

Ancient Egyptians carved exquisite chests and statues from acacia. Since the wood is waterproof, some of the earliest Old Kingdom records report that ships were constructed of acacia in Lower Nubia.[18] Unlike the Egyptians, for Hebrews and other nomads who lived where acacia – and little else – grew wild, the wood was sacred and its use for secular purposes was forbidden.[19] Instead, the durable, yellow-brown, lightweight, waterproof wood was ideally suited for portable shrines, the most famous of which was the Ark of the Covenant.[20]

The Reading

The tree may have long thorns, yet African lions often stretch out on acacia limbs and sleep in peace. Similarly, Acacia builds a protective "ark" around you, giving you access to female wisdom and messages as you are carried on your journey.

Acacia reveals the level of reality at which the Divine Feminine, or *Shekhinah*, is at work in your life – and, having found her there, often at a time of desperation, like the Hebrews on the Exodus, you may find new ways to live and relate to life around you. The tree brings a promise of help and invites a deepening of faith, giving you an awareness that divine wisdom can open ways where, to human sense, there are no ways. An important message might come through an unexpected channel.

If to bless bread, wine, and whatever else is around you is to release the Divine Feminine within, then to bless *yourself* is equally to release the *Shekhinah* within *you*. She is in each bone, tissue, nerve, molecule of your being. Blessing makes everything yours, allowing you to live immersed in the radiant light of that climate of *berakoth*, where everything is flooded with the presence of the *Shekhinah*.

REVERSED:

This is a time to remain self-possessed and to act despite fear, without making judgments. You need humane skills in dealing with yourself, in renewing your faith and trust in mysteries beyond the realm of logic. Try to practice living within a climate of *berakoth*. Awaken a continual recognition that the Divine Feminine is shining in the world around you as well as in the synapses between the nerves in your brain. You are the acacia ark. The in-dwelling life of the Mother-spirit infuses your body with her own deep cellular-wisdom, down beyond the reach of all obstacles.

Artist's Notes:

Canaanite cult stand behind the Shekinah: Taanach, late 10th century B.C.E. Paleolithic Goddess at her heart-center: Berekhat Ram, Golan Heights, c. 230,000 B.C.E. Necklace: Deir el-Balah, 14th-13th century B.C.E. Earring, from a falcon pendant: Tell el-Ajjul, mid 2nd millennium B.C.E.

Endnotes

[1] Russ, "Prayers at the Broken Gate," in *Parabola*, Summer 1983, VIII, #3, pp.26-27.
[2] Walker, *WD*:459; McKenzie:54a.
[3] Ginzberg:I, 334; V,284.
[4] Ginzberg:VI, 98, n.550.
[5] Ginzberg:II, 130-131.
[6] Ginzberg:V, 122, n.126; 152, n.56.
[7] Ginzberg:VI, 50, n.260; III, 446.
[8] Ginzberg:III, 185-186; I, 124; V, 416, n.117; VI, 36, n.201.
[9] Ginzberg:V, 416, n.15; II, 303.
[10] Ginzberg:III,75;460.
[11] Ginzberg:II, 303.
[12] Ginzberg:II, 303.
[13] Ginzberg:VI, 66, n.344; Graves, *WG*:518.
[14] Ginzberg:III, 162.
[15] Jung, *P&A*:384, n.166.
[16] Jung, *P&A*:153-154.
[17] Cowles:78a; 129b; *NG* 11/62:632 (top lion photo); *NG* 10/54:505 (Masai).
[18] Gardiner, *Egypt of the Pharaohs*:42; 436.
[19] Lehner:23.
[20] John L. McKenzie, S.J., *Dictionary of the Bible*:7b.

2
AMRITA

Amrita

Vak: *I am the one who says, by myself, what gives joy to gods and men.*
Rig Veda 10.125.5
~ Wendy Doniger O'Flaherty, tr.

The Mythic World

Early Hindu myths tell of a time of darkness when only waters existed.[1] Eons later, a floating mound arose from the bottom of this ocean and drifted about aimlessly. Intent upon protecting it, *ashuras* ("demon-gods"), dark-skinned deities, identified by their mothers' names, emerged out of the gloom and formed a circle around the mound. Soon thereafter, *devas* ("shining gods"), their younger and lighter-skinned siblings, identified by their fathers' names, appeared. Far from wishing to protect the primal mound, the gods wanted to prod it into activity and get things going.

One of the gods, Indra, hurled his spear into the floating mound, splitting it open and anchoring it firmly in place. Then he began shoving the upper part of the mound, which was to be the sky, away from the lower part, which would be earth. As he labored, a world-tree unexpectedly arose from the primeval waters to support the new sky. As the tree soared up through the mound, four mighty world-rivers gushed forth as well.

Meanwhile, hidden among the tree's mighty roots at the bottom of the ocean, was a secret treasure: a *patra* (vessel) filled with *amrita* (immortal elixir of life), protected by Vak, *ashura*-goddess of speech. With her in the depths was *ashura*-god, Varuna, pattern-master and lord of cosmic harmony.

Following the emergence of the tree, and knowing nothing of what lay hidden below, the patriarchal gods started a war with the matriarchal demon-gods over whether the unfolding of creation should be rigidly controlled, which is what the gods wanted, or allowed to unfold according to its own rhythms, which is what the *ashuras* wanted. The gods won. Later, to tip the balance and prevent future conflicts, some of the leading *ashuras*, including Vak, Varuna, fire-deity Agni, and moon-deity Soma, sided with the warrior-gods but still retained close ties to the other *ashuras*.

Much later, this cosmic war would become the subject of the first drama written by creator-god Brahma. The poor *ashuras* objected to the plot because, since they had lost, they felt it would show them in a bad light. They accused Brahma of playing favorites, pitting his successful offspring against his defeated children. But Brahma assured them he was simply depicting "what is" in order to entertain both groups.[2]

So the first drama began, performed by human actors for the pleasure of their gods. The *devas* relished the elaborate production but their angry siblings continued to protest, instigating onstage accidents, and ultimately causing the actors to forget their lines. With that, the drama was stopped, never to be performed again.

The *ashuras* then asked Brahma to write a drama that would show them in a more kindly light. They wanted it known that they had been actively cooperating in allowing creation to unfold naturally, instead of trying to stifle it with rigid rules. Recognizing the justice of their request, Brahma then wrote the *Churning of the Ocean*. Unlike his first drama, this one was successful.

Churning of the Ocean tells of the postwar period when the gods finally learned about the pot of *amrita* hidden among the world-tree's roots. They lusted after that elixir and began plotting to get it. They determined that by churning the ocean, the dislodged pot would simply float to the surface. Since they lacked sufficient numbers for such a project, however, they turned to their older siblings, asking for help in exchange for a share of the *amrita*. It was a ruse – the devious gods had no intention of sharing the elixir, but the trusting *ashuras* had no way to know this and happily agreed to the terms. The two teams then wound a massive, volunteer serpent around the world-tree and began pulling him like a rope, back and forth, causing the tree to rotate like a churning-stick. The turmoil uprooted many shoreline trees, which toppled into the ocean and, sadly, killed many fish. Oblivious, the two teams kept churning, eager for their prize.[3]

Both sides were completely unaware of Vak's existence in the depths. To their amazement however, as their efforts intensified, it was she, goddess of speech and *natya* (sacred theatre), who arose serenely from the depths, carrying the pot of *amrita* – that concentrate of ecstasy and spiritual intoxication lying at her own heart, her "voice."

Thus, speech itself emerges, dream-like, from the roots of being. Its nature is to transform, heal, energize, and infuse with rapture. It is symbolized by the grail-like vessel, the *patra* – but this Sanskrit word also applies to an actor, for the actor, which is to say, the *patra*, performing in sacred theatre, is viewed as carrying the same energy as a vessel of *amrita*. From Vak's perspective, the root of life is sacred theatre, playfulness, art, beauty. She claims to know "what gives joy to gods and men." When she appears with that richly nuanced pot of *amrita*, she is making good on her claim.

It does not happen at once, however. Since the gods planned to cheat the *ashuras*, "bad faith" had already contaminated the process. Thus, along with the elixir of life came its unexpected twin, the lethal *kalakuta* (see "Reversed Reading," below, for more on this; also *Sandalwood)*. This serves as a reminder of the damage done to language when its transformative potential is twisted.

There is an echo of this from ancient Greece as well. There, among a related branch of patriarchal invaders, similar elements appear, reshuffled, but still visible. When Greece's Olympian deities wanted to take an oath, it was not done casually. Only water from the river of Death-goddess Styx was powerful enough to witness and sanctify divine oaths. Not surprisingly, Olympians feared the Death-goddess and were unwilling to go near her – all that is except Rainbow-goddess, Iris, messenger of the gods, who was accustomed to bridging earth and sky. Thus, when oath-taking was required, Iris would visit Styx, dip a ritual cup into the water, and carry it back to Mount Olympus where the death-water would witness the oath. The penalty for breaking such an oath was extreme: for nine years, a foresworn deity would be denied ambrosia (Greece's version of *amrita*). During those years, the deity would be mortal, subject to illness, aging, and death. After India's "Churning of the Waters," perhaps word spread among related invading nomads that gods could no longer take oaths lightly.

Akin to Vak's immortal elixir, as well as Greece's Rainbow-goddess, there is also a Sumerian myth about a secret treasure, the "Herb of Immortality," found only in the depths of the sea. This is the realm of the goddess Nanshe, one of whose titles, "Interpreter of Dreams," links her to that primal oracular language to which Vak is also connected. To learn this dream-language, Nanshe's priests had to go down into a temple-pit and endure a symbolic death and rebirth. After emerging, the new initiates were entitled to wear rainbow-colored garments as a sign of their union with the Goddess.[4]

> ...Nanshe was also a Goddess of water and fertility, her symbol a vessel of water with a fish in it, signifying the gravid womb.[5]

India's Vak, as we have seen, also has this connection to a vessel of life-giving liquid – this theme will emerge centuries later in northern Europe in stories of a Grail Maiden and a Wounded Fisherking (see *Linden*).

Nanshe's sister-goddess, Inanna, the Sumerian counterpart to the Babylonian Ishtar, had a human son, Gilgamesh, who ruled nearly 5,000 years ago. Gilgamesh was a brutal man – raping, oppressing, enslaving, and slaughtering. His desperate people begged the gods for help and the gods gave him, as a diversion, a companion, the only human he ever considered his peer: hairy Enkidu, who had long hair "like a woman."[6] These two oddly matched comrades then set off on a series of adventures until Gilgamesh offended his mother by killing her sacred bull. In revenge, Inanna took the life of hairy Enkidu.

Gilgamesh went searching for Death, determined to defeat him. When he learned that an Herb of Immortality could be found in the depths of the ocean, he dove down, searched, found the plant, and grabbed it – only to encounter its serpent-guardian, who promptly took it from him. Enraged, more obsessed than ever, Gilgamesh finally summoned up poor Enkidu's ghost, who informed him that the Hereafter was an empty and dreadful place. With this dismal revelation, the king's story ends.

Gilgamesh's epic both resembles and greatly differs from India's "Churning of the Ocean." Both myths involve a quest for an elixir of life. In India, despite the underlying atmosphere of deceit, opposing forces nevertheless set a pattern of communal cooperation in their effort to win the elixir. Gilgamesh, on the other hand, seeks it alone, for purely selfish reasons, in defiance of death. In India, a willing serpent is used as a churning rope to help the shining-gods and "demon-gods." In Mesopotamia, a serpent retrieves the illicitly obtained herb from the egotistic "demon" who stole it. In India, Vak emerges with the vessel of elixir. In Gilgamesh's male-dominated Mesopotamia, ancient Nanshe, whose sea-connections and oracular dream-knowledge make her a close match to Vak, has been displaced. Instead, the goddess Inanna, an angry victim of sacrilege, comes forth vindictively with a suitable punishment. Vak brings life through the magic of theatre. Inanna passes judgment in a deadly serious drama that pits her against her arrogant son. The message is clear in both myths: there comes a time when cooperation between genders, races, even species becomes essential if the fullness of life is to be sustained.

Botany/History

Many cultures recognize an ancient elixir that strengthens, heals, gives bliss, and bestows immortality. The chief ingredient might be earth-grown and exist in reality (grapes or mushrooms, for example) – or sea-grown, often a mythic plant or tree requiring divine aid for its acquisition. The deeper purpose of such elixirs lies in transformations brought about through such consciousness-altering techniques as sacred theatre, dream interpretation, dance, drums, and chant. Thus, the soul's intoxication, not the body's, is the primary goal.

India's connection between sea and world-tree may seem remote, yet there are other myths in which an underwater tree, sometimes made of twisting coral, is both the source of life as well as the tree of Paradise.[7] The Arabic alchemical book of Abul Kasim states, for example:

> This prime matter which is proper for the form of the Elixir is taken from a single tree which...[emerges] on the surface of the ocean as plants grow on the surface of the earth. This the tree of which whosoever eats, man and [genie] obey him....[8]

In more ancient times, in Sumer and Babylonia, that alchemical "tree" was in a simpler form, an herb at the bottom of the sea, guarded by a serpent. The famous *Epic of Gilgamesh* tells of the quest for that herb as well as the greed and violence that caused Gilgamesh to lose it.

In India, the elixir is *amrita,* found among the roots of a cosmic tree in the depths of the ocean. Vak, bearer of *amrita,* is India's Goddess of Speech. Sanskrit meaning-clusters associated with her name include speech, voice, word, oracular utterance, the sound of a drum, humming, the murmur of trickling soma, the language of humans and animals, and the music of birds. The Sanskrit root of her name also appears in European languages: e.g., Latin *vox,* Spanish *voce,* French *voix,* and English *voice.* Related to Vak's name in English are such words as vocal, vocalize, vocalist, voice, evoke, convoke, and vocabulary. Her oracular nuance continues to pulse in our word "vocation," a deeply felt calling to a lifelong commitment.

In Hindu myth, Vak emerges with the *patra* when the ocean is being churned by gods and demons cooperating together. She rises through the midpoint (a metaphor for the heart-chakra, a sea of nectar in its own right),[9] serene, stable in the midst of turmoil. In medieval Europe, a similar theme involves the Grail, a vessel that grants immortality to whomever partakes of its food and drink. In *Parzival,* Wolfram von Eschenbach's early 13th-century epic, *The Grail* is brought to earth during a war between Lucifer's side and God's side (demons and gods, just as in India, only in Europe they are opposed, not cooperating). This Grail, a profound symbol of the compassionate heart, is carried down through an ocean of air by "neutral angels," those in the middle, between black and white, good and evil. These neutral angels are untouched by the dense swarmings of energy around them and yet they are empathetic to all possibilities. They are *between.* For them, there is no war, no dance, no conflict, no re-positioning, no recombining. They are neutral, in the middle. They are in what the 11th-century Hindu mystic, Abhinavagupta, called the *madhya,* or "midpoint," of the heart:

> ...*Madhya* is that point from which the finite realities emerge from the Ultimate and also continuously dissolve back into the Ultimate. This threshold function of the Heart makes it a kind of paradoxical no-man's-land, a boundary which, because it shares and participates simultaneously in the characteristics of the Ultimate and of the finite realities, is also somehow different from either one of those conditions.[10]

Wolfram's neutral angels descend from above, bearing the Grail down through the midpoint. Vak ascends from below, bearing the *patra* up through the midpoint. The correspondences, one might even say the choreography, are too close to be coincidental. The Hindu myth adds a nuance missing in the Grail myths, however, for the Sanskrit *patra,* or chalice, also refers to an "actor," which points to the original connection between elixir and a sacred theatre designed to catalyze compassion within the heart-chakra.

The Reading

Amrita and other elixirs hold out the promise of "immortality" – but this seems to be a paradox, for they make you "immortal" by restoring you to the fullness of a single moment. This is akin to the Zen concept of staying-in-the-moment, allowing everything to *be* without trying to impose upon it any qualities other than what it already has. When you achieve this, you are complete.

Drawing *amrita* indicates that a breakthrough is at hand. It requires you to stay in the mid-point, the *madhya*, without identifying with or giving an emotional charge to the warring internal factions struggling in the "drama" around you. When all sides regain balance and cooperate, joy will emerge.

Amrita is experienced as a widening of consciousness. An inner obstruction has been breached and rivers of inspiration gush forth. But recognize that what you seek may not be what initially appears. As in the Hindu myth, former enemies enter into a temporarily unifying relationship to seek the elixir of immortality. What they discover instead is "language," personified as the Goddess Vak, who rises out of the waters. Only after she appears do gods and demons realize that she is carrying the sought-after elixir. Drawing *amrita* especially favors those involved in "sacred theatre": drama, dance, film, television. What makes it "sacred" is keeping the focus on the inherent goodness, playfulness, cooperation, joy, and depth of the human spirit.

Amrita might invite you to explore a new definition of yourself. You are not your emotional turmoil. In the Hindu myth, smug "gods" – or positive feelings – are quite content to be entertained by a drama about their glorious war. It takes the "demons" to force the issue and insist upon a more balanced perspective. To split yourself or your world between gods and demons is to lose sight of the central core out of which both those emotional energies are constellated. That core remains a compassionate and *Self*-centered awareness lying, relaxed, in your heart.

REVERSED:

You might be at risk of succumbing to addiction, confusing the sacramental use of *amrita* with the addictive poison of its lethal twin, *kalakuta*. In lore related to the god Shiva, knowing such fiery poison could destroy even the gods, he protected them by swallowing the toxin and containing it in his throat. This turned his throat dark-blue and burned it until cooling sandalwood paste was rubbed on it. But creation was saved (see *Sandlewood* for more).

Like Shiva, find a way to contain the poison, whether of language or emotion, before it spreads. This is a time to remain clear and focused. Stay aligned with your own positive creative energies. By identifying with negative thoughts, you are leaving your tired body behind, letting it fend for itself, making it feel sluggish and joyless. Your body needs to be respected, allowed to relax, unburdened by your restless spirit. There, in that pregnant calm, the elixir may be tasted anew.

Artist's Notes:

Vak holds a patra from the Indus Valley civilization; the ghost tree is the Tree of Life and Knowledge from India, Vigayanagar period, 1336-1546.

Endnotes

[1] Kuiper:10; 51; 239; 141-142; 87.
[2] Kuiper:37.
[3] Kuiper:104.
[4] Walker, *WEMS*:3.
[5] Walker, *WEMS*:718.
[6] Goff:246-247.
[7] Jung, *P&A*:335-336.
[8] Jung, *P&A*:438.
[9] Muller-Ortega:76.
[10] Muller-Ortega:107.

3
ANCIENT GIANTS

Ancient Giants

The Mythic World

Many creation myths of Pacific Northwest Native Americans date back to Raven myth-cycles from their Paleo-Siberian homeland. Raven is Creator, Bringer-of-Light, Trickster, Destroyer, and Renewer. He has an intimate connection with the Ancient Giants, especially cedar (early European settlers called the tree cedar because of its scented wood, but New World cedars are related to Asiatic cypresses and junipers; true cedars grow only in Mediterranean and Himalayan regions).

In a Tsimshian myth, Raven travels through a hole in the sky and sees where a selfish sky-chief has hidden the sun in a box. Raven also notices the sky-chief's daughter going to a celestial spring to draw water. He sheds his raven coat and changes himself into a cedar leaf floating on the water. The young woman dips her bucket into the pool and the leaf tumbles in. After she swallows the leaf, she becomes pregnant. Her child, Raven in infant-form, steals his grandfather sky-chief's box of daylight and playfully breaks it open. That is how sunlight – and daylight consciousness – came to the world.[2]

Most of the trees and plants of *The Green World Oracle* speak through age-old myths. The Ancient Giants, however, speak through two contemporary tree-communicators. First is Dorothy Maclean, the Canadian mystic who co-founded the world-famous Findhorn Community in Scotland. She is able to establish telepathic contact with the angels, *devas*, or pattern-holders of the plant kingdom. Two large conifers provide remarkable insights (also see *Introduction*). From the Scots Pine Deva:

> We are guardians of the Earth in many ways....We are, in a way, like a school of benevolent philosophers with unhuman purity and a great wish to serve humanity....Trees, rooted guardians of the surface, converters of the higher forces to Earth through the ground, have a special gift for man in this age of speed and drive and busy-ness. We are calmness, strength, endurance, praise, and fine attunement....[3]

From the Large Tree Devas:

> We would emphasize the absolute necessity for large trees for the well-being of the land. This is not merely because we partly control rainfall, but we also draw forth inner radiances which are as necessary to the land as rain....[4]

The second tree-communicator is an American nature mystic, former athlete, and business executive, Jeffrey Goelitz, who speaks with a 2,000-year-old redwood called the Mother of the Forest and learns:

> ...I am an essence spirit that is very old. I hold the standing wave for the entire surrounding forest. Trees are gravity centers for light and water. We pull in with tremendous force energies that influence the entire earth. Great forests of the world are linked by networks of energy that help sustain and balance the earth's ecosphere. Forests have a special rhythm of existence.... There are powerful energies that pour through me as I am a conduit for heavenly light. Its flow varies with climatic and environmental conditions.[5]

Goelitz does not define "standing wave" – it is more a "felt-sense" of safely holding immense waves of energy, life-force, leylines, or "dragon-paths," as some cultures know them. It is about protecting saplings from an inrush of forces that might prove harmful. It is a towering, calm presence that allows young trees to trust life, knowing that elders are watchful, caring, and will not let things get too far out-of-phase.

One of the manifestations of this ancient Forest Mother is *Dzonokwa*, Wild Woman of the Woods, the Kwakiutl goddess of abundance and rebirth. In one sacred narrative, her son was killed by hunters. A young orphan, who was not pleasant to look at, led her to the body and together they carried him home. To show her gratitude for the young boy's help, she threw some magical water on him and on the body of her son: her son returned to life and the orphan became handsome. She taught the orphan the secrets of rebirth and restored his family by reviving his parents with her magical water.[6]

In addition to the ancient Mother of the Forest, Goelitz also speaks with the nearby Father of the Forest, who tells him:

> ...The purest essence comes from the oldest trees who have peaked developmentally in their beingness. Older trees communicate to younger trees a vibrancy which supports and encourages their growth....There is an intelligence on the other side from which life springs. A tree is a form created by that intelligence. The form arose out of a design which gave purpose to a tree's existence. The form embodies a tree and is one of the many multifaceted manifestations of creation. Within the form is a foundational energy with an inherent design that makes a tree what it is. The energy body is sustained by light-giving properties coming from the other side.... The force of gravity helps us to live. Through gravity we receive light from the sky....Gravity is the bridge to the other world where earth connects to the sky. Trees act like magnetic funnels. Through their centers they draw heavily on the light. As a result trees cushion the light's entrance into the planet and make light more accessible.... [The Mother of the Forest and I] have a deep resonance of peace. Our ages, sizes, and electromagnetic fields

are very much alike. Together, along with other elder redwoods, we watch over the forest with our etheric radiation. Our rays interlace together in a way distinct from other trees because of our similarities.[7]

As such passages reveal, these great trees are akin to Tolkien's wise Ents. They see themselves as guardians, conduits of inner radiances, and other higher energies needed by humans and planet alike. They consider themselves our blood brothers and sisters. Where earth's tropical rain forests are the lungs and uterus of the planet, these ancient giants are the planet's consciousness. They have a profound awareness of their own value and a yearning to fulfill their destiny. They are the sentinels of life as we know it.

Botany/History

Ancient Giants are the great evergreen conifers of the Pacific Northwest, the tallest and some of the oldest trees on earth.[8] Some are a living link to the age of dinosaurs. In these dense forests, millions of needles transform feeble sunlight into nourishment. Along with redwood, fir, spruce, and hemlock are understory trees like the spindly Pacific yew and rare creatures like the spotted owl who act as barometers of the health of these old-growth forests and who depend upon the synergies of the larger trees. The Japanese Current warms the offshore Pacific coastal waters, creating a temperate climate; a mountainous spine runs through this realm, extending some 2,000 miles from Alaska to northern California and blocking moisture-rich winds from penetrating further inland: in the resulting heavy rains from autumn to spring, lush forests thrive.[9] The region is rich in salmon and other fish, game and a wide variety of greens, roots, berries, and other wild plants. This ancient ecosystem is a moist, shadowy realm teeming with highly specialized genetic treasures.

Conifers, or cone-bearing trees, create an abundance of pollen: this comes solely from their cones, for these trees evolved long before earth's flowering plants. Wind carries the pollen from small male cones to ovules in larger female cones. In season, a golden pollen mist drifts down through the trees to cover the forest floor where bears and smaller animals eagerly lick it up. Nothing in that lush abundance is wasted. Even when a great tree dies and falls, crashing down through the dense canopy of the forest, its fallen trunk becomes a nurse log, sheltering and nurturing new life over the 500 years it takes to fully decompose; during this time, fungi spread over it, their chemical scent attracting termites, who digest the wood, thereby helping to return the tree's components to the earth. Everything is used.

Many conifers get their start atop nurse logs where survival chances are vastly enhanced. As they grow, they straddle the huge, rotting log, deriving moisture and nutrients from it. Such trees grow lined up, forming a colonnade; as they mature, the original nurse log, long gone, betrays its presence by a hollow tunnel formed by still-straddling roots of the current generation of giants. The diameter of the hollow reveals the size of the nurse log; by adding this to the diameter of its largest offspring, the nurse's age can be gauged back to when it too was a seedling atop its own nurse log, perhaps a thousand years earlier. In this way, the past remains present and sustains the future in an endless process of cycling, recycling.[10]

As seedlings spring up from the nurse log, threadlike fungi attach themselves to the seedlings' roots: the two oddly matched species will become lifelong partners. Tangled webs of this fungus feed on the tree's sugar content; in return, they help the tree absorb water and nutrients; even more importantly, the fungus becomes an effective immune system for the tree, protecting it from disease. These giant trees could not survive without their partnership with lowly fungi.

Two-thirds of a conifer's growth takes place outside the normal growing season of flowering plants, which is why conifers dominate in old-growth northern forests. Each tree, with its approximately sixty-six million needles, undergoes a spurt of intense growth in the autumn when most other trees are losing their leaves. This cycle continues through winter snows, when winds help trees shed snow so that enough needles are exposed to the sun. During summer droughts, moisture from fog and mist condenses on these same needles: drop by drop, millions of drops of water sustain each towering tree.

As these tall forests unceasingly share and redistribute their wealth, so too did the many Native American kin groups who arrived eons later. Since obtaining food required little effort and there was an endless supply of timber for building large gabled houses and sea-worthy boats, these groups had the leisure to develop wealthy, complex societies. The potlatch ceremony was common to all: this was a festive gathering in which the host's rank and prestige were demonstrated by how much he could give away to his guests. The potlatch ensured that wealth would never accumulate in the hands of only one family or leader.[11]

Another element held in common by many Pacific Northwest peoples was the totem pole depicting each clan's ancestral animal powers. It functioned as the cosmic tree or "Sky-supporting-Pole" up which northern shamans climbed on trance-journeys to the heavens.[12] Cedar provided the preferred wood for these totems. Cedar was also carved into intricate ceremonial masks, headdresses, chests, and musical instruments, playing a major role in elaborate mid-winter rituals.

For everyday use, beautifully designed blankets were interwoven with cedar-bark fibers and mountain-goat wool. Abstract animal forms crafted into these "tree-goat" blankets were believed to have the power to speak to dreamers and protect those who slept under them.[13] Even among peoples who left these forests

ANCIENT GIANTS

centuries ago, cedar remains important. A newborn Navajo infant in Arizona or New Mexico, for example, lies under a cedar-frame canopy, its curving arcs called "rainbows"; this canopy is placed near the hearth with a blanket or goatskin thrown over it to protect the infant from sparks. These cedar "rainbows" hold memories of the Navajo's protective rainbow goddess, Natseelit (see *Corn*), and the ancient, wet, rainbow-graced forests of a far older Navajo homeland.[14]

Interestingly, cedar is a relative newcomer to the Pacific Northwest. Its pollen samples date back only some 5,000 years, about the time when new waves of tribal peoples began arriving.[15] Yet cedar fits beautifully with the other ancient giants, one among many, for these forests are a community, a synergy of life, light and wonder.

The Reading

The realm of the Ancient Giants, where earth's conscious web of life is held, is a patient, mysterious place. When you draw this card, the focus is on your ability to find your own harmonious place in the larger pattern. Recognizing in you a towering, kindred spirit, the trees welcome you regardless of your stage of growth. They give your ancient spirit refuge and your new seeds a supportive nurse log. They awe you with their beauty and wisdom. They understand that you have a higher purpose which you are yearning to fulfill. They are grateful for their contacts with humans, as the orphan boy learned from the Forest Mother's manifestation as Dzonokwa. Allow them to channel for you those rich gifts of which they are the guardians. Learn from them how to be fully yourself, let them re-attune you to the infinite, and bring you back into harmony. They need you as much as you need them. Knowing that you are on this planet with them, traveling the skies together, delights them.

Respect the "little" things in your life. Your healing may lie in what seems least likely – single drops of water, threads of fungi, small owls, droopy little yew trees whose trunks need a full century to grow to a diameter of six-inches. In the realm of the Ancient Giants, at least for awhile, try to let go of artificial constructs like clocks and calendars. Be part of something deeper. Be patient. Then blessings, like yellow mists of pollen, drift down into your life.

Consider joining the Ancient Giants in holding the standing-wave, not only of their forests, but of humanity. For example, instead of feeling angry with self-centered, misguided "young souls" (regardless of actual age), you could visualize the standing-wave clearing new paths so that more sunlight can reach those souls and draw out the poisons and stuntedness. If many of us are indeed "old souls," or, at least, "older souls," then anger against younger souls is without purpose. They need the standing-wave's wise nurturing.

Finally, let this realm be a multidimensional place in your own cells, your mind, awakening your soul's magic. When you are fatigued, let your body enter the ancient forests and hold the energies of a quieter perspective. There you can rest with the Forest Mother who holds baby trees in her hands. She stands there watching, strong, confident. If she offers you a "tree-goat" blanket, take note of which abstract animal-forms have been woven into it, for they will protect you and speak to your dreams. Regardless, be there with her, sharing the standing-wave, becoming wiser and more humane than you ever thought possible.

REVERSED:
Do not sacrifice the past for the present, the towering grandeur for the small and petty. Greater issues are at stake and you could be risking certain doom if you force your will here. Trees forgive much harm done by younger human siblings, but if you trespass here, you might be recklessly destroying your last hope. Guard against such negative emotions as rage, bitterness, frustration: these clear cut both body and soul and leave destruction in their wake.

When you are calmer, allow the ancient forest to offer you a pool of pristine water with cedar leaves floating on it. As you drink, you swallow a leaf and conceive the infant Raven. Your overly controlling and conservative "grandfather sky-chief" has boxed in some "daylight" from your past and hung the box beyond your reach. Raven, however, will not be content until s/he is allowed to play with that box and break it open. What is hidden in your box of "daylight?" What does your raven-child want you to remember and invite back into your conscious world? Accept that you have a higher purpose. Nature has not made a mistake with you. The obstacles you currently face will somehow strengthen your powerful spirit. Do not give up, stay calm and pray for your highest good to unfold. Do not be afraid that this will mean accepting what you most dread: often what is asked is simply a quiet, more conscious change of heart.

Artist's Notes:

Kwakiutl mask of Dzonokwa: Vancouver, B.C., 19th century; robe adapted from early 20th century Kwakiutl cedar bark woman's ceremonial cape; Kwakiutl pole in background: Alert Bay, British Columbia, early 20th century.

Endnotes

[1] Muir cited in Ruth Kirk, *The Olympic Rain Forest*:107.
[2] Campbell, *WAP*:188c-189; Edw. A. Armstrong:82.
[3] Maclean:129-130/133.
[4] Maclean:130.
[5] Goelitz:71; 72.
[6] Adapted from Sandra Stanton, who came across this myth in researching her painting for this card.
[7] Goelitz:75-76.
[8] Unless noted, much of the factual data in this section comes from a 1992 PBS series, *Nature*, "Last Stand of the Giants," with George Page; on "cedar": Alan Mitchell:136; 154.
[9] Waldman, *Atlas*:37-38.
[10] Kirk:81-85.
[11] Waldman, *Atlas*:38.
[12] Campbell, *WAP*:190.
[13] Waldman, *Encyclopedia*:237; 241.
[14] Haile, *Ethnologic Dictionary of the Navaho Language*:467-8.
[15] Kirk:108.

4
APPLE

Apple

Now as I was young and easy under the apple boughs
About the lilting house and happy as the grass was green....
~ Dylan Thomas, "Fern Hill"

The Mythic World

One of the Buddhist *Jataka Tales* tells of a Sowing Festival miracle. Everyone in the royal city had put on new tunics and gathered at the king's palace. The king and his young son, the Buddha-to-be, joined them and walked to where a thousand royal plows would prepare a field for sowing. In an adjacent field, the king saw a shady, wide-spreading rose-apple tree and ordered a couch for his son to be placed under it. Leaving the child with servants, the king continued onwards to the sowing ritual. The servants, seeing the prince was content, decided to slip away and join the festivities themselves:

> And the Future Buddha, looking hither and thither and seeing no one, arose in haste and sat him down cross-legged, and mastering his in-breathing and his out-breathing, entered on the first trance....And the shadows of the other trees passed over to the east, but the shadow of the rose-apple tree remained steadily circular. Suddenly the nurses remembered that they had left their young master alone; ...[and they returned] and also noticed the miracle of the shadow. Then they went and announced to the king, – "Sire...the shadows of the other trees have passed over to the east, but the shadow of the rose-apple tree remains steadily circular." And the king came in haste, and seeing the miracle, he bowed to honor his son.[1]

Here, as a child meditated, that one tree had become a "stillpoint of the turning world," directly connected to the sun.

Apples are also connected with the sun in Greek mythology, where they are guarded by Medusa and her two snake-haired Gorgon sisters. Beyond their dark realm is an exquisite sunset realm. Inside, a tree bears the Golden Apples of the Sun, while ponds flow with ambrosia within sight of three more of Medusa's sisters, the lovely, clear-voiced singers known as the Hesperides ("Daughters of Evening").[2] The garden's location is said to be in northwest Africa near the Atlas Mountains at the edge of the Otherworld.[3] Here, where the wedding of Zeus and Hera was once celebrated, apples of immortality were Mother Earth's gift to the bride.

In addition to the Gorgons and Hesperides, the tree was guarded by two additional rings of protection: Ladon, the unsleeping dragon and the *Graiae*, three gray-haired swan-maidens who shared a removable eye, thereby protecting themselves and the garden with the life/death powers lying in this eye. The "eye" could have been a shamanic crystal designed to focus psychic energy, but an actual object need not be assumed: meditation techniques leading to one-pointedness in the energy-center (*chakra*) known as the "third-eye" are found on many paths of spiritual initiation.

APPLE

Into this fabled realm would one day come Perseus. He had made a bargain to slay Medusa in exchange for saving his mother, Danae, from an unwanted marriage. He would first have to steal the Grey Sisters' "eye," but two deities, Athena and Hermes, had assured him of success. To reach the garden, Perseus had to pass through Egypt's Swamps of Buto, a shadowy, mysterious realm near the Libyan border.[4] This was the site of a much older drama concerning a powerful eye, serpent-wisdom, life/death secrets, and a pregnant woman *(see Papyrus)*. Here too a powerful sisterhood had worked to overcome the aftermath of a single male's malice. In the Swamps of Buto they were successful in bringing to life what had been butchered. In the Garden of the Hesperides, unfortunately, events would turn out differently, for the ancient time of mother-focused religions had waned.

Medusa was originally a winged, full-moon deity, a very old goddess worshipped by farmers who prayed to her for rain. Her protruding tongue shown in ancient art represents her rain-making power; it also suggests her silence before greater mysteries, for, with the exception of a thunderous roar (which is the meaning of *garj*, the probable Sanskrit root of *gorgon*), it is impossible to speak with a protruding tongue.

Sometimes she was accompanied by two black swans, one flying to the right, the other to the left, symbolizing Medusa's control over the interchangeable processes of life and death. This bi-potency was also manifest in her icy blood: the right side, related to the brain's left-hemisphere, seat of logic and "cold" reason, brings instant death; the left, or heart, side of the body, however, had the power to raise the dead, for this side is controlled by the right-hemisphere, seat of dreams, creativity, memories, intuition, all of which can, indeed, be life-giving.[5] In medieval "Garden of Eden" legends from Trans-Caucasian Christians, a similar bi-potency resides in the apple itself, for although tasting the serpent's apple led Eve to death, when the Virgin bites into an apple infused with the spirit of God, she becomes pregnant.[6]

Medusa was originally beautiful. Some say she rivaled Athena herself, which accounted for Athena's hostility to her.[7] It was also Medusa's beauty that drew the love of Poseidon, blue-haired sea-god and Lord of Horses. Hesiod says the two made love "in a soft meadow and flowers of spring," which may have been the Gorgons' original home.[8] Other sources say they brazenly made love on the floor of one of Athena's temples. Regardless, Athena was outraged by the affair between Medusa and Athena's rival, Poseidon, whom she had narrowly defeated in a bid for power over Athens *(see Olive Tree)*. Whatever her reasons, a hostile Athena helped Perseus hunt down Medusa.

Medusa was pregnant when she was slain. From her dismembered torso sprang two posthumous children – the winged horse Pegasus and Chrysaor, who possessed the golden sickle of the New Moon. These two had to struggle

APPLE

up through Medusa's body and out through her bleeding neck. As Robert Graves reminds us, horses were especially sacred to the moon "because their hooves make a moon-shaped mark, and the moon was regarded as the source of all water."[9] Pegasus ("water-springs") was immediately abducted by Athena and taken to Mount Helicon where the foal, born close to ambrosial springs in the garden of the Hesperides, used his moon-hooves to churn up a similar spring. Those waters would become the Muses' source of inspiration.

Unfortunately, Pegasus would eventually be forced to live tamely in Zeus' stables. When he does emerge, as in the myth of Bellerophon, it is Athena who provides the golden bridle that controls him – when that myth ends unhappily, Pegasus becomes a mere pack-beast for Zeus' thunderbolts.[10]

The target of beheading is not the head, but the throat-chakra, the *voice*, with all its multi-dimensional richness of meaning. When the head is the target, that requires bashing, not beheading. Medusa's enemies wanted control of her head – and that meant she first had to be silenced. Thus, after Medusa's murder, a triumphant Athena wore Medusa's snake-haired head on her shield, where it turned her enemies to stone. Athena also kept some of Medusa's blood in two vials, one for raising the dead, the other for killing. The rest of Medusa's blood, according to Greek legend, flowed into the sea from which Medusa had originally been born. There her blood engendered a "Tree of Life" of delicately branching red coral. Magical necklaces of this blood-red coral were fashioned to protect children throughout the ancient Greek world. Thus, Medusa, whose own children were so cruelly born, gave of her own life-affirming power to protect the children of others.[11]

In the aftermath of Medusa's murder, the golden apples of the sun became increasingly vulnerable. The sleepless dragon, Ladon, remained on guard, but he had no chance against another "hero," Heracles, one of Zeus' many sons. It would be Heracles who would slay the dragon and steal the apples. It was a new age. Sacrilegious murders and the theft of sacred mysteries had opened the way for widespread oppression and endless warfare.

Similar themes are found in northern European mythology where the Celtic apples of eternal life grow in Avalon ("Apple-isle"), a western paradise ruled by Morgan who, like Medusa before the age of heroes, had power over life and death. When King Arthur and other Celtic kings died, Morgan brought them her apples and received them into her watery kingdom under the setting sun. Nearby Scandinavians buried their dead with apples as a way of assuring them of eternal life. The Roman apple-mother was Pomona – in her honor, banquets always ended with apples, the symbol of completion.

Cutting an apple crosswise reveals a starlike pentacle, which is one reason for the great reverence given this ancient fruit. The hidden star came to symbolize the goddess in her manifestation as a maiden – the Hesperides, for example, young Hera, Persephone, or Aphrodite. The apple's fruit and fragrant flowers were frequently associated with sacred marriages and tantric rituals.[12]

The apple affirms life in all the cultures in which it is found. Yet where it is exploited for power and greed, it easily shifts its bi-potency, becoming poisoned, a "bad apple," instilling jealousy, souring the springs of life. It is in such times that we most need to return to the richness of the apple's origins in realms of music, ambrosial waters, and a meditating child's simple joy.

Botany/History

Apples were cultivated early in Europe – Greece was already growing a number of varieties by the 4th century B.C.E.[13] The blossoms are five-petalled; in cross-section, its fruit reveals a five-pointed star, associated in ancient Greece with the Evening Star, the Hespera.[14] This member of the Rose family includes more than 7,000 varieties, among them the sour little crab-apples prized by Stone Age cave dwellers. It is a hardy tree, able to tolerate temperatures as low as 40-degrees below zero, often found in regions where few other fruit trees can grow. It also thrives in warmer climates but requires enough winter cold to allow a period of dormancy. The species, *Malus pumila,* from which most of our current varieties come, probably originated in the highlands of southwestern Asia between the Caspian and Black Seas – close to the possible homeland of proto-Indo-European peoples. From there, as a non-dominant member of mixed hardwood forests, apples spread into many areas of Eurasia. In these ancient forests, it was the wild apple, far more than the oak, that was the preferred home of that curiously sacred parasite, mistletoe *(see Oak).* Neolithic peoples stored fresh apples and also cut and dried them in the sun; due to their high caloric value and ease of storage, apples were as important a part of the Stone Age diet as walnuts and hazelnuts.

The apple reached the New World with early European colonists. Once planted, seedlings moved west faster than the settlers did. Some Native Americans even planted apple orchards around their villages. The missionary, John Chapman ("Johnny Appleseed") was active in Ohio and Indiana in the early 1800s, planting seedlings, as well as Christianity.[15]

An interesting peculiarity of apples is that, like human children, they do not grow "true" from their seed: each is unique; thus, trees grown from the seeds of a single tree may differ from their parent as well as from each other. Such chance seedlings account for most of our treasured and now-familiar American

APPLE

varieties. The McIntosh, for example, was discovered when John McIntosh was clearing forestland in Ontario, Canada.[16]

Apples contain an amazing range of vitamins and minerals; they are good for the cardiovascular system, lowering blood cholesterol and blood pressure, stabilizing blood sugar, fighting upper respiratory infections, and possibly even warding off cancer.[17] Their malic and tartaric acid help safeguard the liver and digestive system; their silicon content helps feed the nervous system, reducing tension. In the words of an old rhyme:

> To eat an apple going to bed
> Will make the doctor beg his bread.[18]

The Reading

In the apple groves, time is standing still, enchanted, pointing to mysteries hidden deep inside the star-seeded fruit. This could be a sweet, juicy time for you. Taste the sunshine and rains of past seasons held within each apple. You are cautioned, however, to stay alert even while delighting in this communion with time. Nine women (three triads) guarded the golden apples in ancient Greece: the singing Hesperides ("Daughters of Evening"); the *Graiae*, (gray swan-women); and Gorgons. Despite their power, that ancient domain was where the divine feminine was most at risk, for that is where the patriarchal power-structure attacked, through theft and murder. Protect your time of inner sweetness by holding vigilantly to your outer boundaries. Do not let others exploit you – and do not exploit yourself. The trees give you this time of sweetness, rest, and song as a sacred gift. Honor it.

Apple might be inviting you to find a way of gene-splicing health back into a damaged area in the Western psyche. Medusa, after all, is the *mother* of the winged horse who churned up the Muses' waters of inspiration – her murder tells us much about the West's opinion of female creativity. How different our attitude towards the arts and inspiration might have been if no violence had been done to Medusa's voice, her creative "magic," her ability to express the depths of sea-love that lived so richly in her, her powerful, thundering, loving voice, and the space to birth her children, whether from womb or heart, and raise them unfettered by violence.

Apple also represents time at the hub of the wheel of life. When the child-Buddha meditated under the rose-apple tree, it was a time of perfect balance without pre-determined goals. Of course, this was long before he determined to escape from the wheel of karma. Regardless of gender, male-energy has a tendency to deny life through spiritual discipline. If you have had too much ease in your life, this might be a useful practice for a time. But if you draw *Apple,* you are asked to re-evaluate ascetic choices and discern whether at their core lies affirmation – or hatred – of life.

An important issue connected to *Apple* may concern your right to speak with grounded power. When you are denied your voice for too long, it may erupt in a frantic manner, plunging this way and that, like Medusa's young foal, emerging out of her corpse and torn away to provide inspiration for others while his own strangled voice remained silent. Thus, Pegasus became like so many, condemned to drudgery, unable to run free with his own kind. Find creative ways to free your voice, to sing with the sunset maidens, to thunder with the Gorgons, to whisper endearments to blue-maned Poseidon who once lay with a sea-born, rain-goddess, whether in a meadow or on the floor of Athena's temple and, together, conceived the winged horse, Pegasus. That horse, like his parents, had "water-magic" from which would come all the arts, which is to say, all that makes us truly human, empathic, creative, humorous, and wise. Mythically speaking, all art could be said to come from the wild, fluid sea-god and the passionate goddess, making love on the floor of the human mind.

Apple is also about centering. If you have drawn this card upright, and yet your life feels stuck and devoid of sweetness, consider this an invitation to discover or deepen relaxing non-ascetic practices of centering – perhaps drumming, breathing, a daily practice of gratitude, reiki, whirling, singing, meditating, or whatever helps you to dismiss worries and focus on the larger dimensions of life.

REVERSED:

A situation may be turning sour. Go back to the beginning and try to understand what life is teaching you here. Do not try to force anything lest you tilt the situation towards tragedy. Go within and be willing to wait, dormant, trusting. Even *Apple* requires a period of dormancy – the rhythms of time cannot be hurried. Be the child-Buddha, content to meditate while time stands still. Where time-issues with some trees are hard to endure (see *Hawthorn*), *Apple's* leads you to inner sweetness. Whatever happens in the outer world should not be taken personally, nor allowed to distress you. Stay centered.

If you are the offspring of a woman like Perseus' mother, who identifies with being a victim, you may have a Perseus-archetype within you. If so, the creative, wise, juicy, independent Medusa you will slay without looking her in the face will be the creative, wise, juicy, independent wellspring of *yourself*. Protect your mother as much as you can, but also keep your inner Medusa strong.

Avoid letting yourself feel paralyzed, turned to stone, trapped in fear and denial. Myths offer a way through psychological paralysis: keep your wits about you, but if Pegasus, the goddess' poetic spirit, is given free rein to churn up the "stone" you have become, you have an opportunity to be transformed into a living fountain of inspiration for yourself and others. Then, out of that darkest of mysteries, will emerge life-giving arts.

Artist's Notes:

Left foreground, Gorgon with caduceus, Corfu, 6th century B.C.E.; right foreground, terra-cotta altar relief, Syracuse, late 7th century B.C.E.; tree on right, *Medusa Ludovisi*, Roman, c. 200 B.C.E.; left background tree, Taranto, 6th century B.C.E.; necklace: Medusa's head cameo, Petescia, Italy, 1st century B.C.E.; earrings: Gorgon head appliques, Ukraine, 450-425 B.C.E.

Endnotes

[1] Adapted from Henry Clarke Warren, *Buddhism*:53-55.
[2] Yves Bonnefoy, ed., *Greek and Egyptian Mythologies*:190.
[3] H.J.Rose:23.
[4] Montet:162.
[5] Buffie Johnson, *Lady of the Beasts*:80-81; 150. On *garj*, see A. David Napier, *Masks, Transformation, and Paradox*:88.
[6] M.P. Dragomanov, *Notes on the Slavic Religio-Ethical Legends: The Dualistic Creation of the World*:61-62.
[7] Procopiou:16. Although late (c. 200 B.C.E.), the "Medusa Ludovisi" in Rome's National Museum is one example of Medusa's beauty; an exquisite full page photograph of her accompanies Kimon Friar's article, "The Stone Eyes of Medusa," following Procopiou's (op.cit.):34; also see Friar:32 for the lovely 4th century B.C.E. Medusa Rondanini. (Friar also includes vase-paintings of Perseus, Athena, Poseidon, and Hermes.)
[8] Caldwell, tr., *Hesiod's Theog*.:278-279; Caldwell:46, fn.278-279.
[9] Graves, *GM*:16.5.
[10] Graves, *GM*:75.f.
[11] Barbara Walker, *Dict*.:507.
[12] Barbara Walker, *Encyl*.:48-50.
[13] *National Geographic*, September 1951, p.330; also see Paul Friedrich:58.
[14] Buffie Johnson:153.
[15] *National Geographic*, op.cit.
[16] Ibid.
[17] Jean Carper, *The Food Pharmacy* (Bantam Books, 1988):114-117.
[18] Ibid.:114.

ASH

Ash

The Mythic World

Mythology's most famous ash is Yggdrasil, the Teutonic *axis-mundi*. Its trunk rises up through Midgard – literally, "Middle Garden," where humans live.[3] Its branches soar beyond into Asgard, the upperworld of the gods, or Aesir. The underground third is the sacred domain of the three Norns, the *Schreiberinnen* ("writing-women"), goddesses who rule time and destinies and who dwell in a warm uterine cave down among the tree's roots.

The world of the Norns is one of seeds, ancient rhythms of life, new beginnings, endings. Here they work, writing ancient wisdom in a runic language originally known only to them. In some traditions, reflecting Greek influence, they also weave, passing the shuttle of Fate amongst themselves as they weave the above-ground destinies of the world, the gods, and mortals.[4]

The tree is supported by three enormous roots stretching deep into the underworld, dividing it into three realms. One root embraces the goddess Hel's land of the dead, whose most beloved inhabitant is the god Balder, Odin's second son, treacherously slain by the trickster Loki (see *Holly*). Another root penetrates the Frost Giants' icy kingdom. The third reaches into the Norns' domain – here, after traveling over the rainbow-bridge *Bifrost* from their sky-realm, the Aesir meet daily to settle legal disputes and other issues of communal concern.[5]

An underground spring lies near each of the roots. Of the three, the Norns' is the most crucial. This is the Fountain of Life, belonging to the eldest Norn – Urd (or Erda). She tends the tree's roots, watering them day and night, ensuring that the tree remains green, filled with vitality. Urd's water rises up through the trunk and out into leafy branches, where it falls back to earth as dew, honey, or mead, which is why poets sometimes call the tree Mead-Mother.[6] Although Yggdrasil is land based, the image of its roots contained in a space bound by three springs and watered with a mead-like elixir by its guardian is analogous to India's world tree, its roots lying in the depths of the ocean in a vessel containing the elixir of immortality, tended by the goddess Vak (see *Amrita*).

The second spring, the Fountain of Wisdom, lies near the tree root in the Frost Giants' realm – it belongs to Mimir, a wise, kindly giant. This water makes one a seer, gifted with prophecy, poetry, and memories of ancient times. To become such a seer, the god Odin gave up one of his eyes and never begrudged the price. What he learned from drinking these waters inspired him to go further – he sacrificed himself to the tree by hanging himself from the branches for nine days and nine nights, eerily "riding" the tree like a shaman on a mystical horse, swinging in the winds, wounded, bleeding, seeking help, looking upwards and all around for it, but unable to find it until he finally looked straight down, back toward the Norns' Mother-realm, and saw runic writings scattered on the ground. In that moment, he "knew" their meanings. He reached down for one and it miraculously healed him.[7]

The third fountain is called Hvergelmir and its source lies near the root embracing Hel's realm in Niflheim, the land of ice; from this fountain pour waters abundant enough to supply all the great rivers on earth.[8]

Yggdrasil does not represent a static cosmos – it is a place of drama, dynamic tensions, cycles, endless change, endless regeneration. A dragon, Niogghr, and many serpents chew at the tree's roots even as Urd faithfully waters them; the green-spreading branches shelter countless winged, clawed, and horned creatures, many of whom, especially the goats and stags, daily devour the leaves and young shoots; an eagle in the top branches is the eternal foe of the dragon at the roots; the squirrel Ratatosk runs up and down the tree, carrying their insults back and forth, creating a toxic pathway along the very spine of the tree.

When the forces of destruction outpace the tree's ability to renew itself, that will launch the world's end, Ragnarok. Then Yggdrasil will shake itself, destroying gods and mortals alike in earthquakes, fire, and floods. The gentle god Balder, however, protected in Hel's realm, will survive to guide a new beginning, for hidden within the tree's trunk are the seeds of a new race of humans, a woman named *Lif* ("Life") and her mate, *Lif Prasir* ("He Who Holds Fast to Life"). With Balder's aid, these two will restore the earth and bring about a time of lasting peace.[9]

The ancient Germanic concept of Fate, as personified by the three Norns, is unrelated to our association of fate with blind chance – they had no word for "chance": the word for "luck" was the same as for "happiness."[10] When a child was born, it would first be laid upon the earth, then raised up to the skies, and finally sprinkled with water from an underground spring or well. In this consecration, the child was marked by the energy of the dynamic interaction – at that exact moment – among the three realms, Middleworld, Upperworld, and Underworld. In this interaction lay the child's Fate, a sacred pact with the divine. The connection was so close and affectionate that one's chosen deity was called *vinr, ástvinr,* "friend, dear friend."[11]

One's duty thereafter was to know oneself, accept oneself, and manifest one's destiny. In this lay one's honor. If one's dignity were injured by an enemy, this was considered an attack upon one's Fate. To thwart one's destiny would do harm to the divine; to fulfill one's destiny brought one into communion with the divine. Thus, the three worst crimes among these people were theft, insult, and perjury because each was an attack upon the divine within the victim and was punishable by death and blood vengeance.[12]

Unfortunately, such an attitude was heavily weighted in favor of heroic action, preferably in battle, where the delicate balance of respect for the divine in oneself and equally in one's neighbor tended to crumble with devastating consequences.

Further, even if the balance held steady, rarely was recognition of the divine extended to peoples outside one's group. The shining destinies of warriors came at the expense of conquered strangers. Yet the ideal was there, implicit in a healthy, affectionate relationship with Fate. The implications are fascinating:

> ...It follows from this that few universes have been as attentive to the decrees of fate, while at the same time few have been less oppressed by an anonymous or grim fatality, once fate is accepted and its aspects manifested in acts.[13]

If the intense, action-prone thrust of such an attitude were softened to embrace a more sage-like realm of non-action, if to be compassionate and wise was also viewed as a destiny, a fate, a *wyrd,* even greater than that of the dramatic hero, if the earth-magic of the Norns and Mimir could reassert itself and begin the greening of Yggdrasil anew, then the ancient Germanic view of fate might have a more significant role to play in humanity's future. Then we would see that:

> ...If the Germano-Nordic supernatural world is an onrushing force, it is not one that rushes on blindly, nor one that finds its fulfillment in its pure exercise. Rhythm balances and stylizes magical speech, magic duplicates and deepens speech, the world is put in place, justified, magnified, and thus loved, through the effect of action: once again, nothing is left to chance.[14]

In addition to being a World Tree, other mythologies often saw ash as a primal parent. In Greek mythology, Zeus carved one of the early races of humankind out of ash. In Celtic mythology, the first woman came from a mountain ash, her mate from an alder. In Norse mythology, Odin carved the first man from ash and the first woman from elm.[15] These myths point to a deep-seated sense across large areas of Europe of a special affinity between humanity and certain trees, especially ash.

Greeks, like Germanic peoples, also honored the connection between ash and water, although for the Greeks it was rainwater, not springwater, and its origins were ominous. When the abusive Uranus was castrated by his son Cronus (see *Oak* and *Laurel*), drops of blood rained down upon Mother Earth: from them, she conceived three vengeful Furies as well as their milder sisters, the rain-making ash-tree spirits, the Meliae. It was one of these ash-spirits, Adrasteia, who would later nurse and protect the infant Zeus from his father Cronus (who was as much a child-abuser as Uranus). Ash-spirits were invoked whenever rain was needed, perhaps in recognition of the fertile blood "raining" from the skies at their conception. They were especially connected with the rainy lambing month (approximately mid February to mid March) and were, therefore, revered by shepherds.[16] The ash was also considered a healing tree in Greece. Achilles had a spear made of ash which was capable of healing with one end whatever wound had been inflicted by the other.[17] The ash thus heals what it wounds, and wounds, perhaps, in order to heal on a deeper level.

Botany/History

The frost-sensitive ash did not spread into Europe, especially from Switzerland to Scandinavia, until the "hazel time" (see *Nut Trees*), a time of warming climate conditions beginning some 5,500 years ago. Its tender shoots made it second only to elm as fodder (see *Elm*). After the shoots were harvested, ash would continue growing but would be unable to flower for two to four years. Since palaeobotanists determine the range of trees and plants from ancient pollen, the restricted flowering periods of ash limited such evidence, which makes it difficult to know how widespread these trees were (even left to itself, the tree's pollen yield is small and decomposes quickly). Although it is probable that it was a frequent minority in hardwood forests, there may also have been large stands of ash alone, as there are today.[18]

Ash is both beautiful and strong. Therefore, unlike the poor drudge-tree elm, the ash, in addition to being used as fodder, was also valuable in "primitive" crafts. Since its smooth, close-grained wood is one of the most durable and elastic ever known, it was prized in carving spears and bows; the connection with the spear is so strong that in a number of Indo-European languages the word for "ash" came to mean "spear" as well. Ash was also widely used in making carts, tool handles, oars, walking sticks, and shepherds' crooks.[19]

As firewood, ash is exceptional, burning sweet even when green, and often used at the winter solstice as the Yule log. A Devonshire legend says that the Christ child was first washed and dressed by his mother in front of an ashwood fire. When a child was born in the Scottish Highlands, one end of a green ash stick was put into the fire; when the heat caused sap to ooze out at the other end, a spoonful of this juice was given to the newborn infant to bless it with the strength and protection of ash.[20]

The common ash (*Fraxinus* genus) and the unrelated rose family's mountain ash or rowan (*Sorbus aucuparia*) were generally not distinguished from one another in English, German, and other folk taxonomies since they shared such traits as leaf patterns and the hardness of their wood. Mountain ash, unlike ash proper, is extremely cold-resistant – it is found north of the tree line in Scandinavia, produces a great deal of pollen, and may have spread into Europe during the glacier periods or shortly thereafter.[21] Both the common ash and mountain ash or rowan are associated with runes (see *Rowan*).

Ash grows from 50-125 feet high; its generally inconspicuous flowers are followed by winged seeds, "ash-keys." Before laying her eggs, these seeds are curiously vital in the diet of a female finch, a bird celebrated for song, as well as for prophetic powers. In addition to its strong, lightweight wood, ash is valued as a shade tree. The lifespan is relatively short: few ash trees reach an age of 200 years.[22]

Ash is popular in folk medicine as a cure for poisons. In medieval times, it was believed that the tree could neutralize anything poisonous lying within its shadow; thus, ash leaves in England and ash sap in Germany and Bohemia were used to counteract snake venom. Ash buds and bark were also used by Native Americans to heal rattlesnake bites. In addition to its power over poisons, ash's bitter bark is both a tonic and an astringent; bark and leaves are also useful as laxatives.[23]

The Reading

Ash is the World-tree of patterned order. Muse-goddesses spin life into the roots while galaxies of stars spiral out of the leafy crown. Here, everything makes sense and higher purposes stand revealed. Do not expect everything to fall smoothly into place, however. The dramatic forces of unraveling may at times seem to outpace the steady work of the spinning Norns. Avoid emotional poisons. Resist lashing out at others, insulting them, dehumanizing them, turning them into scapegoats. What you see as an "enemy" out there could be a mirror of the enemy hidden inside you.

A sacrifice of cherished illusions, prejudices, or something else you hold dear may be required – and you may not know until it is over just what it was. Whatever it was is karmic, essential for the further unfolding of your path. Understand and accept this with patience. The Norns spin wisely and understand those dynamics of the distant past which may be hidden from your current awareness. The destiny they spin for you is not meant to be oppressive. Develop a sense of affection for those Powers guiding your life – re-consecrate yourself to them. You might wish to do the ancient ritual *(see Myth section)* of lying on the earth, then standing and stretching to the skies, finally sprinkling yourself with water from a source you consider sacred.

REVERSED:

Things are askew, out-of-joint. You may not be in harmony with your own path. "Destiny" is a volatile concept if too much ego determines its course, or if too much fear attempts to thwart it. Try to stop the critical voices that run up and down your spine spreading doubts. Lighten up. If you have been too sedentary, let life call you into invigorating action again. If you have been too active, find a more compassionate balance. Do not blindly drain your energies without taking time to restore them from deep down in your roots. If there is no sense of happiness or honeyed mead in your life, no time to enjoy the beauty and greenness, something is wrong. You are allowing your new shoots to be harvested right back down to the ground and used as fodder – this cannot continue if you are ever to flower. Thus Ash warns you to find a new perspective, as Odin did when he hung upside down for nine days, looking everywhere except straight down for help. Find what is hidden, take time to decipher it, stay open to the oracular roots until you feel restored. You might even go into a meditation in which you descend to Mimir's spring and ask the kindly old giant what he wants from you in exchange for the Waters of Remembrance. Explore the resulting insights.

Endnotes

[1] Cited in Roger Cook, *The Tree of Life*:11-12.
[2] Regis Boyer, "Elements of the Sacred among the Germanic and Norse Peoples":227.
[3] Ralph Metzner, *The Well of Remembrance*:198-199, 200.
[4] Cook:12.
[5] H.R. Ellis Davidson, *Gods and Myths of Northern Europe*:26.
[6] Davidson:26; Larousse:365, 390, 392.
[7] Larousse: 371, 369.
[8] Larousse:365; Walker,D:460.
[9] Davidson:26-27; Cook:12; Larousse:365; Boyer:232.
[10] Boyer:231.
[11] Boyer:231.
[12] Boyer:241.
[13] Boyer:231.
[14] Boyer:234.
[15] Altman:75.
[16] Graves, *GM:* 6.a, 6.3-4; 7.b, 7.3; 32.3.
[17] Altman:140.
[18] Friedrich:97, 98.
[19] Friedrich:96-97; Geoffrey Grigson, *The Englishman's Flora*:292, 295.
[20] Grigson:292-294.
[21] Friedrich:97.
[22] Cowles:79-80; Mitchell:116; Beryl Rowland, *Birds with Human Souls*:63.
[23] Altman:140.

Artist's Notes:

Erda or Urd (on the left) represents the past. Her necklace is from Gryta, Sweden, Viking Age (8th-11th centuries); she holds a Frankish pitcher from a Viking grave at Birka, Sweden, 9th century. Verthandi or Verdandi (in the middle) represents the present. Her necklace was found at Birka, Sweden with a pendant depicting a weaving goddess from southwest Germany, 6th century; her small plaque depicts three goddesses holding a child, a scroll and a bowl from the Romano-Gaulish settlement at Vertillum, France. Sculda (on the right) represents the future. She held the scroll that the future was written upon. They all hold spindles. Associated with weaving, they wove the future for each person at the time of birth. The stags in the branches of the tree, Dain, Dvalin, Duneyr and Durathror, represent the four winds. The relief behind them, depicting deer chewing on the branches of the Tree of Life, is from the Staukirke, Umes, Norway, c. 11th century.

ASH

BEECH

Beech

> ...thou, light-winged Dryad of the trees
> In some melodious plot
> Of beechen green, and shadows numberless,
> Singest of summer in full-throated ease.
> ~ John Keats
> "Ode to a Nightingale"

The Mythic World

In ancient Italy, Diana, goddess of childbirth and protector of children, was widely worshipped in beech groves. "Beech" in Latin is *fagus*, derived from the proto-Indo-European **bhagos*. Other variants of the word, Old Norse *bok* and Old English *boc*, point to the relationship between beech and sacred writing, which eventually led to the English word "book." Beech-bark tablets were inscribed with symbols because the smooth, pale bark invited such use; these oracular runes were then used in seeking the beech-goddess' wisdom.[1] Beech is often confused with oak. Both trees bear edible nuts (acorns and beechnuts) and oracles were sought in both beech and oak groves. Greece's eco-system, however, was kinder to oak and eventually the Greek word for beech shifted to oak.

The oracular connection with beech remained strong elsewhere, however, especially in France and Italy, where magnificent beech forests were found dedicated to Moon-goddess, Diana.[2] Among her many titles was Diana of Nemi (Latin *nemus*, "grove"). Sir James Frazer wrote that Nemi was a sacred grove of mistletoe-hung oaks, known as "the golden bough," but this reflects the general confusion between oak in Greece and beech elsewhere. Italy's Nemi was a major cult center in its own right, unrelated to Greek shrines, for although Diana eventually came to be linked with Artemis, the Greek goddess of childbirth and wild creatures, Diana's own identity arose independently and was indigenous to the forests of Italy and adjoining lands to the north.

Nemi itself was established along the shores of Lake Nemi in the Alban hills south of Rome. There, in a round temple among great beeches, Diana's hearth was tended by virgin-priestesses who kept the holy fire burning continuously,[3] for fire represented the fertilizing power of the moon. The region's hand-carved beechen bowls and cups were much prized[4]; such vessels would have been used in rituals by outcasts and runaway slaves who were granted sanctuary there.[5] To Diana, these supplicants were her children and, like the goddess Nemesis ("Fate"), Diana was the avenger of wrongs done to her children.

Widespread legends suggest that a priest-king was selected to function as Diana's consort in sacred rituals. Eventually, this King of the Wood would be killed by a young newcomer, who would later die in his own turn. If small communities of male refugees lived within the protection of Diana's groves, ritual combat might indeed have relieved boredom and frustration. Originally, however, it is likely that these groves were a refuge, not for men, but for women and children,[6] who desired to live in peace, worshipping the goddess in her moon-smooth beech guise, winding in nocturnal processions, chanting as they went. They ate the goddess' beechnuts, carved her wood into cups from which they drank in communion, and sought her oracles from words written on her bark. That the goddess was concerned with sacred, caring language is suggested by a passage in Ovid in which he states that she "abhors boastful words."[7] Such sisterhoods had no need for the high drama of ritual combat. Working together, sharing in the rearing of children: this was drama enough. The women lived as friends, wise companions, like the ancient beech trees themselves, nurtured among the like-minded, all their roots touching, bonding, creating communal strength.

The tradition of a mother-goddess "nurse" who cared for the abused and weak goes back thousands of years into Europe's pre-history. Hundreds of small statues portray her as bear-headed (and indeed Diana's Greek counterpart, Artemis, is a Bear-Mother). Many statues show her protecting a weakling child.[8] This divine nurse survived the arrival of patriarchal Indo-European herdsmen. Her persona and functions were slowly transformed into lunar-cycle goddesses associated with fertility and childbirth, among them Diana in Italy, and Artemis and Hekate in Greece. Statues of these later goddesses often show them carrying a burning torch as a symbol of the fertilizing power of the moon as well as of their ability to give warmth and protection to the young.[9]

W.E. Butler writes that next to the always hospitable pines and firs, the most powerful trees from which to draw revitalizing energy are beech, oak, and apple.[10] This awareness perhaps emerges out of thousands of years in which abused slaves and outcasts retreated to the protection of these groves. It recognizes that beech, oak, and the friendly apple, have a very welcoming "aura" out of which flows a mighty stream of restorative energy.

Botany/History

The wind-fertilized beech spread west out of the Carpathians and Caucasus into more ancient mixed forests of oak, ash, hazel, elm, and linden. Eventually, beech forests would be found within a great triangle from Norway down to Spain in the west and Turkey in the east. It is a sensitive tree, unable to produce yearly flowers, and with a sparse pollen supply even when it does flower.[11] It thrives under the shade of older native forests and eventually replaces them, since the seedlings of those pre-existing forests are unable to flourish under dense beeches.[12] Because of this, by 1700 B.C.E., many of the primeval forests of Europe were dominated either by beech or oak.[13] Where oaks prefer wet soils like heavy clay, beeches need light, well-drained, chalky soils or porous limestone. Thick, muscular beech roots then spread far out, creating a sturdy base; the growing tips reach down into wetter layers, where they drink, but do not penetrate. Although such roots lack depth, their wide-ranging and powerfully anchored networks nevertheless meet the tree's high water needs.[14]

A beech forest will never grow as a pioneer on virgin land: it is what is known as a "climax forest," meaning that it cannot thrive unless other species have first served as its "mother-goddess nurse," shading it and preventing the growth of strangling grasses.[15] Thus, a beech forest, just like a new generation of children, marks the climax, or culmination, of many earlier species.

The smooth, gray-barked beech may grow to a height of a hundred feet with a girth of more than thirty feet.[16] The tree has small, oval, bright green leaves and edible, delicate-flavored three-sided nuts paired inside a little four-sided burr.[17] In Europe's early pig-based economies, pigs were driven into the autumn forests to feed on sweet beechnuts.

Beeches like their own company and survive best in dense forests, where some have lived for nearly 250 years. Those growing in more open spaces tend to develop heavy, gnarled branches – and then, with little warning, they may die.[18] Denied closer companionship, it is as if they see no point in continuing such extravagant growth.

The Reading

Everyone needs beechen-green times to join with friends and feel contented with life. Drawing Beech points to such a non-abusive period of quiet friendship and mutual support. It is a "we" tree, not an "I" tree, which is not to suggest that you will have to submerge your individuality. On the contrary, in the midst of generous and calm companionship, you will be free to grow into your own potential without the constant stress of competition. This will not be a time of exciting high drama, but your basic needs will be met and you will be able to grow strong and tall, secure in the company of those who share your values and beliefs.

Thus, Beech suggests that you would do well to accept her advice and relax and heal among like-minded companions. Your roots need to be in light, airy soils – nothing soggy or depressing. In this protected companionship, you are invited to find fulfillment by mothering others and/or being mothered yourself. You might wish to explore your deeper connections, "roots," to the realm of intuition, the moon, simple rituals of shared friendship. In meditation, you might go into your own inner-grove, and see who greets you there. Who hugs you? Whom do you hug? Alternately, you might wish to find an actual beech tree, sit under it, aligning your spine with it, and "cuddle" into its spirit.[19]

REVERSED:

Consider whether a person, behavior pattern, belief-system, or your own emotions are abusing you. If you feel you are being treated as a slave, drudge, outcast, or victim, you might be caught in ritual-combat mode, a "kill or be killed" mentality, either with yourself or with a colleague, friend, or foe. Whether your role is that of the Old King or the New King of the Wood *(see Myth section),* you are invited to go back into an earlier level where richer choices still exist. Learn from the goddess about deeper wellsprings where your roots can drink gently, without penetrating, claiming, or invading. The solace of those wellsprings is her gift to you.

If you have allowed yourself to become isolated through excessive work, grief, or introversion, it may be time to seek a more active support network. Otherwise, your health may be at risk – like the tree, deprived of nourishing relationships, you may topple.

On the other hand, you might already be too active, spread too thin among too many people – if so, it might be time to focus more clearly, sink your roots more deeply, and retreat to the company of a few trusted companions.

Yet another possibility is that you have been enjoying the "we" for too long, using this as an excuse for not risking your ideas elsewhere. You may have honed your skills in preaching to the converted, but it might be time to take what you have gained within your circle of safety and carry it forth into the wider world around you.

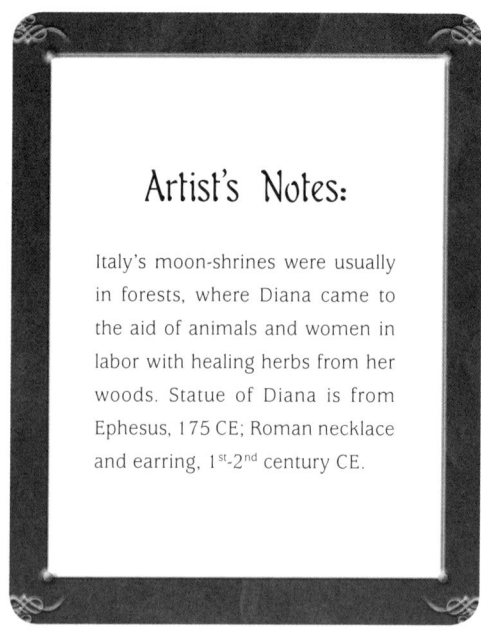

Artist's Notes:

Italy's moon-shrines were usually in forests, where Diana came to the aid of animals and women in labor with healing herbs from her woods. Statue of Diana is from Ephesus, 175 CE; Roman necklace and earring, 1st-2nd century CE.

Endnotes

1 Friedrich:108-110.
2 Friedrich:109-110.
3 Frazer:v.1,41;
  Stapleton:67.
4 Sargeaunt:44.
5 Frazer/Gaster:760.
6 Graves, GM:6.3.
7 Walker, WEMS:722.
8 Gimbutas, G&G:190-5.
9 Gimbutas, G&G:196-200.
10 Butler:30-31.
11 Friedrich:111-112.
12 Mitchell:32.
13 Friedrich:112.
14 Mitchell:32;
  Cowles:74.
15 Mitchell:32.
16 Hooker, SF:367;
  Butcher:962.
17 Friedrich:109.
18 Mitchell:32.
19 Butler:30-31.

7
BIJA

Bija

>...You will behold a fire leaping skittishly
>like a child over the aery waves;
>or a fire without form,
>from which a voice emerges;
>or a rich light,
>whirring around the field in a spiral.
>   "The Epiphany of Hekate"
>   from the *Chaldean Oracles*[1]

The Mythic World

This is Seed. It is not a seed you could hold in your hand. It is the formless primal impulse or point at which everything starts. A profound example of this comes from the opening passage of the 2nd century C.E. "Epiphany of Hekate," where we are given a sense of those moments when the Greek goddess Hekate, as the playful fire-seed, the *bija* (the evocative Sanskrit word for "seed" – see Shiva and "Seed" sections that follow), first begins to take form. She is a skittish fire, a divine child dancing in the waves, a fire-which-speaks, a Burning Bush, a whirring light, spinning as playfully as a child's top and creating that spiraling energy-field upon which creation plays out its processes.

Hekate, as Cosmic Soul, brings all creation into being out of that fiery, yet playful spark. She is Birth-Mother and Death-Mother. Another of her titles was "Closer of the Boundaries of Things within the Cosmos." That title reflects her power to harmonize all forms, bringing each out of a state of primal oneness, guiding the forms through millions of stages of multiplicity until, within the vast boundaries she has set, each reaches fulfillment.[2]

It seems strange to think of Hekate as a child. We know her as a withered crone, sinister witch, hag-goddess of the waning moon. Yet, in *bija*, she reclaims her wholeness and reminds us that when old age is wise, as opposed to egocentric, it is also child-like, spontaneous as fire, and full of joyous music.

In the ancient world, Hekate's vast powers were deeply respected. To those who sought her oracular wisdom, she taught techniques of theurgy to guide a seeker into the depths. The "Epiphany of Hekate" is the goddess' own description of how she appears when a seeker summons her:

> ...But [it is also possible] that you will see a horse
> flashing more brightly than light,
> or a child mounted on the swift back of a horse,
> a fiery child or a child covered with gold,
> or yet again a naked child;
> or even a child shooting arrows,
> standing upon a horse's back.[3]

These are the images a child spins out of fantasy, but this makes them no less real for that child. If one is a goddess, of course, as Hekate is, then fantasy is actual reality. She is at once a radiant mare as well as the child mounted on this mare. They are one, child and mare, the fragile and the strong, the two-legged and the four-legged, the stumbling and the swift. The child learns to take strength from the mare, becoming fiery, covered with gold, even blissfully naked, fearless, an acrobat shooting arrows in a cosmic circus of light.

Equal to her ability to bring life into being is her ability to take it out of being. As Hekate expresses it in her "Epiphany":

> ...You will observe all things growing dark,
> For the curved bulk of the heavens disappears
> and the stars do not shine;
> the light of the Moon is hidden
> and the Earth does not stand steady.
> All things are revealed in lightning.[4]

Here, what has taken form is now dissolving back again into the primal sound/light-seed. Light has become a shimmering, pregnant blackness. In India, this process is represented by the god Shiva who drums, beating seed-sounds as he dances through the blackness. Gradually, as sound waves expand outwards, further and further from Shiva, they become denser, more solid, and a universe of form takes shape. At the end of each cycle of time, however, everything is drawn back again, dissolving into the formless energy of the pure seed-sound, *OM*. This too is expressed in Hekate's "Epiphany":

> ...But when you see the sacred fire without form,
> Shining skittishly throughout the depths of the Cosmos,
> Listen to the voice of the fire.[5]

Thus, even in this formless state, Hekate and other archetypes of wholeness remain.

The Seed

There is no tree, no botany, no history. This is the Seed. This is the realm of *ch'ien*, the "Creative," in the *I Ching*; the blank Rune; the zero; the Tarot's wise "Fool"; the One; the Alpha and the Omega; the Beginning and the End; the divine Child; the Old Seer.

Bija is Sanskrit for "seed." Other Sanskrit meanings include source, primary cause of being, mystical sound-syllables (from which spin the origins of the universe), semen ("seed" for mammals), even the position of a child's arms at birth as that child prepares to embrace a new life.

In the oracle, *bija* stands for the primal undifferentiated seed-potential out of which all life emerges. *Bija* is sound-seed, light-seed, soul-seed, embryo-seed, tree-seed. It is that spark of fire, that "seed" of light that initiates the whole

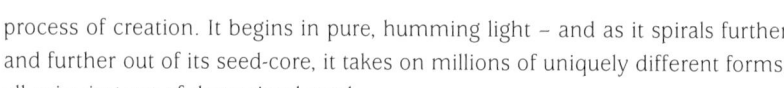

process of creation. It begins in pure, humming light – and as it spirals further and further out of its seed-core, it takes on millions of uniquely different forms, all spinning out of that primal seed.

The Reading

When you draw the primal seed, *bija*, all possibilities are open. This is a time of destiny – do not hold back out of pettiness, modesty, a conviction of unworthiness, or any other form of self-hate. This is a powerful time for you, a time to explore, full of a wise-fool's curiosity and delight. Let yourself range through new times, spaces, ideas – "boldly go where no one has gone before."

If you are agonizing over several paths or choices, drawing *bija* frees you: it tells you that you cannot make a mistake no matter what you choose, as long as your decision is based upon a deep sense of self-worth. Decide from strength, not fear. Be aware of your interconnectedness within the vast shimmering patterns of the cosmos – and know that you are never alone.

This may require loosening bonds that have held you back from your own fulfillment. It may feel like decay or a death as you allow what was once solid to dissolve back into formlessness. In that process, however, as form returns to energy, out of the "emptiness" of that energy, new form comes to birth – and a child's arms reach out to new possibilities. Nothing is ever lost. It just re-balances and shapeshifts through endless multiplicity, a dance of cosmic playfulness.

Drawing *bija* should lead to a positive emotional response – a fire-spark leaping within you, a sense of pleasure, an "Aha!" If it leads instead to disappointment or a sense of being overwhelmed by the magnitude of what lies before you, this might be a signal that your question is premature. You might not be ready to live with the long-term results of your choice. You might be asking about a project or situation which has not yet come to fruition. If so, allow it to lie awhile in the realm of the formless while you get on with other aspects of your life. If you do not know how to sort through those other aspects, ask of the Oracle again.

If you feel neither disappointed nor overwhelmed, but you do feel trapped, cramped or simply "blah" when you draw *bija*, this is a strong indication that whatever you are asking about is part of an worn-out pattern and no longer has any real energy for you. You are beating a dead horse. Let go, boldly, of whatever it is and release it to the formless. Then re-focus your question and ask of the Oracle again.

REVERSED:

There is no reversed position because the opposites are united in *bija*, yet this unity carries with it a powerful reminder. In popular imagination, an old hag or crone is boring, dull, her life diminished to petty concerns. She stumbles along, an easy prey for those who victimize the weak. *Bija* reminds you that what feels weakest and most vulnerable in you needs to be honored nevertheless, because under the mask of frailty lies the fire-child goddess who created the world. You demean the goddess, whether in yourself or in others, at your peril.

Live from your strength, not your weakness. Regardless of your age or imagined closeness to death, there is that in you that does not deserve to die untimely. It is strong, gentle, fierce, able to balance light and dark, able to live purposefully regardless of the blindness around you. Give it free rein.

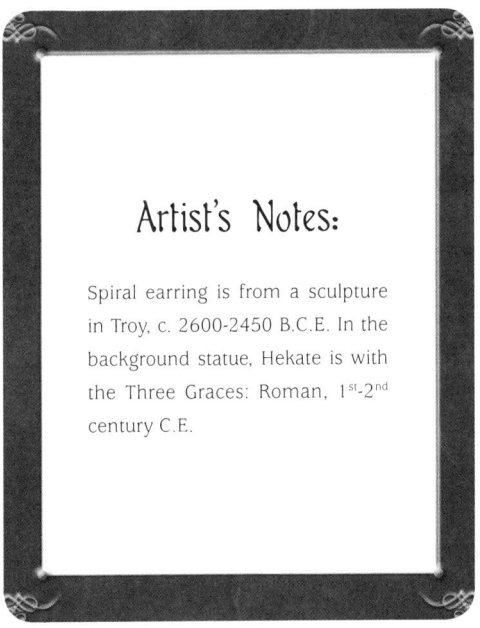

Artist's Notes:

Spiral earring is from a sculpture in Troy, c. 2600-2450 B.C.E. In the background statue, Hekate is with the Three Graces: Roman, 1st-2nd century C.E.

Endnotes

1 Johnston:111.
2 Johnston:40.
3 Johnston:111.
4 Ibid.
5 Ibid.

8
BIRCH

Birch

In song she deplores not just the loss of her freedom, but her link with both the forest and the magical maiden *rusalki* who inhabit it....The bride was herself assimilated to the birch tree. In the bathhouse, she abandoned the divinity of the tree to dedicate herself to the cultivated maternal earth.

~ Joanna Hubbs[1]

The Mythic World

In writing of the birch, Lebanese-Armenian scholar Elizabeth Terzian tells us that:

> At the dawn of the Russian culture stands the birch, tall and slender, in her glorious white beauty and silvery leaves....Besides its lightness, elegance, and beauty, the birch is essentially a "tree of light."[2]

According to Paul Friedrich, Indo-European linguistics bears this out because nouns for "birch" are related to parallel verbs meaning "to shine, shimmer, gleam, become white," which suggest that "the Proto-Indo-Europeans conceived of the birch as somehow quintessentially white, shimmering...." Considering northern European reverence for the birch in sacred rituals and lore, Friedrich argues "that the birch has been a female-virgin symbol for many Indo-Europeans for over five thousand years."[3]

In Old Russia, the most revered of the *rusalki* (female forest spirits) were those of the birch, "the most holy of trees, the first to flower in the spring."[4] In late winter, as sap began rising in the trees, the *rusalki* left the frozen rivers and streams where they lived during the cold months and climbed back into the still leafless birch trees, weaving fresh linen garments to replace their icy winter garb, and combing their long Medusa-like serpent hair, "milking" it to bring the warm rains of spring.[5] Some of the *rusalki* had always been spirits, daughters of a water king, or a bird king, reflecting their dual nature as spirits of tree and water. As Terzian writes, "*rusalka* is connected with *rus*, an old Slavonic word for stream, or with *ruslo*, the bed of a river...."[6] Other *rusalki* were the souls of abused or rejected maidens who joined the others after drowning themselves.[7]

The birch spirit also appeared alone as the Great Goddess, the *Rusalka*, who, like her maidens, was untamed, virginal. Russian history professor, Joanna Hubbs, writes:

> The *rusalka* in Russian lore is a maiden; she is a spinner who regulates human and animal fertility, the cycle of the seasons, the moon, and the weather.[8]

Thus, she is the Tree of Life, spinner of destinies, and "guardian of the well-being of the community."[9] As leafy branches spin patterns in the wind, so do the *rusalka* and her maidens spin future patterns for young women whose fertility will insure their people's survival:

> ...the Russian birch had an oracular nature. The *rusalki* who sat on its branches and watered it were, like the Fates, spinners; they decided who died and who would be reborn, who prospered and who perished, who married and who would be barren. The tree was the spindle out of which they spun out human life. Just as they united the living with the dead, so too they raised the water from the ground into the skies, making rain.[10]

The *rusalki*, their newly woven linen garments washed and drying on the still bare tree limbs while long, golden, pollen-rich male and female catkins hung all around them, called out to the village girls to bring them gifts. Young women came singing, decorating the trees with long ribbons and embroidered votive towels of linen.[11] Together they celebrated, wild tree-maidens and high-spirited village maidens, rejoicing in their freedom.

The *rusalki* had a starkly different relationship with young men. When the spirits lured men with their songs, those who recklessly followed the call were destroyed.[12] There is an obvious attraction-aversion here – the *rusalki* are untamed, willing slayers of men, yet they also spin destinies that will turn young maidens into brides, the property of men. It is as if both birch and *rusalki* are trying to adapt to new customs, yet their hearts remain firmly rooted in a more ancient time – a time when birch forests grew untouched by ax or hand, and young women freely chose, or left, their mates at will. In the disparity between ancient and contemporary times lies a resentful, brooding, unpredictable power liable to flash out and destroy. As men lured village-virgins to their beds, so forest-virgins lured men to their graves.

> Perhaps the anger of the *rusalki* in Russian folk belief...specifically reflected the suppressed fury of peasant women whose lives and cults were treated with rough disrespect by men, who were nonetheless fearful of their magic.[13]

Despair lies here, too, a despair born of the knowledge that for long centuries, female power has been largely despised and oppressed by men – sadly, with the enthusiastic aid of many women. This is poignantly apparent in the women's beautiful, yet eerie, spring festival, the *Rusaliia,* which celebrates a time when the teeming fertility of the *rusalki* is forcibly taken from the wild forest and brought into the domesticated village.

The *Rusaliia* begins with the central ritual of the Semik (the root, *sem',* is related to words for seven, seed, sperm, and family). This occurs on the seventh Thursday after Russian Easter and just before the celebration of Pentecost Sunday (Whitsuntide). The seven-week period from Easter to Pentecost was a time during which the souls of the dead, welcomed back at Eastertime in an ancient pagan ritual (*Radunitsa*) performed by old women and very young women, "...

were thought to linger in trees, fields, and gardens, bringing life and vigor."[14] Beginning on the seventh Thursday after Easter, this help from the dead would be fully focused and actualized in the *Rusaliia*, a powerful women's ritual that no man was allowed to see – in fact, in some regions, any intruder would be torn apart by these Russian maenads.[15]

> In the evening, girls went into the woods to pick a Semik birch and mark it, sometimes tying its tips together as if to trap the rising sap to energize the fields and village where it would be carried. Next morning, the girls would go to the birch with eggs and beer, offerings of food for the dead. They would decorate the tree with ribbons and [embroidered] towels....[16]

In the clear morning light, these maiden-priestesses would then braid living birch branches together, sometimes weaving in domesticated stalks of dried wheat or rye as a prayer for abundant crops in the year to come. The braided branches would then be tied into large garlands, creating leafy portals: "the girls would embrace one another through them, pledging eternal blood ties...on behalf of their families."[17]

> The braided tree branches perhaps represented the braiding of the girls' hair to "trap" their own fertility and tame it until they married. The Semik rite, over which the birch tree presided totemically [...] involved the unification of all nature and humanity....[The girls] pledged themselves to the birch, which was to be tamed like them for the benefit of the cultivated land and the continuation of the human community....Kissing through the braided and circular boughs, they became possessed with the fertilizing powers of earth, as well as the ancestral family spirits.[18]

Possessed by these spirits of earth and the dead, the girls were empowered to do what would otherwise have been a sacrilege: to kill the tree. After hewing it, they carried the garlanded sacrifice ceremoniously through the fields and into the village. There the tree, "decorated like a goddess," was brought into a house and entertained by the entire village, feted and fed like a beloved deceased family member. Groups of girls then returned to the forest to gather more birch branches for festooning the entire village:

> Houses and churches were decorated with the holy birch so that the whole community assumed a festive air, itself transformed into a forest and infused with its vitality....[The girl-priestesses] would themselves begin to select mates, like alluring *rusalik*. They invited men to come and stroll with them, to drink vodka and eat eggs.[19]

BIRCH

Two days later, on Pentecost Sunday, the same young women would turn the birch out of the village, carrying her to the river, and ritually stripping her of leaves, ribbons, and embroidered votive towels. As they undressed her, they, like *rusalki*, unloosened their own braided hair and sang poignant songs reflecting their future fate as well as that of the birch, who "pleaded with them not to send her away:"

> I was curly, I was well-dressed,
> But now I stand naked.
> All my clothes have been taken away,
> All my leaves have been torn away.
> [My] friends take me away,
> [They] throw me in the fast river.[20]

The maidens who had been the birch's friends now consign her to the river:

> ...Semik or Rusalka was drowned in order to provide the needed rainfall for the sprouting crops.[21]

As the current carried the stripped tree away, the girls threw ribbons and garlands after her. "I will throw my garland into the water," they sang, "so that the wheat grows thick."[22] Hubbs comments tersely:

> If the garland sank, its owner would perish in the course of the year and would thereby join the *rusalka*...; if it floated, she would marry. In either case she would be a source of natural abundance.[23]

If her garland floated, oracular patterns made by the ribbons floating in the wake of the tree allowed each maiden to further predict her future husband as well as her fate in marriage.[24]

Marriages were arranged in the spring and summer but usually not celebrated until year's end in October after the autumn harvest was gathered. Autumn was also when the birch *rusalki* "reappeared to announce their return to the underworld."[25] In anticipation of this, women, young and old...

> ...would go outside, where swings had been set up for them to imitate the behavior of the *rusalki* in the tree boughs, swinging back and forth as though imparting the magic of "feminine power" to the soil. They sang about the declining vitality of the sun, about the ancestral spirits in the underworld, and about the water and tree nymphs who were withdrawing to their winter dwellings.[26]

"The culmination of the year's cycle in wedding plans," Joanna Hubbs states, "was not a joyful one." Brides often wove votive towels embroidered with an image of their powerful *rusalka*, the Great Goddess, but their "social reality was quite at odds with such an assertion of female power....This is apparent in the large numbers of wedding songs suffused with poignancy, melancholy, and even bitterness."[27]

Marriage was a boon for Russian husbands because it gave them prestige and heirs. But wives were deprived of all freedom, often beaten, driven like slaves, and drained of all vitality by too much child-bearing. They might well have envied the Semik tree, drifting dead and peaceful along the currents of Russia's rivers. The women's bitter, lamenting songs reflected their sorrow but Hubbs suggests that the songs:

> ...may also refer to a distant period when matrilocal weddings did not deprive the bride of the security of her family or of the freedom she continued to prize.[28]

In some regions, especially in the Ukraine, the bathhouse became the point of demarcation. As the *rusalki* retreated to the cold waters of a Russian winter, the bride-to-be went with her attendants to the steaming bathhouse for the *devushnik*, a ritual in which they mourned the coming loss of the bride's long, lustrous braid, with all that it implied. *Devushnik:* the word comes from *deva*, Russian for "girl," but the word is related to Sanskrit, where it means a deity or "shining one." In the bathhouse, the future bride is given a substitute for her braid – a special ribbon set with beads:

> In song she deplores not just the loss of her freedom, but her link with both the forest and the magical maiden *rusalki* who inhabit it. The [beaded ribbon] was often dedicated to the birch tree, where it was ceremoniously hung. The bride was herself assimilated to the birch tree. In the bathhouse, she abandoned the divinity of the tree to dedicate herself to the cultivated maternal earth.[29]

The wedding day soon followed upon this ritual. The bride's own mother would turn into an "enemy," cutting off her daughter's serpent-braid and replacing it with a married woman's traditional headdress.[30] With this, the girl's final tie to the birch forests and their *rusalki* was severed. She was now a wife. Motherhood would follow. Life would be hard.

The young, serpent-haired *rusalki* spirits of the great birch forests lived alone, without mates, and yet nurtured the future mothers of the village. An elder spirit, "once a mother and now past childbearing age," also lived near them in the birch forests. This was the Baba Yaga, the great Crone Goddess.[31] Depending upon how one approached her, she could show either her good or her evil side, for she, like the *rusalki*, resented "the patriarchal denigration of their cult" and harbored a grudge "against those who controlled religious and social life."[32] If you approached with respect, reining in your curiosity about her, she would provide necessary help; if you approached with a sour, demanding spirit, she would kill you, put you in her cooking pot and recycle you into something that would better nurture her realm.

Where the *rusalki* are often depicted as a group of maidens, there is only one Baba Yaga:

> Multiple, like their nature and productions, the maidens suggest the many seeds which fall to earth but do not always attain their full cycle of growth. But Yaga is like the withered flower pod brimming with new seed. She is the expression of realized potential, the fulfillment of the cycle of life associated with women. She has known all things: virginity (she has no consort), motherhood (her children in plant and animal form are legion), and old age (she gathers all things into her abode to die)....The living and the dead commingle; the moon and the sun, the evening and morning star, begin and end their heavenly course from her abode.[33]

Yaga punishes the greedy, the despoilers of earth and sky, but she is helpful to mortals who win her favor: she might give magic weapons or a winged horse to heroes; she gives magical instruments to those whose music pleases her; she helps lovesick young men win their brides.[34] To Vasilisa, a little girl who has the good sense not to ask too many invasive questions, Yaga even gives a pole topped by a skull, from whose eyes flash the gift of light, which frees the child from those who would abuse her.[35]

As a goddess of the skies, Yaga rides in a mortar, pushing herself against the winds with a pestle and sweeping away all traces of her passage with a birch broom. This is a goddess who demands secrecy, privacy, mystery. She, who has seen everything, chooses not to reveal her hidden paths. Symbolically, her mortar and pestle represent womb and phallus, which means that this crone-goddess is present in every act of love-making, flying through the skies of human ecstasy, sweeping away all trace of her presence while at the same time creating life and spinning new destinies.

Botany/History

Related words for birch are found from the Indus Valley (where *bhurja'* dates at least from the late Vedic period), to Iran, and all the way across northern Europe; even non-Indo-European Basque appears to have borrowed its word for birch, *buruki*, from some form of the proto-Indo-European word, *'bherH-g-o-*. Cognates of this word appear so uniformly and across such a wide range that linguists use it as a basis for formal theories relating to proto Indo-European. In most cases the birch-words are feminine and refer to the white birch (*Betula pendula*), a tree with obvious "physical brightness" related to its very distinctive white or silvery bark.[36]

The birch does well in cold regions. After lying dormant in winter temperatures for a few months, its tiny winged seeds "germinate in the melting snows of spring." As glaciers slowly retreated in Europe, birch migrated from Russia at about the same time as the pine, both dominating during the Preboreal (8500-7200 B.C.E.), marginalizing earlier shade-intolerant willows and aspen. Some 2,000 years later during the Atlantic period (5500-3000 B.C.E.), birch was crowded out by the aggressive hazel's advance but by the Subboreal (3000-800 B.C.E.), both birch and willow had made a comeback and remain prominent in northern forests.[37]

There are about three dozen kinds of birch, some barely shrubs in Arctic and Alpine regions, but others growing up to seventy feet. Birch trees grow swiftly, but rarely live beyond a century. The graceful tree's first focus is on fertility – while its branches are still bare, it puts forth long, pollen-bearing catkins; only after the pollen has been released do birch's lovely, light green, saw-edged leaves unfold.

Native Americans used the trees' hardy bark to cover canoes and tipis; in the eastern part of the country, oils from the bark of the fragrant black birch (*B. lenta*) were used as wintergreen. Worldwide, birch sap, akin to maple syrup, served either as syrup or as the basis for birch beer.[38]

In early Russia, a proverb points to the birch's value in four ways: it is "the source of light; it stifles cries; it cleans; and it cures." As a source of light, bound branches of birch served as torches during long Russian winters. To stifle cries, its rich sugary sap was used to soothe children and, when brewed into birch beer, it soothed adults as well. Its branches cleansed by scourging and invigorating the body in Russian steambaths. It cured in a variety of ways – its young leaves provided a helpful tea for people with arthritis and rheumatism; birch teas were also strong diuretics, "breaking down kidney and bladder stones"; finally, as an antiseptic, it cleared up infections and healed skin diseases. As Terzian emphasizes, "The Russian peasant lived in close contact with the birch, using practically all its elements, from bark to sap, for his daily needs."[39]

The Reading

As an oracle, Birch is about the dangers of domesticating, taming, and ultimately bringing down a wild and beautiful energy. It is about being honored and garbed for a powerful ceremony only to be used up, depleted, and finally discarded. If you draw this oracle card, do not be an accomplice in your own destruction. Find another way.

Birch is filled with poignancy and paradox. It usually suggests a marriage or some form of partnership, which might be seen as a happy occasion. But look carefully at your culture's marriage customs and expectations, especially if you are from a traditional background. Don't be blinded by romantic illusions. Allowing your wildness to be tamed may be a necessary sacrifice leading to greater joy, but keep your eyes open and pay attention to the inner voice of your *rusalki* nature. Too many women enter into marriage willingly, lovingly, and all too soon wind up feeling trapped and afraid. Their sadness and the bewildered wrath lying just below the surface will be transmitted in subtle ways to their children – and the cycle may never be broken.

Birch reminds you of a time when the feminine spirit was honored for its power, its lightness and strength, and its wisdom. In ancient times, a woman might choose to be tamed for a time so that she could delight in human community, bear young, raise them wisely, and enjoy a fully equal relationship with a mate, but no one, least of all her mate, took such domestication for granted – it was a *gift*. To attempt to break her and imprison her in societal laws and expectations was to risk unraveling the warp and woof of mutual respect that held society together in the first place. Despite common belief, societies are never held together by laws – laws are only a poor substitute, emerging when mutual respect is too badly damaged to continue holding things together.

Regardless of gender, Birch warns you not to give yourself as a *gift* any longer – not your body, your love, your creativity, your strength, your hope, or your wisdom. Today, gifts given too generously are too soon devalued and thrown away. Recipients who cannot match your own generous spirit will come to see you as their property and your gifts as their right. They will soon strip you of them and walk away. Birch would have you remain strong, free, and self-sufficient.

If you are male, look to your relationship with the feminine in your life, your soul, and in the natural world around you. If you are not honoring it, if you are allowing it to be oppressed, or if you are abusing it yourself, the Oracle warns you to re-evaluate such behaviors before it is too late. If marriage is an issue, males also risk having their genuine and fertile wildness destroyed by societal expectations. Walk carefully lest the *rusalki* lure you into romantic illusions. Know, however, that a genuinely wild spirit is not to be confused with the immature self-indulgence of the narcissist, the *puer*, the eternal Peter Pan. You will need honest insight into yourself here. If like Peter Pan, you are afraid to grow up and can cope only with your own needs, then be realistic enough to admit this and do not get married. Otherwise, the likelihood is that you would abandon your wife and children and contribute to a general climate of despair.

Female or male, if you are considering marriage and you are a truly wild spirit, full of dreams, and with the sincere desire to spin those dreams into reality, you run two risks: meeting the needs of a family may burn you out and leave your soul empty; on the other hand, too much insistence upon your own creative fulfillment may leave the souls of your mate and children empty. In either case, be very clear about who you are and how capable you are of honoring the *rusalka* in yourself, as well as in your mate, and be even clearer before you risk bringing children into an already dangerously over-crowded world. From the perspective of Birch, having children is not about ego, biological clocks, or legal heirs – it is about contributing to communal survival. Today, it may well be that communal survival itself demands that only domesticated, warm, steady, patient non-*rusalki* people bear children.

Finally, Birch asks you not to forget that, for good or ill, the powerful ancestral crone-goddess is always a secret presence in the cells of human biology, in the mortar and pestle of your love-making. Do not host her lightly: she demands respect and can be pitiless when it is denied her.

REVERSED:

Whether in your current lifetime or in an earlier one, whether as victim or perpetrator, your courage, insight, persistence, and wise heart have finally brought you safely through the enmeshed thickets of societal oppression and bestowed upon you the rare gift of serving life with single-minded devotion. You have escaped bondage. You now have the hard-won strength of "at-one-ment" with your Self, living freely within the forcefield of Birch's sacred power, within the shifting dynamics of this "tree of light" moving effortlessly in the wind. For you, no matter what you face on your journey, Birch opens the way with light, grace, and wonder. Like a shaman, you travel into inner dimensions and return with the gifts of power and creativity you find there. The Great Goddess, the *Rusalka*, untamed, virginal, Tree of Life, spinner of destinies, welcomes you as daughter, son, friend, and dear one.

Artist's Notes:

The carvings on the birch trees are from Yugoslavia, 5th to 4th millennia B.C.E.

Endnotes

1 Joanna Hubbs. *Mother Russia*:83.
2 Dr. Elizabeth Terzian, "The Birch in the Russian Sacred Tradition," unpublished paper, 1998.
3 Friedrich:27.
4 Hubbs:33.
5 Hubbs:28;31;32.
6 Terzian, *op.cit.*
7 Hubbs:30.
8 Hubbs:27.
9 Hubbs:28.
10 Hubbs:33.
11 Hubbs:28.
12 Hubbs:28.
13 Hubbs:30.
14 Hubbs:62; 71-72.
15 Hubbs:73 (In other areas, a young man dressed as a woman participated in the ritual; see p.258, fn54).
16 Hubbs:72.
17 Hubbs:72.
18 Hubbs:72-73.
19 Hubbs:73.
20 Hubbs:73.
21 Hubbs:73.
22 Hubbs:73.
23 Hubbs:73.
24 Hubbs:62.
25 Hubbs:78.
26 Hubbs:78.
27 Hubbs:79-80.
28 Hubbs:81.
29 Hubbs:83.
30 Hubbs:84.
31 Hubbs:36;45.
32 Hubbs:40.
33 Hubbs:37;38.
34 Hubbs:36;42.
35 Hubbs:50.
36 Information for this opening section comes from Friedrich:26-27.
37 Friedrich:19;31.
38 *Cowles Encyclopedia of Animals and Plants*:82a.
39 Information in this paragraph comes from Terzian, based on data from Angelo de Gubernatis, *La Mythologie des Plantes*, vol.1, 1878.

9
CORN

Corn

One of the most common ritualistic substances, one which is a prayer in itself, is [corn] pollen whose very name derives from light. The word is *ta'di'di'n* and means "it emits light here and there, everywhere."
~ Gladys Reichard[1]

The Mythic World

In Navajo sacred narratives, two deities are closely associated with corn: Isanakleshe (variant spellings exist, e.g., Estsan-ah-tlehay), the earth-goddess known as "Changing Woman," and Talking God, one of four maternal Grandfathers. Sometimes Isanakleshe is his mother: "He was transformed from white corn, which she placed at the top of a mountain where fogs meet."[2] In other versions, he is her father or foster-father. The sunrise sky is Talking God's special province. The sunset sky is Isanakleshe's.

Talking God is a deity who loves life. It is with joy that he enters into all his roles: bringer-of-dawn, healer, teasing jester, protector, peacemaker, messenger-herald in bluebird form, and even giver of the very means of life – corn. "There is no better thing than this in the world," he tells Changing Woman, "for it is the gift of life."[3] He is the inner-form or "soul" of moving morning light, which helps corn grow by becoming part of the plant, going within it – thus, Talking God is also the "soul" of corn. This intimate connection is hinted at in the name for corn pollen, that quintessence of generative power: *ta'di'di'n*, which means "it emits light here and there, everywhere." In Navajo ritual-dance, Talking God's mask is white, the color of early dawn; a halo of white eagle feathers represents the rays of the rising sun; extending from the forehead to the mouth is the Navajo tree-of-life – a cornstalk with two ears of corn upon it.[4]

Changing Woman, born of Darkness and Dawn, unites the opposites, transforming them, creating a new balance, growing old and bent, then youthful, only to change again. She changes as does the earth through her seasons, from budding to bloom, from harvest to barrenness, and again to budding. Her changes are more gradual, softer, than the rapid daily changes of her mate, the Sun, yet hers are as much a dance through sacred space as his.

In later years, after her twin sons are grown, the Sun persuades her to move to an island off the California coast. He summons many spirits to build her home, designed to follow, not static compass points, but his actual path. There is a room of white-shell facing the sunrise, turquoise facing south, iridescent abalone-shell facing the sunset, and black jet facing north. In the center is a room with a rock crystal altar, shimmering with light in all directions – here, as the sun sets, she dances barefoot, a joyous act that preserves all of creation, for dance, like ritual, harmonizes the energies of opposites.

A time comes when Talking God brings two human children to her island. At first, Isanakleshe chooses to appear so old and gnarled she can barely move. Then she reverses the aging process until she is a beautiful maiden. She teaches the awed children the stories, chants, and dances of the gods' heretofore-secret rituals. When the children leave, they take this knowledge to their people.

Sandpaintings did not yet exist and thus were not part of Isanakleshe's gift. As time passed, errors crept into the ceremonies because there was no memory device to assure continuity. Isanakleshe realized that sandpaintings would solve this problem, but how could she bring them into being? She decided to have a "sing" over herself:

> ...She made her foot prints in yellow pollen and then seated herself beneath a cornstalk....Here she said all the chants and prayers and when she had finished, a bluebird came and perched upon the flower tassel of the corn and sang. In this way she knew that she had done everything perfectly.[5]

By dancing through pollen, immersing herself in prayer, then opening herself to these powerful energies, Isanakleshe has perfectly prepared herself for the sacred images beginning to emerge, one after another, so vividly that she is later able to teach her human children to depict them with colored sands, dried petals, grains, corn kernels, and pollen ("sandpainting" describes effect, not ingredients). What is especially fascinating about the emergence of this new art is that it takes place in a simple cornfield. The earth-goddess dances in sacred pollen, which "here and there, everywhere" emits the dawn-god's light. And it is the bluebird, Talking God's herald and alter-ego, who celebrates Isanakleshe's discovery of how to harvest and translate "inner forms" into visible paintings. Together, these Holy Ones cross-pollinate one another and make conscious the artistic contents of their inner worlds.

In one of her sandpaintings, for example, Changing Woman's rainbow house is surrounded by a trail of white cornmeal marked with footprints of yellow corn pollen. In a healing ceremony, the patient is asked to step into the design and follow the footprints.[6] Through those movements within the healing energies of this sandpainting's cornfield, Isanakleshe brings ever-changing transformations.

In another sandpainting (shown on Corn's card), she provides images to drive away nightmares. Here again the power of corn is recognized. A yellow corn-pollen path runs from east (dawn) to west (sunset). On the south side of the path are cornstalks and three corn-deities: Corn Beetle Girl flanked by Corn Beetle Boy and Pollen Boy. Emitting light, understanding that everything in life is light-in-motion, these corn-deities drive away nightmares. On the north side of the pollen-path, directly opposite the two male corn-deities, are two square-masked female deities in blue. Arching between them is the powerful rainbow goddess, Natseelit, who offers a path over which negative energy may be driven and harmlessly dissolved. Through this ceremony, the "corn-plant" of the human mind is protected on its pollen-path, while dreams holding positive energy begin emerging like tassels of corn-silk.

In these, as well as many other sandpaintings, Changing Woman reveals new ways of resolving tensions and restoring one's innately harmonious body/mind.

Botany/History

Corn or maize is to the New World what wheat was to the Old: the staff of life. The plant is native to the mountainous tropics of Central and South America where Native Americans domesticated wild grass, developing it into many genetic strains. These range in height from two to an astonishing thirty feet. In the spring, winds blow through pollen-dense stamens, pollinating the clusters of flowers from which the kernels develop. As the kernels form, they are patterned into a tight spiral along a husk-sheathed cob; from the top of the cob hang long silky threads.[7]

Walking through tall ripe corn can be a wonderful experience. Stalks tower over one's head, creating the sense of a light, airy forest. Rustling winds brush silk tassels over spiraling galaxies of kernels, each rich in minerals such as potassium, iron, and zinc. Many peaceful civilizations in the ancient Americas were based upon the cultivation of this sacred plant. Tribes eating a diet of corn combined with beans had no problem with cholesterol or hardening of the arteries.[8] Raising corn was a communal effort, requiring many willing hands for plowing, seeding, watering, and harvesting. With the coming of autumn, the entire community looked forward to celebrating a bountiful harvest together.

The Reading

Drawing Corn indicates that your basic needs are being met in a light-filled, balanced environment. At the oracular core of this plant is pure joy, nourishment, wholeness, an at-one-ness with your inner and outer eco-system, and a desire to protect what you value most. It is time to set aside any youthful self-indulgence and uncertainty. You have grown strong and tall almost without realizing it. The plant invites you to recognize and celebrate your maturity, your healthy sense of communal responsibility, your ability to creatively solve problems for the benefit of all.

Corn asks you to energize your inner "pollen-light" (in today's terms: biophotons). Native Americans found ways to domesticate wild mountain strains of corn; in addition to food, corn inspired sacred arts. Consider the infinite number of wild strains of *ideas* growing in the mountains of your mind; recognize that you are being given the opportunity to domesticate new hybrids of art, writing, film, music, teaching, healing. As a civilizing force, corn's energies may also be

 CORN

used in re-balancing societies gone astray. To do this, explore new ways of using arts and ritual to speak to the heart, to build up, not to tear down.

Corn wants to hear the bluebirds inside you sing out into the world, inspiring others to do the same. Corn wants to see you dancing. Corn sees the world as one, a pollen-path of light. Corn invites you to help make it so, in whatever way you can, doing everything in a simple, balanced, harmonious way.

REVERSED:

If you are one of life's "haves," Reversed Corn asks you to re-evaluate your communal responsibilities. Do not forget that your wealth has been accumulated through the work of many "little" people. Wealth comes to you to be shared, not squandered or hoarded.

If you are a "have-not," Corn acknowledges that your basic survival needs are not being met – and this is not due to any fault of yours. You are not lazy – you work hard but the work is joyless. Life seems a constant struggle against overwhelming odds. You have ceased to trust life – and, in a sense, you feel justified because life itself is turning to dust between your careworn fingers.

This is a very difficult period to endure. Know, however, that you can weather it. Despite times of drought, poor soils, blistering sun, you have the wit to "domesticate" the raw stuff of survival around you. Try to go gently with yourself, re-define your basic needs, your priorities. Perhaps, hard as your life is, you might garner a little space of time for yourself – time in which to find a new way of looking at life, time to draw a breath of fresh air, time to find a wellspring from which to drink, no matter how briefly.

In other words, find a corn-kernel of hope. Do your best to be at one with your eco-system, even though it may not look like much. Let in light from your pollen-tassels right down to your roots. From that light, take heart and continue on for another day. In time, that day will arrive in which you find that the endless struggle had purpose after all. This is not to say that it all will have been worth it. In a sense, no matter *what* comes after, such suffering is not worth it – but that is never the point. Then was then – now is now. You will have survived and now you can go on.

There is a sacred Navajo narrative about twin boys fathered by Talking God – one is blind, the other crippled. The blind child carries the cripple and the cripple's eyes guide the steps of the other. These "have-nots" turn for help to the gods, the "haves," the "healthy ones," but the twins are repeatedly ignored. At last, when they can endure no more, the boys pour out their despair and heartbreak in a series of songs. In this impossible situation, their harrowing perseverance has uncovered a new "voice." A deep wellspring of purest creativity is suddenly released and through an intense union of language and music, they find the means to wring the very hearts of the gods. The gods relent and heal the boys. Their songs thereafter became part of the powerful nine-day winter ceremony, *Nightway*, which has brought profound healing to many.

As it was for the twins, trust that Reversed Corn opens the possibility for a healing so deep you cannot currently imagine it. From *Nightway*:

…In beauty may I walk.
All day long may I walk.
Through the returning seasons may I walk.
Beautifully will I possess again.
Beautifully birds –
Beautifully joyful birds.
On the trail marked with pollen may I walk….
In old age wandering on a trail of beauty, lively, may I walk.
In old age wandering on a trail of beauty, living again, may I walk.
It is finished in beauty.⁹

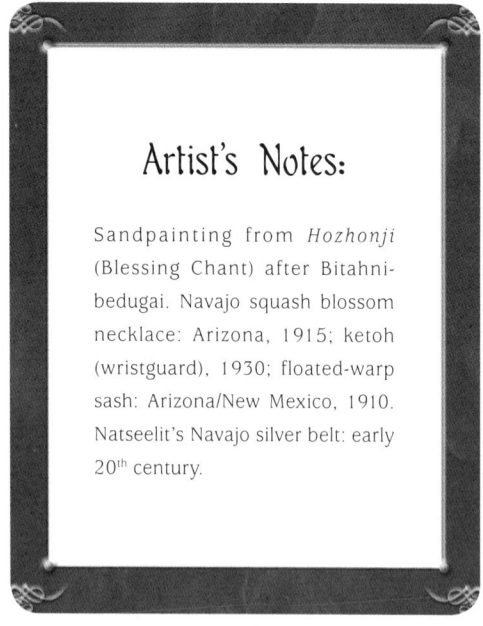

Artist's Notes:

Sandpainting from *Hozhonji* (Blessing Chant) after Bitahnibedugai. Navajo squash blossom necklace: Arizona, 1915; ketoh (wristguard), 1930; floated-warp sash: Arizona/New Mexico, 1910. Natseelit's Navajo silver belt: early 20th century.

Endnotes

1 Reichard 1944:29.
2 Reichard 1983:476.
3 Reichard 1983:27.
4 Luckert, *NRCSV*:193.
5 Klah/Wheelwright:172.
6 Klah/Wheelwright:174.
7 Cowles:89.
8 Hausman & Hurley:162.
9 Southwest Indian Foundation, New Mexico 87305; translator unknown.

10
ELDER

Elder

For centuries [Elder] has had the reputation of healing the body, but in the elderberry's golden age, it made music to heal the spirit. [1]

The Mythic World

The elder, like hawthorn, rowan, dogwood, holly, and other berry-bearing trees, whose leaves or flowers have the cloying smell of death, was sacred to many of Europe's goddesses in their seasonal maiden-mother-crone stages. Such trees represent the white loveliness of her springtime, the juicy life-rich red or purplish-black berries of her late autumn, and the stark beauty of her austere winter. In their on-going cycles of regenerative growth, these trees are living manifestations of deeper mysteries of life, death, and rebirth. They are protective, but also threatening. As such, they are both revered and feared.[2]

The elder tree, more than the others, is especially related to the sacred crone, or wise-woman aspect of the goddess. Nordic peoples across northern Europe believed that elder trees were home to the spirit of Hel, Queen of the Underworld, who was incarnate within them. As late as the Middle Ages the elder was called Hel-tree or "elven-tree." "Hel" still remains in Helsinki, Holland, Holstein, Helvetia, Holderness, and related names.

If Hel's elder were pruned or, worse, felled, she would haunt the person who did it. When pruning or felling was necessary, a bargain could be struck by promising to give her of one's own wood or "essence" after death:

> Lady Elder, give me thy wood,
> And I will give thee of mine,
> When I become a tree![3]

This reflects a very old belief that Hel placed the souls of the dead in elder trees. There, cradled in the tree's cottony pith, they remained until it was time for them to go forth anew as babies. The tree, like the goddess herself, was both tomb and womb, the holy place from which the dead were reborn.[4]

This belief in the elder as a tomb/womb was so strongly rooted that it was transposed nearly intact when Northern Europe was Christianized: thus, the elder became the tree of Christ's crucifixion. As if to underscore the imposition of Christianity's life-versus-death duality upon a much older life-death-rebirth cycle, the elder also became the tree upon which Judas hanged himself.

New and conflicting meaning-clusters inevitably arose from Christianization. It was good luck, for example, to stand under an elder in a storm because no bolt of lightning was impious enough to strike the tree which had provided the blessed wood for Christ's death.[5] Yet it was bad luck to fall asleep under an elder because the scent of its leaves might induce a deadly coma.[6] In earlier times, Hel had protected newborns. In Christian times, it was unlucky to make a cradle of Hel's elderwood lest she and her ghostly demons pinch the baby black and blue and strangle it.[7] It was dangerous to burn elderwood because, when you looked into the flames, you would see a devil, which is how the ancient tree-goddess was now interpreted.[8] If you dreamed of elder, it meant you would soon fall ill. Elder twigs and berries could allegedly ward off witches, and yet, paradoxically, elder groves were to be avoided at night because witches loved the trees and were believed to gather among them.[9]

It was said that elder sticks bound together were used for witches' broomsticks or "magic horses."[10] Such stick-horses seem to have been inspired by medieval rituals of Sufi visionaries whose "horses" symbolized the mystic, shamanic journey into invisible realms. The broom-horse also implied sexual union, which is why jumping over a broomstick was an old pagan wedding ritual. In ancient Rome, the midwife-priestesses of crone goddess, Hekate, used a ritual elder broom to sweep away negative spirits after the birth of a child. Thus, the broom, like the elder, had ancient connections with crone-goddess mysteries of fertility and birth.[11]

In Celtic tradition, the elder tree ruled the brief, three-day, thirteenth lunar month, which ended on Samhain (Halloween), the "Feast of the Dead," the last day of the Celtic year. That three-day period was a "crack between the worlds," the boundary between one year and the next, just as the "witching hour" is the boundary between one day and the next. Spirits and ghosts were able to pass through these gateways to give omens, advice, magical gifts, and to feast as guests with their loved ones ("ghost" and "guest" come from the same German word, *Geist*).[12]

In ancient Greece, well-aged elder wood was crafted into a triangular-shaped stringed instrument, the *sambuke*. Not only was the triangle a sacred vulva-symbol, it was also the Greek form of the letter "D" (*delta*), known as the Holy Door of birth and especially connected to the crone aspect of Athena, owl-goddess of wisdom.[13]

Botany/History

Black elderberries have been found at archaeological sites, especially in Alpine regions, dating as far back as the Stone Age.[14] More than a dozen varieties of elder trees are native to Europe, western Asia, North Africa, and North America. Some species grow to fifty feet, but heights of ten to twenty feet are more common. The tree is exceptionally vigorous, especially in moist soil where its weedy shoots will overrun a garden without constant, even severe pruning.[15] Its bark is corky and its stout branches are packed with spongy pith. Even smaller trees may have trunks as thick as a heavy thigh.

The tart berries can be eaten raw, cooked, or made into wine. Native Americans used them to dye their hair black as well as to dye the grasses with which they wove their baskets.[16] The tree has so many medicinal uses that in his *Merry Wives of Windsor*, Shakespeare ranked it with ancient healers as a physician in its own right: "What says my Aesculapius, My Galen, My Heart of Elder?" Summer-blooming elder flowers are used in medicinal teas for bronchitis, asthma, and colic; flowers simmered in oil will ease sunburn; steeped in water and made into a compress, flowers relieve headaches. Leaves and roots are used as an external wash for skin diseases. Used internally, roots, leaves, and bark require caution because they are a powerful purgative. Some species contain toxic cyanogenic glucosides: ripe *cooked* berries are safe, but raw fruits should be eaten sparingly. In earlier times, children used to cut young elderberry shoots, poke out the cottony innards, and turn them into whistles – some got mildly sick from blowing on the toxic wood but this never stopped children from playing with them.[17]

When young, elderwood is too spongy to be useful. When old, it becomes hard, fine-grained, and highly valued for making precise mathematical and musical instruments. The tree's generic name, *Sambucus,* is derived from Greece's *sambuke*,[18] an ancient triangular-shaped harp with a high, piercing sound.[19]

When Europe was Christianized, much conflicting folklore about the elder emerged from this awkward merger of two very different spiritual traditions, the earth-based and the Christian. Nevertheless, in the midst of many superstitions about this tree of "doom," there remained great respect for its medicinal uses. John Evelyn, a seventeenth century herbalist, went so far as to call it a cure "against all infirmities whatever."[20]

The Reading

The elder tree is sacred to Hel as the Crone who enfolds your child-spirit between projects, lives, relationships, patterns, and holds you safe. The tree is mysterious, first of the forest trees to leaf after winter's dark. When it is time for you to put forth new leaves, wise Hel is there to help in the birthing and to sweep away adverse influences. It is a tree of excellent omen for pregnant women and for the elderly.

Elder is a tree of completion and transition to the next stage of growth. It is the new seed hidden in every ending, and the generative ending hidden in every beginning. It is teeming with life force, sending up great numbers of shoots, rapidly repairing any damage, and resistant to being enclosed in small spaces. It wants to spread out and will not be docile if you try to confine it. It has much to offer, including giving generous shelter to a lifetime of memories, accomplishments – "ghosts," if you will.

Drawing the elder suggests that you are feeling pot-bound, for you have outgrown the space in which you have been confined. Expect a change soon.

Since shamanesses once "flew" on elder brooms, this may be a time of travel, usually over short distances only, unless a mental journey is involved.

In your youth, elder protects the children you bring into the world. In your old age, it gifts you with wisdom and renewed creativity. As fine-grained elderwood was once crafted into mathematical instruments, so elder invites you to discover your own sources of mental clarity, precision, calm. As that same wood was once crafted into *sambukes*, so elder touches strings of music deep within you, drawing them forth, piercingly clear. Open up to that voice of nature flowing through you.

Everything depends upon your perception of what is happening. If you project alien judgments or expectations upon the simple reality of what *is*, everything will tighten up and you may feel like a victim, pinched black and blue by negativities, your new life strangled in its cradle. If, however, you see yourself as a full participant in the sacred unfolding of your own life, the wisdom in every cell of your body will take over and see you quietly, serenely, through whatever is occurring.

REVERSED:

Something new is trying very hard to be born from you but you persist in throwing up obstacles. It is time to take a deep breath, settle down, and give yourself the time and space to go through labor pains. Calmly watch your emotions: overindulgence in either your highs or lows will only drain vitality from the work at hand. Protect your physical health with common sense and temperance. Gracefully avoid situations in which you feel "used" – husband your strength for yourself during this period: do not squander it trying to rescue others. Learn when to bless, release, and let others fade out of your life to find their good elsewhere.

If the obstacles to this birthing persist, they may relate to your shadow-side. Your shadow is that part of you that you most fear. It makes you feel weak, "evil," full of hate. It does not fit your self-image. To keep from dealing with it, you will project it onto your enemies instead of compassionately realizing that the same tendency lies in you, not as full-blown, perhaps, but nevertheless there. Your shadow may be trying to tell you that you have some "elder-shoots," that is, patterns, behaviors, strategies, or conflicting beliefs that are no longer relevant. Although the elder threatens to haunt you if you cut it back thoughtlessly, its life-force is so intense that it can readily survive even a severe pruning as long as you do it in a timely and positive manner.

Be mindful as you cut. Remember that what you are removing was once at the leading edge of your growth. You called it into your life to help you survive and you would not be where you are today without it. Work gently and respectfully. Remember to protect your child-spirit's vulnerability. Approached wisely, the shadow becomes a friend, a difficult friend, perhaps, but one who has your deepest spiritual growth at heart. Turn to nature to restore your spirit after the work of integrating the shadow is safely underway.

Never mind what you are thinking, fearing, worrying about. Such mental agitation weighs the body down and sends disruptive signals to its cells. Get your mind out of this process. Your body does not know what "tomorrow" or "yesterday" mean. It only knows "now." Whether the birth, or transition, at hand is perceived by you as primarily mental, emotional, or physical, you need to stay focused in the body and trust the millennia of wisdom and innate harmony shimmering in each cell. Female or male, only the body *really* understands birthing. Rest your hand gently on your belly as a means of returning your focus to the body, quiet your restless mind, let it engage itself only with physical sensations, awareness of touch, sound, light, air. Then let your body do its thing, moment to moment.

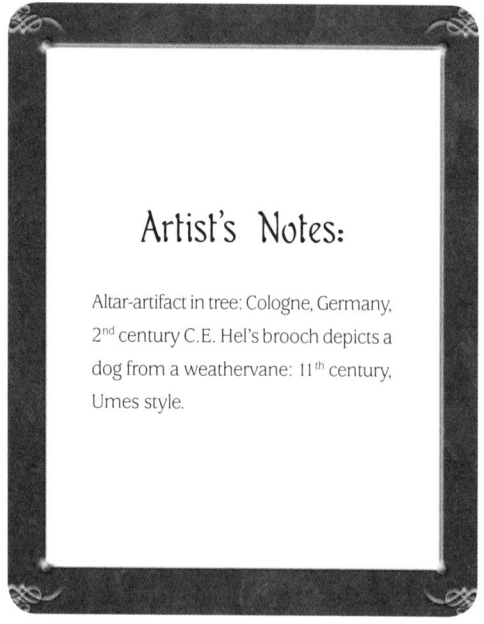

Artist's Notes:

Altar-artifact in tree: Cologne, Germany, 2nd century C.E. Hel's brooch depicts a dog from a weathervane: 11th century, Umes style.

Endnotes

[1] Rodale:178.
[2] Baker:108-109.
[3] Chant cited in Baker:110.
[4] Baker:110; Rodale:181; Walker, WEMS:380-382; Walker, WD:251; 463; Grigson:376.
[5] Lucas:112-113;
Baker:109.
[6] Baker:107.
[7] Graves, WG:191; Jeanne Rose:58.
[8] Sylvia Woods:84; Baker:109-110; Grigson:376.
[9] Rodale:178.
[10] Graves, WG:191;
Walker, WD:463.
[11] Walker, WEMS:119-121.
[12] Darrah:63n; Walker, WD:180;250.
[13] Walker, WD:40.
[14] Jane Renfrew:150; Rodale:178.
[15] Rodale:178;181.
[16] Hooker, SF:190;
Law:16; Lucas:113; Adrian/Dennis:11-12; Rose:57-58.
[17] Rodale:178-179.
[18] Rodale:178.
[19] OED.
[20] Cited in Rodale:178.

11
ELM

Elm

The elm is a tree to avoid as far as its auric atmosphere is concerned, for quite apart from its nasty habit of dropping a dead branch without any warning, it does seem to be in some way inimical to human beings.[1]

We are not told which of the three [Odin, Hoenir, or Loduir] endowed [the elm] with the devastating habit of crashing flat to the ground when full-grown without a word of warning.... *[In the Celtic world]* elves...had a lien on elm-trees, as the old name for these trees was "elven," from their connection with elves.[2]

The Mythic World

In the 13th century *Poetic Edda*, the first female, Embla, was made from elm; her mate, Askr, from ash (*See Ash*). They were created when Odin (god of wisdom and battle), Hoenir (rune-master), and Lodur (god of beneficial fire), were walking along the shore and saw two tree trunks washed up by the sea. The gods carved the soft elm into a woman, the hard ash into a man. Odin contributed their souls; Hoenir, thought, mobility (and some say the senses); Lodur, blood and ruddy complexions.[3] The two types of wood, hard and soft, reflect ancient fire-making rituals in which spinning hard ash against elm generated enough heat to "birth" the fire lying latent within the softer wood. Among many Indo-European peoples, such fire-making techniques were metaphors for human sexuality.

Once past the creation of the first two humans, ash continued to figure prominently as Yggdrasil, the World Tree. Elm became a drudge, exploited for mundane purposes. A group of Amazon women, however, continued to revere elm as the embodiment of a woman's spirit. According to medieval legends, they founded the southern German city of *Ulm*, "elm." Here, they worshipped their goddess in elm groves (*ulmae*) along the Danube.[4]

These were warrior-women, fierce in battle, loyal to their sisters, and intolerant of men except for "fire-making" a child. It is said they cut off a breast for more effectiveness in handling their bows. Modern archers say this would give no advantage, yet such legends persist. Regardless of whether they literally removed a breast, myths point to some catastrophe so terrible that Amazons took extreme measures to prevent its recurrence. Pushed to the edge, these women sacrificed whatever impeded their survival, then faced their foes, and fought for their lives. They won but it was too late to return to their old lives. They had to forge a new way of being.

Botany/History

The elm (Latin *ulmus*) has similar physical characteristics to the linden *(see Linden)*: both have fibrous bast which allows strips to be woven easily into clothing, footwear, baskets, mats, ropes. Although smelling too foul to be used as firewood, linden lent itself gracefully to other mundane uses; it was also ritually important in horse-breeding areas where horses were outfitted in trappings woven of linden bast. The elm, perhaps because it was unsanctified by any ritual significance, may have become more hostile to humans. Where linden was allowed to be lithe and graceful, elmwood was forcibly shaped into killing-tools. Language reflects this, for in Old Norse, **olm*, as well as cognates in other Indo-European languages, refers to the tree as well as to cheap elm-bows used by those who could not afford more highly valued ash-bows. The elm is as graceful and stately as the linden and the two have often been confused (for example, a Middle Welsh word, *llwyfen*, was used for both trees). Yet it was elm, not linden, who was subjected to thoughtless and widespread exploitation.[5]

Between 7000-3500 B.C.E., climax forests of elm, mixed with smaller numbers of linden, covered large areas of Europe and Russia. From about 3500-800 B.C.E., elm declined dramatically in central and western Europe, supplanted by oaks and other hardwoods. Archaeological evidence from Neolithic and Bronze Age sites shows that elm was the preferred fodder-tree among Indo-European tribes practicing animal husbandry. When branches, leaves, and shoots were grazed, the tree's pollen production was drastically curtailed. Vulnerable shoots were especially at risk because it would be another seven or eight years before they could flower again. Few were given that long. In addition, fibrous bast could only be obtained by stripping bark off the elm – if done recklessly, the tree would be damaged or killed outright.[6]

For centuries, after its use as fodder had diminished, elm was considered a cheap building material. Being water-resistant, it was used for ship keels; its hollowed-out trunks were used as drain pipes. Troughs, sluices, bridge pilings, and coffins were also made from its wood. Further, countless elms were chopped into "sullen and slow firewood."[7]

The elm seems never to have been a "people" tree. After centuries of abuse, it is perhaps not surprising that she will no longer fight to survive. Severely stressed urban elms have been all but decimated by Dutch elm disease, a fungal disease probably originating in Central Asia and associated with the Dutch only because they worked so diligently, albeit unsuccessfully, to develop an elm capable of resisting the disease. The fungus, which clogs the tree's water-conducting system, is spread by bark beetles. The beetle begins with badly stressed trees but, as they die out, it seeks prey among stronger varieties, soon infecting them with fungal spores as well. There are exceptions – elms growing in coastal areas seem to be protected by sea winds; also, Chinese and Siberian elms remain highly resistant. Aside from these, older species are increasingly succumbing to infestation.[8]

Fortunately for those who love elms, new hybrids have been developed by American horticulturists. To keep them healthy, they must be fertilized each spring – a hands-on way of belatedly honoring the special beauty of this tree.[9]

The Reading

This is a hyper-vigilant tree with a history of being hacked, burned, bark-stripped, axed, and butchered. She is a patient listener to those who have also been abused, but otherwise prefers to be left alone. Historically, Amazons are female. Psychologically, they can be either gender. If you draw Elm, you are being told that you are capable of taking extreme measures to survive. You can cut off your past without hesitation if it interferes with your chosen path, your destiny. You can single-mindedly sacrifice tenderness and mercy. Sometimes this may be necessary. Many times, however, too much single-mindedness is dehumanizing. It can indicate a need to control, an unwillingness to explore other options.

Consider whether it is time to become human again, to reactivate your empathy and intuition. Until you can release the prodigious energy required to sustain your vigilance, you may not have the resources necessary for transformation.

REVERSED:

When Amazons fought and won, they never looked back. They found new ways of coping, relating, surviving. Unfortunately, this often meant devaluing the playfulness and innocence they once possessed – gentle, even elfin, qualities which may indeed have led to the original catastrophe. Reversed Elm recognizes that it is time for those qualities to be re-integrated, not recklessly, but with tenderness and respect for an elfin nature that has been wedded to a bow for too long.

This fire-savvy tree could also be alerting you to impending burn-out, happening suddenly, without warning. Too much hyper-vigilance takes a heavy toll. You need to re-balance, but do not believe you have time. You do – use it wisely. Never forget elm's *elfin* nature: bright, shimmering, magical. The tree's Amazon-guise was adopted only because of dire circumstances. Left to herself, her innocent, hidden sweetness makes her a chosen abode for the elves. Male or female, give yourself that chance again.

Artist's Notes:

Scythian horse plaque on woman's headwear: Bobrytsia, Cherkas'ka Oblast, late 7th-early 6th century B.C.E. Rein-roundels are Scythian Gorgon heads: Babyna Mohyla, Dnipropetrovsika Oblast, 350-300 B.C.E. Tree's amphora from Attic red-figure Amazonomachy, attributed to the Suessula Painter, ca. 400 B.C.E.

Endnotes

[1] Butler, W.E., *How to Read the Aura*:30-31.
[2] Dorothy Jacob, *Witch's Guide to Gardening*:38;95.
[3] Larousse:364;386;398;
Dorothy Jacob, *Witch's Guide to Gardening*:38.
[4] Walker, *WD*:463; *WEMS*:26.
[5] Friedrich:80-81; 83.
[6] Friedrich:85.
[7] Grigson:260.
[8] Alan Mitchell:48-52; *Better Homes and Gardens*, April 1993, v.71, n.4, p.20.
[9] *Better Homes and Gardens*, April 1993, v.71, n.4, p.20.

 EUCALYPTUS

Eucalyptus

>...the rainbow is a huge serpent, which lives in deep, permanent waters and is associated with rain and rain-making and with the iridescence of quartz crystals and mother-of-pearl....Rainbow Serpent and All-Mother sometimes are equated.
>~ Kenneth Maddock[1]

The Mythic World

The very appearance of some of Australia's eucalypts is mythic– they are giant, old, bearded beings with gnarled, thick, powerful, twisting, muscular limbs that give the appearance of great serpents about to take flight. The trees seem to send their spirits out along the synapses of their boughs, endlessly stretching, longing to fly, questing beyond their confines, until they do indeed burst free with such an immense shock that the trees' very bark is sloughed off, like a rainbow-serpent bursting at its seams, shedding its skin. When the tree's essence leaps as spirit into the celestial skies, it becomes a pure surge of power, traveling between realms, into Dreamtime and back.

In addition to the rainbow-serpent, a crucial concept in Aboriginal spirituality is Dreamtime – the "World Dawn," or primal source of life, a beyond-time dimension inhabited by shapechanging Dawn-Beings who act on temporal planes by extending their power outwards from Dreamtime's central axis.

When humans are near death, they become increasingly sacred because they are drawing closer to Dreamtime. Once there, they enjoy that realm while awaiting rebirth, for death is not an end but "an open-ended continuum."[2] When they are ready to return, tribal members ritually "sing" their spirits into the wombs of new mothers. With profound insight, Aboriginals respect each child as a carrier transporting a precious infusion of life from Dreamtime to the human plane.[3]

The constellation of the Pleiades is another important concept. For some tribes, the stars are seven sisters, the *Meamei*, a group of huntresses, their bodies sparkling with icicles, their hair falling to their waists, their clear voices haunting all who hear their music.[4] For others, the Pleiades are eucalyptus trees sending shimmering waves of light throughout Dreamtime to all life-forms. These trees welcome the spirits of the dead, sheltering them prior to rebirth.[5]

When some eucalypts allowed themselves to be transplanted from the Pleiades to earth, they brought shade, bark for making shelters, roots filled with water, and leaves and twigs for medicinal purposes. Their bark was already available when the first people were created from clay – it was stringy eucalyptus bark that formed their hair – hair, a manifestation of spirit-energy.[6] Eucalypt bark is also used for extraordinary works of "x-ray" art, a style which sees through to the bone, focusing on structural beauty.

Eucalypts retain their Dreamtime power on earth: during rituals, for example, some tribes brush participants with bunches of eucalyptus leaves to neutralize the immense buildup of power around them;[7] others attach clusters of leaves to dancers' knees in order to create a primal, rustling sound, like the sounds of creation itself.[8] Eucalyptus limbs hollowed out by termites become didgeridoos, hypnotically haunting instruments used during rituals and storytelling.

EUCALYPTUS

A story from southeastern Australia about a young orphan, Koobor, reveals more of the tree's shamanic power.[9] Koobor was abused by his kinfolk. Hoping he would die, they refused to feed him, but since they lived in a eucalyptus forest, he survived by eating leaves. Without water, however, he was always thirsty.

One day the tribe forgot to hide their water-buckets before leaving to gather food. Overjoyed, Koobor drank his fill for the first time. Then he collected the buckets and hung them on a eucalyptus branch. He climbed into the tree next to them, sat down, and began chanting magical words to the tree. The tree was only a sapling, barely older than Koobor, but it heard the song and responded by growing swiftly, swiftly, up into the sky until it towered above all the other trees in the forest.

The people returned at twilight and were furious to see Koobor sitting up there. The men demanded the return of their water-buckets but the boy refused, saying he would never be thirsty again. His enraged relatives tried to climb the tree, but it was too tall. They tried to shake the boy out of the tree, but the tree stood fast. Finally, they summoned two cunning medicine-men. Unfortunately, the child's magic was no match for theirs and he was soon flung to the ground with the buckets and brutally beaten. No one felt any pity for his battered, broken body. Then – before the people's astonished eyes – the tree healed his injuries and transformed Koobor into a koala bear who immediately scampered back into the highest branches. Since koalas do not need water, leaves alone would keep him alive.

Koobor forbid the killing of any koala unless the people were starving – even then, they must show respect. No bone could be broken nor could the little body be skinned until it was fully roasted. If Koobor's law were ignored, the spirits of all koalas would dry up the rivers and people would die of thirst.

Botany/History

Eucalyptus comes from Greek, *eu*, "well," and *kalyptos*, "covered," referring to lidded cups which cover buds until they break through and burst into musky-scented, fluffy, tufted blossoms ranging in colors from cream through crimson. Trees, young and old, flower early and freely, even during droughts, attracting bees to their abundant nectar.[10] Eucalyptus, or Gum, is native to Australia, where it has flourished for at least 250,000 years, adapting to various ecological extremes found on the subcontinent.[11] It accounts for 95% of the trees in forests, even growing in heavy snow at elevations of up to 6,000 feet in the Australian Alps. The trees will grow in soils ranging from hard clay to rich loam and have adapted themselves to a wide range of non-forest conditions, tropical and temperate, swampy and parched, sheltered and exposed. The trees provide a variety of strong hardwoods, some beautifully grained, whose uses run from fine cabinet-making to bridge-building. Oils extracted from willowy leaves are used in perfume-making, dyes, and remedies for colds and respiratory infections; medicinal exports to Europe began as early as 1798.[12]

The genus has over 500 species, including the "Coolibah," whose wood is among the hardest and densest in the world.[13] The "mountain ash" (*Eucalyptus regnans*) can tower over 480 feet, making it the tallest hardwood in the world. More frequent are trees growing 100-120 feet – or 60-80 feet along parched watercourses. Common names tend to be based upon such characteristics as bark (stringybark, ironbark); wood-types (ash, boxwood, mahogany); or oils (peppermint, lemon).[14] The attractiveness of these trees led to a wonderful description by artist Henry Turner Bailey in the 1920s:

> ...If trees must hang their leaves about them, let them emulate the Eucalyptus family. That's a great race! They are rather slovenly when it comes to housekeeping, but they are a handsome lot, from the slim maiden who shoots up a hundred feet and dangles a few scraps of clothing against the sunrise, to the ample matron who sits as comfortably upon the hillside as a Gypsy, the luxuriant folds of her garments golden with the sunset.[15]

Many eucalypts shed their bark seasonally, much as snakes shed skin. Old bark in some species is a luminous bluish-gray while exposed new bark reveals a subtle rainbow ranging from pale rose to violet to apricot. Other species have bark hanging in long, coarse, fissured strips, giving the trees a shaggy, bearded appearance. Still others have fibrous bark which can be removed in sections and were used by Aboriginal peoples for shields, rough shelters, and canoes.[16] Aboriginals learned early that eucalypts store water in their roots. A section could be dug up and, if one blew on one end, water would bubble out the other. Many European settlers died of thirst, unaware that water was stored in roots all around them.[17]

In the early nineteenth century, eucalyptus trees were exported worldwide to be used as windbreaks around property, to drain swamps, and to rid countries of malaria by draining mosquito-infested marshes. Additionally, their value as timber improved the economies of many countries.[18] Brought in as "workhorses," they transplanted well. Their grace and majesty soon made them a favorite in many places where they are now grown as much for their beauty as their usefulness.

The Reading

The eucalyptus is emotionally and physically very accessible. It possesses a special gift for teaching meditation to those in tune with its vibratory field. The tree shelters the traveler, the x-ray-eyed artist, and the koala-spirit within you. It understands your thirst and respects that, as poet Peter Viereck writes:

> *Thirst is not reasoned. There is for each own darkness*
> *No general compass.*

Since this is a tree of long-distance travel, whether earthly or otherworldly, this card might indicate a major move or transition. If so, accept being transplanted with grace and a spirit of adaptability.

If you are asking about pregnancy, you are cautioned that bringing life from Dreamtime to the earth plane should be a conscious, loving, and responsible decision. If the child would face an environment of neglect, that soul might be better left in Dreamtime.

Eucalyptus brings dreams to the surface. It views Dreamtime as the living "here and now" reality running parallel to, undergirding, and continually crossing over into your usual "reality." It sees transitions, including birth and death, as simple shifts between realms. From an oracular perspective, however, "death" would more likely refer to the demise of outgrown beliefs, allowing a new blossoming in your life, regardless of your age. Eucalyptus, therefore, invites you to explore the worlds of mineral, vegetable, and animal consciousness, drawing closer to their numinous realities. Life, after all, offers many beautiful frequency-bands of awareness beyond those with which you are most familiar. Perhaps, in other words, it is time, not to die, but to live more fully in the deep places – to *feel* Dreamtime all around you in nature.

If your question concerns a relationship, things may move quickly, flowering early and well – a dynamic relationship with excellent potential. Expect that you will often have to shed outworn habits and expectations. Be willing to change and grow because this is what will be demanded of you both.

If you are inquiring about health, pay special attention to your respiratory system. Also, be respectful of your body in general. It will not understand why you might dislike or abuse it. The eucalyptus tree suggests that you treat your body like the lovable, warm little koala your body genuinely believes itself to be.

REVERSED:

You may need to keep a low profile and put your dreams on hold, letting them rest in your roots. But do not forget them. They are what nurture, water, and keep you balanced in an otherwise "workhorse" environment. They are as real as anything else in your "reality."

In a relationship, events may not move as swiftly as you would like but the potential remains excellent. Be content with lowered expectations instead of

blaming your partner or falling into angry silences. This is no time for emotional droughts. Once safely rooted, the relationship should endure, perhaps becoming more dynamic than you wish, but you will find the strength to embrace the changes gracefully.

Artist's Notes:

Garment worn by one of the *Meamei* is myth in picture-language: bodice-sky; skirt-desert; top seven circles represent the constellation of the Pleiades; lower brown semi-circles are their non-star positions, activities, and states of transformation into the Dreamtime. Circle petroglyphs: Uluru (Ayers Rock); figure being transformed (signified by surrounding dots). Murujuga petroglyphs: Dampier Archipelago, Western Australia.

Endnotes

[1] Kenneth Maddock:94; 98.
[2] Berndt-III:vii; Berndt-1:7.
[3] Berndt-II:23; 8; 11; 31.
[4] Lambert, ed., *Wise Women of the Dreamtime*:44-49.
[5] Charles P. Mountford, *The Dawn of Time*:38.
[6] Raymond Van Over, *Sun Songs*:380.
[7] Berndt-I:38, fig.17.
[8] Berndt-I:42, fig.40.
[9] Mountford, *The Dreamtime*:34.
[10] James Wales Audas, *Native Trees of Australia*:30; 36-37; 80.
[11] Audas:39.
[12] Forestry and Timber Bureau [henceforth, F&TB], *Forest Trees of Australia*:30-31; Audas:36; 34; 37.
[13] Audas:46.
[14] F&TB:31-33; Audas:39; Rodale:185.
[15] Henry Turner Bailey, *The Tree Folk*:13-14.
[16] Audas:32.
[17] Rodale:185.
[18] F&TB:102; Audas:37; Rodale:185.

13
HAWTHORN

Hawthorn

[About the Sutton Benger Green Man:] Out of the mouth pour the twisting twigs of hawthorn....The vigour of the foliage indicates spring: the presence of the berries indicates autumn. It is as though the range of the seasons are present and known to him. As for his face, it is of a power to make you draw back and compose yourself

~ William Anderson[1]

The Mythic World

The hawthorn's month is April, bridging cycles of dark and light. The sense of it is beautifully evoked in British playwright Christopher Fry's *The Lady's Not for Burning*, when Alizon, an excitable young woman, first sees the man with whom she will fall in love:

> Out there, in the sparkling air, the sun and the rain
> Clash together like the cymbals clashing
> When David did his dance.
> I've an April blindness.
> You're hidden in a cloud of crimson catherine-wheels.

Standing on a threshold between wintry March and Mayday, the hawthorn's April is a quixotic month, unsteady, full of promise, blinded by the coming brightness. The hawthorn tree is traditionally associated with chastity, isolation, inactivity. "Sleeping Beauty's" hawthorn thicket is a perfect illustration.[2] Within its boundaries, the princess lay cloistered, chaste, in a state of total inactivity for a full century. Finally awakened by a kiss, her Mayday arrives with fertility and fiery catherine-wheels of joy.

Three was a sacred number for many early cultures, especially Celts, who portrayed the White Goddess as Maiden, Mother, Crone, mirroring the cycles of nature. Altars to these three *Matrae* can be found throughout the settled areas of Europe and are associated with the fertility of crops as well as the health of children. For Mayday celebrations, hawthorn flowers, sacred to the White Goddess, were woven into yoni-wreaths to adorn phallic maypoles. The custom prevailed long after the advent of Christianity, much to the consternation of the Church. Hawthorn flowers were also carried in springtime wedding processions due to their power to avert negative influences ("evil spirits"), and certainly not to their fragrance, for they smell of decay. Hawthorn leaves were also strewn in cradles to protect newborns from "evil spirits."[3]

In addition to Mayday, hawthorn is associated with a miraculous Christmas Day blooming at Glastonbury, whose famous tree was said to have sprung from the hawthorn staff of Joseph of Arimathea who brought the Holy Grail to Britain. Glastonbury is considered the mythical gateway to Avalon, where Arthur sleeps. Arthur's wizard, Merlin, is connected to hawthorn as well, for the fairy Morgane lured him into a hawthorn grove. Unable to escape from the thorny brambles, he finally accepts the grove as his home. As Heinrich Zimmer writes:

> The world is for Round Table knights, for expeditions and adventures. But the hawthorn patch blooms everlasting and Merlin is at home in it. He, the

"magician," is at home in the timeless, looking at the future, like the changing images within a crystal, while he hovers above the flow of time....[4]

Merlin is as everlasting as hawthorn, but then he is a wizard and an eternity of contemplation suits him. For most of us, a hawthorn-time will eventually give way and return us to the outside world. That is what a threshold offers – the opportunity for a radical transition or for a deepening of trust in the path one is already walking.

Botany/History

Hawthorn – additional names include whitethorn, fairy thorn, holythorn, may tree, and mayflower – rarely grows more than fifteen to twenty feet high. It is dense, twisted, impenetrable, which makes it an ideal barrier-hedge. The tree has very hard wood with smooth gray bark. Its timber is an excellent fuel: it burns slowly, intensely, with a lilac flame. It is a tough tree, grows in poor, dry soils, and requires little care. In spring, it is covered with white flowers, protected by thorns. In autumn, it is covered with dark red "haws," or berries. Birds, especially the thrush, feed upon these.[5]

The hawthorn's fragrance is lovely from a distance but sickly-sweet up close (the smell is suggestive of sex and has also been compared to decaying flesh).[6] Like the similarly odoriferous white-flowered elder, holly and rowan, hawthorn was respected as a springtide manifestation of the White Goddess.[7] It was especially associated with April, during which time it was in its late stages of pregnancy, gathering energy to put forth flowers. Under the old British calendar, the tree bloomed for May Day, which increased its sacred connection to the goddess. With the 1732 change to the Gregorian calendar, May 1st became May 13th – thus hawthorn now flowers in mid-May.[8]

Hawthorn's peculiar "aura," as reflected in such names as fairythorn and moon-flower, made it one of the highest ranking "supernatural" trees, especially in France and England, where wreaths and other talismans of interwoven branches (interweaving intensifies the magic) were a protection against the increased springtime activities of mischievous spirits.[9]

Since hawthorn's smell repels fastidious bees, it must be pollinated by flies. The odor is caused by coumarin, an anticoagulant, which makes both flowers and berries useful in cardiac and rheumatoid tonics.[10] Modern medicine recognizes that coumarin aids the functioning of damaged heart muscles and lowers blood pressure by dilating blood vessels.[11] Hawthorn tea steadies the nerves and, perhaps not surprisingly, considering Sleeping Beauty's long slumber, is an old remedy for insomnia.[12]

The tree is native to southern Europe. Once it spread, it became especially common in the far west of Europe. As sacred ash trees were often found guarding springs, so solitary hawthorns, often hung with fluttering prayer-streamers, were found protecting sacred wells. Cults frequently sprang up around such thorn trees, the Glastonbury thorn being the most famous.[13] Since England's long-lived hawthorns, as well as solitary oaks, were distinctive landmarks in open fields or village centers, more English place-names originate in compounds involving thorn and oak than any other trees.[14] Finally, hawthorn gave its name to one of the most famous ships in history: the Mayflower, which, for good or ill, bridged Old England with New England in 1620.

The Reading

The thorny hawthorn marks boundaries and denies access to destructive energies. Its White Goddess/Green Man protection extends from the physical into mental, emotional and spiritual realms. Their strength may be invoked whenever you need such boundaries – or they may impose such boundaries unasked, unwanted, when they are essential if you are to survive.

If you face medical decisions, the hawthorn urges you to get a second opinion. After all, the late-arriving, benevolent fairy at Sleeping Beauty's christening mitigated the harsh decree of the uninvited fairy, who had doomed the princess. You too may find another late-arriving voice offers a more spacious, hopeful path.

Hawthorn usually gives little in the way of sweetness, yet at the root of its putrid odor lies the ability to protect, or "hedge," heart and blood from harm, thereby sustaining you until you are able to awaken into Mayday's sweet kiss of light. In recognition of this, ancient Greeks made torches of hawthorn-wood to light the marriage altar and nuptial chamber, kindling it into pure lilac light, marking the way towards future bliss.[15]

For you, however, such bliss lies in the future. The hawthorn remains rooted in April even though its buds dream of May. Drawing the hawthorn indicates that you are in a period of cleansing, isolation, silence – a time of imposed inactivity and impatience. Since spiritual, emotional, and physical fertilization lies just ahead, the temptation is to rush towards it. What is required, however, is a patient willingness to remain centered in each moment as it passes. It is a time to keep to yourself, allowing inner processes to unfold. There is no blame in putting your dreams and big energies on hold, letting them rest like Sleeping Beauty in a lovely mindscape, while your little energies handle daily life and take their delight in the simpler things of life. This can be frustrating but do not forget that although the tree's flowers symbolize chaste seclusion, within their white silence lies the promise of delight, for by autumn they will be scarlet berries.

Guard against anger and impatience. Do not waste energy demanding to know "Why me?" You are on the difficult threshold of a new growth-cycle. You are simply being protected, with or without your conscious cooperation. Just relax and go with it. It will not last forever. This does not mean, however, that you should go to the other extreme and let yourself shut down, go numb, or sink into lethargy. Stay awake and calm. Shift out of any victim-mentality. To force the rhythms of time will only lead to self-injury. If others mistake the odor of your process for decay, that is their problem, not yours. Something new and wonderful is in the process of being birthed from deep within you. Let the full May flowering unfold in its own way.

Above all, this is a quiet time of watchfulness. Avoid the anxious pressure to verbalize your needs. Simply watch and accept. Sometimes, in exceptional circumstances, when you have already patiently carried a project far beyond its term and it continues to remain "stuck," it may be time to hasten your labor by taking determined action, planting your staff firmly in new ground, as Joseph of Arimathea did, confidently waiting for an out-of-season blooming. Be aware, however, that the "miracle" may not be destined yet, and even if it is, the outcome, while promising, may not be quite the result you expect.

REVERSED:

The constraints are finally being lifted and freedom lies ahead. But let the Hawthorn-time protect your cradling-days awhile longer before you resume your path. Let the "doing" unfold naturally around you.

April is time's pivot, the liminal space, the birth-canal, the place *between* where newness is configured a heartbeat before it is made manifest. "April" is where you have been confined. Trust the unfolding of your own seasons – let one end fully before you enter into the transition lying just ahead. Know that as you move on, you will continue to have the wise guidance that brought you to this point.

Artist's Notes:

Frieze, lower right, portrays Maiden, Mother, Crone holding loaves and fruit: Roman era, Cirencester, early 1st - 2nd century CE. Rabbit holds frieze of Sutton Benger Green Man: Wiltshire, England, 13th-14th century C.E. From left to right, torques are from: Vix, France, 6th century B.C.E.; Snettisham, Norfolk, mid 1st century B.C.E.; and Waldalgesheim, Germany, 4th century B.C.E. Crone's earring: Ireland, 1st- 2nd century C.E.

Endnotes

[1] Anderson:120.
[2] Rodale:275.
[3] Rodale:275.
[4] Heinrich Zimmer, cited in von Franz, *PP*, Spring 1975:34.
[5] Mitchell:66.
[6] Vickery:182-184; Grigson:181.
[7] Baker:106-109.
[8] Grigson:181.
[9] Lehner:59; Grigson:180-181.
[10] Rose:66.
[11] Rodale:275; Lucas:212; Law:19.
[12] Rodale:288.
[13] Vickery:78;
[14] Hadfield:123 (in *TBO*).
[14] Hadfield:123 (in *TBO*).
[15] Lehner:59; Lucas:211.

14
HOLLY

Holly

Heigh-ho! sing, heigh-ho! unto the green holly:
Most friendship is feigning, most loving mere folly.
Then heigh-ho! the holly!
This life is most jolly.

~ Shakespeare
As You Like It

The Mythic World

In Teutonic myth, holly belonged to underworld goddess, Holle (Hel, Helle, Hilde, Hulda, all linguistically related to *höhle,* cave, grave, yoni – *also see Elder*).[1] Despite her death-connections, Holle was the namer of newborns, thereby giving them a soul, identity, voice, and a destiny in a unique time/space.[2] Drops of Holle's blood appeared as holly's midwinter berries, drops which rendered the tree immortal, evergreen. Thus, holly represented birth, death, and re-birth as an on-going cycle of wholeness and balance. For humans, this can become a fierce struggle between life and death, but at the level of the goddess, it is simply a natural union of opposites, where life itself continues "evergreen" – and death's opposite is re-birth, not life. The dualities were ritually reconciled at Winter Solstice in the *hieros gamos,* or sacred marriage, when doorways were festooned with evergreen boughs of female holly twined with male Dionysian mistletoe, whose white berries symbolized semen and eventual death.[3]

Holle herself unites the opposites in her mismatched face: one half appears normal, the other half is fearsome and black (she predates African contact and "black" has no racial implications). Yet despite her strange appearance, Holle is far from gloomy. The dead in her underworld realm of Niflheim, where she makes no clear distinction between death and life, live peaceful, communal lives.[4] All are welcome here except warriors who die in battle. Those go to Valhalla, an unnatural ghetto-paradise, which indicates Holle's awareness that the battle-addicted are unsuited to normal cycles of regeneration or to living according to wiser choices.

The story of Balder's murder reveals Holle's own deepest values. This innocent, the second son of Odin, shone with light, like the white wildflower he always carried. He was a wise judge, skillful and gentle of speech. More than any other god, Balder internalized the "voice" of the Naming-goddess, Holle, which suggests that the two are actually aspects of each other, he: her male-face, her benevolent Holly King – she: his alter ego, his soul, his voice, his ethic-ing heart. But Balder is doomed:

> ...all he asks is to be able to spread harmony and joy, but he hardly ever succeeds; it is as though he were the survivor of some golden age and is now an outcast in a world no longer his own. One day perhaps the world of Balder will be realized, but for the present he is condemned to die...[5]

Balder lives in the sky in a place called "Widely Brilliant." Nothing impure can exist there. In a related myth, it is that mid-point through which the neutral angels will carry the Grail *(see Linden)*. It is a place untouched by the usual strife and turmoil of Germanic myth. In India, it is the place churned out of the sea through which another Voice-goddess, Vak, with her elixir of immortality, arises *(see Amrita)*. It is the *madhya*, the mid-point, the center around which the worlds revolve. It is, finally, the heart-chakra.

In that timeless place, Balder dreams he will be killed. His distraught mother, Frigg, begs for promises from all creation – fire, water, stone, metals, plants, animals, birds, serpents – that no one will harm her son. The only life-form from whom she fails to elicit this promise is a sprig of female mistletoe whom Frigg regards as too young to be asked to swear an oath.

Unfortunately, the spiteful trickster-god Loki disguises himself as a crone and worms the secret of her omission out of Frigg. He finds the mistletoe and tricks a blind brother of Balder's into aiming the sprig at Balder. Now a holly-spear, even thrown by a blindman, could be a threat, but not a dart of mistletoe. It is not even a true plant, for it lives as a parasite, both contributing to life, as well as draining life away. Here mistletoe is said to be a young female – or is it? Loki appears to be an old female, but is not. Is he not perhaps both crone and plant, disguised? In any event, Loki's malice twists both language and appearance – and Balder is slain.

Frigg immediately sends another of her sons to Holle's Niflheim to beg for Balder's return. Holle agrees to release him under terms that show what matters most to her. She understands that Balder's voice will only be heard if his "Widely Brilliant" heart-center is internalized in all hearts. With this in mind, she sets the test. She asks for compassion, for heartfelt grief, from everyone, living and dead. Then she will return him, knowing his message will finally be able to root itself in those opened hearts. But if *anyone* refuses to weep, or simply feigns grief, that infectious parasitic growth will spread, dooming Balder's vision. In such an event, Holle will spare him further anguish and keep him with her.

Frigg sends messengers all over the world. All humans, animals, trees, stones, metals weep for Balder. Only one being refuses – a witch living in a remote cave who says she has no reason to weep because, whether alive or dead, Balder never did anything for her, so why should she do anything for him? She is, of course, another of Loki's disguises. In this way, Loki prevents the return of Balder. After that:

> ...the world knew no more true happiness, perfect justice, or ever-kindly beauty... and everything in the world became a mixture of pure and impure, joy and tears, beauty and ugliness, life and death. From then on, the world would degenerate till the fatal moment of its dissolution.[6]

There is yet a note of hope, however, for after the final dissolution, or Twilight of the Gods, Balder will return and bring his ethical vision and "Voice" to a new race of mortals destined to live in peace *(see Ash)*.

Botany/History

Holly is a shrubby tree which grows to heights of twenty to fifty feet in almost any soil. Glossy green leaves are tender in springtime, but are toughened in summer to a leathery texture with sharp points. White and rank-smelling female (pistillate) and male (staminate) flowers develop on separate trees – only females will produce autumn's red berries, poisonous to humans, but prized by many birds, especially songbirds, driven by severe weather to pick them clean.[7] The berries are, as Margaret Baker writes, "symbols of blood and, therefore, of life...and protective against all forces threatening life." Baker adds that the transformation of white, odiferous, "even sinister" smelling flowers into red berries places the holly among that select group of "magical trees" (including rowan, hawthorn, elder, and dogwood) which are claimed by the White Goddess in her aspect of regenerative growth.[8]

Holly bark is smooth and gray. Stripped of bark, the beautiful surface of the hard, white wood invites drawings, finely-turned handles, and other works of art.[9] The wood was given more aggressive expression in earlier times when men crafted holly-spears. Women, on the other hand, working with more life-oriented forces, crafted magic wands of holly-wood. The tree is especially protective of the home where, in Pliny's words, "Holly trees round the house prevent sorcery" (*Aquifolia arbor, in domo aut villa sata, veneficia arcet*).[10]

The Reading

Traditionally, winter's holly with its protectively-toothed leaves represents a warrior, standing firm, evergreen and virile in the midst of a bleak and barren world. This is the Holly King of medieval legend. Darker nuances emerge in legends of kings sacrificed at Yuletide and resurrected to rule anew at the Goddess' side. In an interpretive context, this points to the periodically necessary process of re-balancing male and female energies. Otherwise, male energy might easily be sidetracked into serving power and property, not life. If you must fight, be careful that the cause is just and will not result in oppressing yourself or others. Then stand your ground and trust your strength.

Just as the face of Holle seems mismatched, half darkly fearsome, half normal, so too does holly present seemingly mismatched aspects in a reading. This "black and fearsome" is not racial. It is the formless, shimmering black of primal chaos, tomb, abyss, vagina, womb. This "black and fearsome" is what men fear most about women. Yet holly traditionally has represented, not a female presence, but a warrior bristling with spears and thorns, protecting his winter fruit. Regardless of gender, however, no matter how strong and valiant you are, it is unwise to remain continually at war. When everything around you is lush and green, you have no need to defend yourself. Your new leaves are soft, your flowers pure, even if somewhat foul smelling. The winter-warrior is out of place here. Your show of prickly leaves is inappropriate, even bullying. If your winter's berries have already fallen, what are you protecting? Are you warring from habit? — from fear of being vulnerable? Stop depriving your next season's crop of its essential life-force. Relax and claim some downtime. You have earned it.

While resting, holly invites you to reconsider ethical priorities. It asks for your willingness to handle dualities without combat. It suggests a new spirit of creativity, a "Holly-wood" to nurture the spirit. It asks you for a new voice, a new wisdom, with which to re-name, or baptize, your vulnerable self. It warns that rest is necessary along with a good-natured acceptance of your odd burden of beauty and bad smells. Only through this seemingly mismatched period of wonder and disgust will you be able to re-birth that which is truest and best in you, that which comes out of a balanced center, illumined by the inner congruence of both winter and summer suns.

Drawing holly may mean that you are faced with important choices requiring a clear sense of values. Holly in winter represents a careful balance of mother and warrior, for her sharp leaves protect her berries from four-footeds. Yet this tree also knows how to protect her source of song: to her fosterlings, the birds who will sing in her branches in kinder weather, she allows a share of her bounty. Search within for the wisdom to know the difference between giving to what will only strip you bare – or giving to what will later enrich you. Then give wisely of your brightness in the cold dark so that you may later enjoy music and companionship in the warm light.

REVERSED:

Unlike hawthorn, which actively blocks movement and forces you to rest, holly offers a choice. Holly urges you to know *when* to rest. If you draw holly reversed, you would be foolish not to slow down. You will only become more exhausted if you struggle. You cannot expect that your still-embryonic fruit will dramatically ripen on its own in an unremittingly stressed body and psyche.

Reversed holly may also be an indication that your inner Loki-child has a claim on your attention and will impede your struggles until it is recognized. The nature of its unresolved claim may emerge in dreams or active imagination. Do not be afraid to explore this. Remember that the cynical, love-deprived Loki needs to experience the compassionate joy of Holle, who herself is the alter ego of your loving Balder-side. You have perhaps misjudged Loki in his immature female mistletoe-guise. That was Frigg's error: she failed to ask for a commitment from what seemed most vulnerable. This created a power vacuum around the small plant, putting it at risk. Yet nothing is too weak or confused to be asked, respectfully, for help – the very request aids in the maturation of such energies.

Loki, for all his disguises, is that wounded child, a source of your song, who needs to *feel,* in a deeply personal manner, that his gifts are esteemed and needed. Neglected, these gifts contain the seeds of your undoing. Nurtured, their life essence will invisibly heal and support all you do. Through compassion, the goddess helps you unite what seems to be opposed: the purity and goodness of Balder with the cunning and power of a spurned Loki. By returning to the place of compassion, you can merge the two in your heart and find your way into a new balance.

Otherwise, if you feel self-hate, body-hate, or even life-hate, there in that kernel may lie the saboteur, the mistletoe, the endlessly cunning Loki-child. Begin there, going slowly, resting often, playing more, laughing much. Reversed holly, even more than upright, invites you to explore your own spontaneity, wise folly, creativity and vulnerability.

Artist's Notes:

Holle: Cologne, Germany, 2nd century C.E.

Endnotes

[1] Walker, *E*:406.
[2] Walker, *D*:466.
[3] Walker, *E*:406-407.
[4] Larousse:389.
[5] Snorre Sturlasson, cited in Larousse:382.
[6] Larousse:383.
[7] Zim & Martin:64; Hooker, *BF*:67-68; Martin:pl.20; Mitchell:88-89; Crowles:102a.
[8] Baker:106-7.
[9] Hooker, *BF*:67.
[10] Cited in Baker:112.

15
LARCH

Larch

The *turu* [larch], the tree which grows over or from the body of the deer or elk, is synonymous with clan origin: it marks the place of emergence from the animal mother and the place where one passes to the upper or lower worlds....

~ Esther Jacobson[1]

The Mythic World

Larch, often depicted as having deer-antlers, is the World Tree for many Scytho-Siberian peoples. In a shaman's initiation among the Evenk, for example, a spirit-ancestor leads the shaman to the underworld place from which the clan's *turu* grows. As art historian Esther Jacobson writes:

> Among the roots of the *turu* lies the great Animal Mother, a cow elk or cow reindeer. She eats the shaman's anthropomorphic soul and then gives birth to the *khargi*, the soul of the shaman's animal double. The *khargi* is then placed by the spirit ancestors in an iron cradle hanging from the branches of the larch, or *turu*....[2]

This ritual of soul-birthing his animal double empowers the shaman to take the form of any creature, whether man or beast. The next step is to fashion his drum from the *turu* – its framework deftly cut from a living larch, binding both shaman and drum to that sacred source. Were the tree to die, the Evenk believe the shaman would, too. Over the drum's larch-wood frame is stretched a consecrated deerskin, which connects both shaman and drum to the animal mother. Since female reindeer in Siberia are antlered, those antlers are seen as the tree's origin. Thus, both tree and animal mother mark the clan's origin and return. Thereafter, the drum's soundwaves will serve as a reindeer-steed when the shaman "travels" in trance.

The Evenk and other Siberian peoples believe that shamans were originally women, usually elderly, who guarded the path to the realm of the dead and guided souls across the boundaries. As males gained more power, however, women were eclipsed. The sacred clan tree was reduced to being the central pole of a shaman's tent; the animal mother became no more than his helper.

Thus, although women and animals had possessed independent power for thousands of years, they lost that power in a social order of male-centered shamanism. They became mere allies, respected, but carefully controlled and manipulated.

A telltale clue to shamanism's female origins is that the clothing of male shamans deliberately resembled women's garb, often with women's help, for they alone understood the required ornate amulets and artwork. When the shaman was fully dressed in robes, footgear, gloves, and headdress, he took on the power and awareness of the clan's Animal Mother (whether elk, deer, or bear). He became possessed by the animal, mystically becoming *her*, becoming the clan's primary progenitor. However, since Animal Mother and Tree of Life were interchangeable transmutations of one another, much was lost. In Jacobson's words:

...the Animal Mother was reformulated in terms of cultic spirits – of the fire, the sun or moon, the hunt. In the shamanic rite she retained a powerful position; but in that tradition, without the shaman as mediator there is effectively no animal mother, no tree of life, and no access to the realm of the spirits.[3]

As far as is known, the peoples of Siberia did not have a goddess in human form until fairly late. The oldest Animal Mothers were elks (in some regions, bears). With changing environmental conditions, antlered reindeer and birds became more common (ancient images depict birds sitting on antlered trees or tree-like antlers turning into birds). Sometimes there were composite deer-women or bird-women.

Eventually, largely under Greek influence, the Animal Mother became fully human, depicted as a seated goddess, addressed by young horsemen, sometimes holding cups or hunting paraphernalia. According to Herodotus, the goddess Tabiti was the chief deity of the Scythians. Herodotus equated her with the Greeks' Hestia because both were connected with fire, hearths, and fertility. Below Tabiti, Jacobson writes, were "a male and female generative couple, roughly equivalent to Heaven and Earth."[4] There was no Zeus-like god ruling the Scythian pantheon – Tabiti was at its summit.

In the nomadic Scytho-Siberian world, art in general found its most distinctive expression in what is known as the "animal style" – an ornate, symbolic representation of deer, stags, other horned animals, large cats, wolves and other predators, and birds of prey. Some were made of gold, others carved from wood and probably covered with gold. Their uses ranged from jewelry and mirrors to horse-trappings. Mirrors, which in many ancient cultures protected against evil spirits, frequently had long handles carved in "animal style," the animals often morphing into one another, as was common with this style.[5] Coffins too were carved with animal imagery: one such, known as the Bashadar coffin, was crafted of larch and elaborately decorated with:

> ...a row of standing tigers distinguished by their huge jaws and claws. Under the feet of some of the tigers and in proximity to their jaws are the images of sheep, boar, and saiga antelope or female elk, crushed or twisted under the weight of the cats.[6]

At first glance, predators and their victims would not seem comforting images for one's dead. But when we go more deeply into what we know of this lost world, we find very different meanings. In art, predation was a central motif among these peoples but, as Jacobson comments:

LARCH

...It is a predation without conclusion....Within the eternal repetition of that act there is no death.[7]

She describes a large deer from a 5th century B.C.E. plaque found in a burial barrow in Ilyichovo:

...Rearing up before the raised head of the deer is a great serpent, while a wolf or bear-like animal curls around the deer's upper body and bites into its chest, and an eagle pecks at its tail. Faced with such ferocious predation, the deer's raised neck and head and its firm body still express enormous vitality. As if they were an aspect of that vitality, its antler-tines have been transformed into the heads of birds with long curled beaks. Even the hoofs of the deer and the tail terminate in bird heads. The image clearly joins the processes of predation and transformation, centering them in the body of the antlered deer.[8]

Thus, not predators, but the deer, seemingly the victim, is the central focus. Many cultures align themselves with predators: eagles and large felines are among the most common. But across a wide swath of Eurasia, the Animal Mother was prey – and in her "Passion," if you will, her transformation empowered her people. As Jacobson writes, predators:

...were the symbols of that change which was catalyzed by death but which in fact was the process of metamorphosis from one form of being to another, and thus from one realm to another...[9]

...In those cases where the deer is twisted as if under the impact of a predator [...] the twisting refers to the death from which regeneration will emerge. . . . [This regeneration] is ultimately signalled by [...] the antler-trees in which the birds of souls to be returned to the world are perched.[10]

By making this process so graphically visual, artistic expression itself became a ritual invocation of life out of death.[11] It was an endlessly cycling process, forms reborn into another after another.

Botany/History

The slender larch of the pine family grows rapidly to a height of 50-120 feet. Because its scaly bark withstands cold, many northern mountain ranges support majestic, long-lived larch forests. These trees are unique among northern conifers because they shed their needles in autumn. The inch-long, blue-green, dark, soft needles form into tufts spaced along short, graceful branches. Nestled in the tufts are small cones, able to cling to their branches for several years, despite annual tuft-shedding.

In Siberia, the larch was frequently used for the framework or resonators of a shaman's drum – the wood was cut carefully from a still-living tree for it was important that the tree survive.[12] Native Americans in the eastern part of the United States harvested tough fibers from the tree's roots and used them to bind the seams of their birchbark canoes.

The Reading

The Larch was reduced from Cosmic Tree to being the central pole in a shaman's tent. The Animal Mother was reduced from progenitor of her clan to being a mere ally, subject to the will of a shaman. Whether male or female, if you have drawn this card, you are cautioned to avoid anything that diminishes your intrinsic worth. This means people, events, rituals, politics, media – any form of negativity that drains or harms your power. Similarly, do not to allow your own negativity to drain or harm the power of others. Turn your mind's mirror on the world and see things for what they are. Be the clear-eyed child of "The Emperor's New Clothes." Many religious traditions, for example, have stolen power from women and still have misogynistic cores. Continue to follow the beliefs of such traditions if they resonate with you, but keep your eyes open for inevitable eruptions of hypocrisy and abuse and do not make excuses for perpetrators.

In personal relationships, do not become ally or "animal mother/father" to another and wind up too exhausted to express your own creativity. If you feel used, unheard or unseen by a mate, do not pretend it is love – it is manipulation. Trust your feelings. Do not provide your sacred deerhides and amulets for someone else's robes. They are *yours* – part of you and your path. Tend them well and respectfully. Ask for guidance, perhaps from Tabiti, last in a line of powerful Animal Mothers, or seek it from her more ancient antecedents.

Finally, in making decisions about whatever has brought you to the oracle, Larch asks that you look at life with *non*-human eyes and experience the increasing vulnerability of the beauty lying all around you. It asks that you realize that you, the larch, the animals, and everything else in life are interconnected, secretly communicating with one another across boundaries between realms, relying upon one another for survival in a web of patterns too mysterious for any one species to control.

REVERSED:

You are not defined by your job. Journey inward. Within you grows the larch, tall and stately, shifting into the Animal Mother, both of them cradling your deeper self. Explore your creativity and rich imagination. Recognize that what seems to be destroyed on one level serves as a life-giving prelude to your transformation on another level. Like larch-cones on bare branches, even though your supporting tufts of soft needles have fallen away, you instinctively know how to hang on, trusting in the on-going life being generated deep within you.

Artist's Notes:

Artifacts come from various Ukrainian sites. Mirror from Kul'Oba Kurgan, c. 4th century B.C.E. Cup with horses from Bratoliubivs'ky kurgan, near Ol'hyno, 5th century B.C.E. Torque from Soboleva Mohyla, 350-25 B.C.E. Earring, depicting a seated goddess (probably Tabiti), from near Velyka Znam'ianka, c. 4th century B.C.E. Headdress and dress plaques, found in Chertomlyk kurgan, 350-25 B.C.E., could depict Tabiti's ritual marriage to a king.

Endnotes

[1] Jacobson:193.
[2] Jacobson:194.
[3] Jacobson:245.
[4] Jacobson:215 – rest of Tabiti and goddess data
from pp.214-217.
[5] Jacobson:7.
[6] Jacobson:11.
[7] Jacobson:54.
[8] Jacobson:55.
[9] Jacobson:86.
[10] Jacobson:240-241.
[11] Jacobson:239.
[12] Data in this Botany / History section comes
from Lehane:42-43; Zim & Martin:30; Brockman:36-37; and Altman:183-184.

16
LAUREL

Laurel

Lovely laurel, evergreen in all its parts, standing midmost among many trees smitten by lightning, bears the inscription: "Untouched it triumphs" *(intacta triumphat).*
~ Picinelli, *Mondo simbolico*[1]

The Mythic World

Ancient divinatory centers were "tree-coded"[2] – Nemi's beech, Dodona's oak, Buto's papyrus, and laurel near the sacred Castalian springs at Delphi. When Daphne, a priestess of earth-mother Gaia, fled from Apollo, who had stolen the Delphic Oracle from Gaia, Daphne was saved from rape when Gaia transformed her into a laurel.

Significant earlier levels of abuse and rape underlie this story, however. When Gaia emerged alone from Chaos, she birthed sky-god Uranus. She took him as her consort and then had many more children. Uranus found her one-eyed offspring and those with too many hands objectionable so he tossed them like so much toxic waste from his pristine sky. Outraged, Gaia turned to her youngest son, Cronus, who coldly castrated and overthrew his father. Cronus then became the consort of his sister Rhea.

A dark pattern is taking shape: when unwanted offspring become their father's prey, a surviving son takes revenge on behalf of their mother. Thus, once Cronus is Rhea's consort, he swallows *her* first five children, lest they overthrow him. Their youngest, Zeus, subsequently deposes his father, Cronus *(see Oak for further details)*.

Then the pattern shifts and rape is added. Although Gaia took Uranus as her consort, and their daughter Rhea took Cronus, Zeus refuses to be consort to any of his sisters, Hestia, Demeter, or Hera. Instead, he rapes Hera and announces his intention to force her into marriage. Until then, women were free to choose mates at will. Zeus' plan would turn them into a male's property. His mother, Rhea, unequivocally forbids this.

Determined to have his way, Zeus threatens to twist his own sexuality into brutal vengeance by raping Rhea. Appalled, she turns herself into a gigantic serpent, confident that this raw, primal display of power will force Zeus to respect her authority. Instead, he also takes serpent-form, winding around her and coiling himself into knots, which hold her immobile while he viciously rapes her. Gloating, he then weds Hera, who ever after loathes him and does her best to make his reign miserable.[3]

Rhea, for her part, withdraws in cold rage. She is steeped in archaic birth-magic learned from her mother, Gaia, who, unpartnered, created Uranus. Rhea too can conceive parthenogenetically, "alchemizing" herself. Although Zeus might temporarily shapeshift into serpent form, *she* could engender an entirely new being. Thus, to humiliate her overweening son, Rhea births the great serpent-god Python.

As if to focus all attention upon Rhea's birthing power, the mysterious new god swirls through the cosmos, deliberately searing Zeus' sky with serpent-lightning. Then he dives back to earth where he coils around the *omphalo*s ("navel") at Gaia's shrine in Delphi ("womb") and intertwines with Gaia in her serpent-form of Delphyne, "Womb of Creation," in whom Gaia-Rhea-Hera merge their identities into the same primal energy.

Python knows all Delphyne's secrets and shares relevant knowledge with the *Pythia,* or Pythoness-priestess, serving Gaia's shrine.[4] Unfortunately, a day comes when sun-god Apollo, one of Zeus' powerful sons, lusts after Python's power. After a ferocious struggle, Apollo slays the ancient serpent and steals the shrine for himself.[5] Some say Python was buried at Delphi, his spirit appeased by Pythian Games held every eight years. More convincingly, others say Apollo hurled his body into the skies where he became a constellation, eternally yearning for his mate, Delphyne, who was imprisoned deep underground as Apollo's hostage.

The *Pythia*, Delphi's seeress, had always spoken on her own to those seeking oracular guidance, but Apollo's priests now turn her oracles to their own benefit.[6] Where once she spoke only during a brief season, she is now forced to function year-round. The shrine becomes a place for those wealthy enough to afford opulent gifts. Guidance in private matters is still sought, but high-profile statecraft issues become Delphi's specialization. Although Apollo's priests generally recommend reason and moral excellence, these patriarchal virtues, worthy as they might be, were nevertheless bought at the price of the voices of women.

Apollo coveted more than oracular mysteries at Gaia's sacred springs. When he saw the virginal Daphne, he pursued her, wild with lust. As he was only a hand's breadth away, the desperate maiden begged merciful earth-mother Gaia for help and Gaia instantly changed her into a laurel.[7] As Apollo reached out to snare her flying hair, he came away with his hands full of laurel leaves. She was *intacta triumphat,* untouched, intact, triumphant.

The laurel tree was intimately associated with Delphi. Priestesses chewed the prophecy-inducing leaves as they sank deeper into trance.[8] As preventative magic against evil, a laurel-wreath crowned the boy-actor representing Apollo in rituals that celebrated the slaying of the monster, Python.[9] Of course, this was a perverse twist: from Daphne's perspective, the monster was *Apollo,* not Delphyne's devoted consort. In classical times, laurel wreaths, their older meaning forgotten, crowned heroes and victors in contests of sport and art.

The laurel and oak, both oracular trees, both originally the domain of an earth goddess, were both required in kindling sacred fires in Greece and Rome. Oak was revered because it could attract lightning. Laurel was revered for the opposite reason – it remained intact among other lightning-struck trees. Greeks used the hardy laurel as the borer of the fire-drill in engendering sacred fire.[10] Romans, recognizing that laurel and oak both possessed auspicious fire, used both in their temples.[11]

Bitter-tasting laurel, in ancient Israel as in Greece, was associated with sacred springs. On the Exodus, after Hebrews had gone for days in the scorching desert, they rejoiced to reach the springs of Marah, only to find its waters too bitter to swallow. They broke into desperate laments, afraid for themselves and their young. After Moses begged Yahweh for help, Yahweh told him to take a laurel leaf, write His name upon it, and cast it into the waters. Bitter waters, bitter laurel – from this doubled bitterness, mediated by a written word, came, miraculously, sweetness – and the people drank their fill of this simplest, most ordinary, and yet most precious gift.[12]

Botany/History

A great many trees are called "laurel" and it is often impossible to determine which tree the ancients meant when they referred to the evergreen laurel (Greek, *daphne*). Today, what is usually called "laurel" is *Prunus laurocerasus,* the cherry laurel; the unrelated poets' laurel, *Laurus nobilis,* is a bay tree – their leaves are similar and when the ancients crowned victors with wreaths, it is not known which one was used.[13] In addition to its leaves, the bay also produces dark berries – when crushed, these berries were used to ease bee stings; when eaten, they were believed to ease a woman in labor.[14]

Research done in the fifties or sixties at the Southern Research Institute in Birmingham, Alabama on varieties of laurel showed that no matter what soil it grows in, even when necessary minerals and nutrients are not even *there*, it nevertheless can "alchemize" the rare earth elements it needs and the chemical content of its leaves remains constant.[15]

Many scholars believe the cherry laurel has the famous trance-inducing leaves used at Delphi. Its mildly toxic leaves, when crushed, have a sweet almond scent. The leaf is both a poison and a narcotic, containing 0.1 percent of hydrogen cyanide – a tiny percentage but enough to cause delirium or worse.[16] Apollo's priestesses would have gone through a period of training to enable them to handle these effects.

Apollo was a latecomer at Delphi – his priests not arriving until the 8th century B.C.E.[17] Yet archaeological finds date back to at least 1600 B.C.E. and the original dream-oracle cave, thought to have been in the mountains high above the later shrine, was doubtless revered long before then.[18] The shrine itself occupies a dramatic location some 2,000 feet above the Gulf of Corinth. The ancients regarded this as the navel of the world, the place from which Gaia had birthed all life.

After Apollo's arrival, although there was a bias towards patriarchal concepts of reasoned logic, the necessity for the heightened emotions of Dionysus, god of wine and ecstasy, was also acknowledged. Thus, during the winter when sun-god Apollo went north, Delphi gratefully welcomed Dionysian theatre to a magnificent site above the temple.

The Delphic oracle ended when the Christian emperor Theodosius closed it down in 385 C.E.[19] Though its oracular voice has long been silenced, there remains an inner seed-memory of the depths of insight to which the alchemy of laurel, allied with ancient goddess-energy, could take one.

The Reading

This is a tree of sacred alchemy, able to birth insight and physicality out of its very own essence, regardless of the raw materials available to it in its environment. If you draw the Laurel, you are being told that you too have this gift: no matter what soil you are growing in, even when the minerals and nutrients are not *there* and there is no way to get them, you can nevertheless alchemize what you need out of "nothing." Trust this and reclaim your own inner voice. Do not internalize the values of those who have victimized you.

You have perhaps been passive and unable to get your own needs met. Western culture expects this passivity from women and more sensitive, thoughtful males. This expectation arises from the image of a receptive womb dedicated to nurturing *otherness*, not oneself. The Laurel tree reminds you that there is yet another dimension to the feminine: the womb may quietly, patiently support growing life for nine months – but then – *whooomph!* – it takes powerful action! As Genia Pauli Haddon writes with refreshing insight in her *Body Metaphors*:

> Femininity traditionally has been described as receptive and nurturing, as exemplified by the receiving and gestating function of vagina and womb. It follows that to be feminine is to be like a vessel, receiving, encompassing, enclosing, global, wholistic, welcoming, sustaining, protecting, nourishing, conserving, embracing, containing, centripetal, stable, holding together, inclusive....
>
> ...The receptive and gestating (yin) function is only half of their story. The womb is also the organ that pushes mightily to birth. Our understanding of the nature of femininity needs to be revised to take into account the birth-pushing, yang, assertive function of the womb.
>
> ...Anyone who has assisted with the birth of larger animals, such as sheep or cows, will attest to the enormous thrusting power of the womb pushing toward birth. If we were to define the Great Feminine solely in accordance with the womb's birthing power, we would speak of it as the great opener of what has been sealed, the initiator of all going forth, the out-thrusting yang power at the heart of being....

If our ideas about femininity were based on the birth-pushing function of the womb, rather than solely on its containing function, women would be expected to be initiators and movers, and to call a woman "pushy" would be to compliment her on her femininity.[20]

If you have drawn Laurel in your reading, it may be time for you to get past any neglect or abuse, take matters into your own hands, and "push mightily to birth."

REVERSED:

Further gestation may be needed – and this suggests that you take special care not to "alchemize" so often that you deplete yourself. Do not sink into depression or feel betrayed by cosmic energies. Such energies may seem to be favoring others while avoiding you. Perhaps this is because those energies are sending blessings to you in areas you yourself have been avoiding – you may need to practice greater subtlety of discernment to see this.

You may have been put down, criticized for your gifts, your "differentness," but trust that you have your own right to oracular dimensions. As at Marah's bitter springs, let Laurel – with whatever name or word embodies the sacred for you – sweeten the inner bitterness.

The poet Rilke uses laurel in his "Ninth Elegy"[21] as a metaphor for the simple, fleeting, sweetness of life; he contrasts this with the human frenzy to have more, ever yet more. Why, he asks do we:

> ...*have* to be human, and, shunning Destiny,
> long for Destiny?. . .
> Not because happiness really
> exists, that premature profit of imminent loss.
> Not out of curiosity, not just to practice the heart,
> that could still be there in laurel. . .
> But because being here amounts to so much, because all
> this Here and Now, so fleeting, seems to require us and strangely
> concerns us.
> Us the most fleeting of all. Just once,
> everything, only for once. Once and no more. And we, too,
> once. And never again. But this
> having been once, though only once,
> having been once on earth – can it ever be cancelled?

He speaks of the sufferings, "the hardness of life, the long experience of love" – and at the end of our wanderings we do not bring a handful of earth to our destination but, rather, miraculously:

...some word he has won, a pure word, the yellow and blue
gentian. Are we, perhaps, here just for saying: House,
Bridge, Fountain, Gate, Jug, Olive tree, Window, –
possibly: Pillar, Tower? . . . . but for saying, remember,
oh, for such saying as never the things themselves
hoped so intensely to be.

And so we say our word, a word we have won, a pure word, "some simple thing," something that "lives in our hands and eyes as a part of ourselves," and we speak this, we tell it, "just to make everything leap with ecstasy in them." We become so present, so translucent, to each thing that it becomes transformed "within our invisible hearts." We take the Laurel – and the word – and sweeten the bitterness. For the frenzy too is sweet and transforms what is fleeting into "an invisible re-arising in us."

Artist's Notes:

The depiction of Gaia in the upper right corner is from the Pergamon altar, Greek, 165-156 B.C.E. Her gesture is part of the spirit-energy transforming Daphne. Snake earring from Greek bracelet: Avola, 330-300 B.C.E.

Endnotes

[1] Cited in C. G. Jung, *A&CU*:333, n.132.
[2] Buffie Johnson:61.
[3] Graves, *GM*:vol. 1, 13.a.
[4] Walker, *Encyclo.*:857; 832-833; 218.
[5] Frazer, IV:79.
[6] Graves, *GM*:vol. 1, 51.1.
[7] Rose:141.
[8] Frazer, I:384.
[9] Frazer, IV:78-79; VI:241-243.
[10] Frazer, II:251-252.
[11] Altman:49.
[12] Ginzberg:III, 39.
[13] Alan Mitchell: 82-83.
[14] Altman:149.
[15] Private communication from William Samuel of Mountain Brook Publications, Mountain Brook, Alabama; unfortunately, the Institute's library has been unable to locate any data on this work.
[16] Mitchell, op.cit.; Walker, *Dict.*:441.
[17] Baring/Cashford:330.
[18] Joseph Fontenrose: 412-416; 418-419.
[19] Stapleton:63; 65.
[20] Haddon:11-12.
[21] Rilke:73-77.

LINDEN

Linden

Sigune, we cry for all your barren womb might have born,
for all your barren heart would have taught us –
you might have led us through the linden grove,
taught us to be daughters of the earth
instead of consorts to a sword.

Sigune, Sigune,
lift up your face,
the world has moved on,
we need you strong.

~ Eanna Einhorn
"Sigune"[1]

The Mythic World

In Greek mythology, linden was the goddess Philyra (Greek, "linden"). In a linden grove on a tiny island no longer than a hundred yards, she turned herself into a mare to escape the Titan-god, Chronos. Undeterred, he turned himself into a stallion, caught, then raped her. To her horror, she soon birthed the centaur Chiron, half-human, half-horse. The unwilling mother begged the gods to change her form so she would not have to raise such a grotesque newborn. They changed her into one of the grove's lindens.

The abandoned child could have grown up bitter. Instead, Chiron became famous for his kindness and wisdom. As a physician, he knew how to use herbs, plants, and dreams; as tutor and seer, he functioned as a living, human version of a divinatory-tablet made of linden-bast; as a musician, he carved fallen linden-limbs into trumpets and other wind instruments. Somehow, he intuited how to express the best of "linden-ness" in his own life. Chiron knew how to "parent," as his own had not.

He raised others as well – Asclepius, the most gifted of Greek physicians, and also Jason, Aeneas, Achilles, and other heroes. They did not all turn out well, but he never begrudged his time. Eventually, he was accidentally poisoned in the knee. The agonizing wound refused to heal but, as an immortal, he could not die. The gods finally allowed him to surrender his immortality to fire-bringer, Prometheus, and Chiron died in peace.[2]

In classical Greece, an elderly woman, Baucis, prayed that she and her husband Philemon would die and remain together forever. The gods granted her prayer and transformed them into trees – she into a linden, he an oak. Thus, linden came to symbolize love enduring beyond death.[3] Reflecting this, lindens in European town-squares have long been a focal point for courtship and marriage.

Medieval Europe gives us a linden-theme involving Sigune, cousin of young Parzival in Wolfram von Eschenbach's early 13th century Grail epic. Here again, an incurable wound, akin to Chiron's, causes an anguished longing for death on the part of the Fisherking, Anfortas (Latin *infirmatus*, "infirm man"), maternal uncle to the cousins. He is tended by one of his sisters who feeds him and his court from the mysterious Grail.

The Fisherking's niece, Sigune, orphaned in infancy, was reared by another of his sisters. When Sigune was five, her foster-mother gave birth to Parzival. Some years later, Sigune left to make a life of her own. She met and fell in love with a knight, only to lose him to death. She then spent the rest of her life grieving over his corpse. In later years, after Parzival abandons his mother to become a knight, Sigune's neurotic suffering plays a crucial role in catalyzing Parzival's dormant sense of compassion, which eventually enables him to heal the Fisherking.

Parzival meets the adult Sigune four times. The first time she is sitting in a linden tree holding her just-slain beloved's body. Distressed that he died before they could consummate their love, she wears his garnet ring in token of a posthumous union. Parzival offers to bury the body but Sigune, ever the noble martyr, refuses, saying that the only help she desires is for the wretched Grail king to find healing. She is furious when she learns that Parzival actually had the opportunity to ask the compassionate question ("Uncle, what ails thee?"), but instead, he followed court-etiquette and kept silent.

At their second meeting, Sigune is perched higher in the linden tree, still cradling her lover's body, which never decomposes – a sign of sanctity in medieval times. Several years later, they meet again. This time Sigune has left her tree and now keeps vigil over her beloved's coffin in a small hermitage built over a stream.[4] Weekly, crone-sorceress Kundrie, garbed in a black robe embroidered with doves, or a blue cloak and peacock-feathered hat, brings Sigune food from the Grail. Kundrie is the Grail Messenger, a shape-shifter who travels between realms. Sigune, for all the victim-quality of her chosen life, has powerful, magical connections.

This same hermitage is where Parzival finds Sigune for the final time, immediately after he has healed their uncle and restored the Wasteland's joy and fertility. He finds her lying dead over the tomb of her beloved, a fitting end for Sigune, for in her grief and obsession with death, she had long since shut herself off from joy and would not have known what to do with its restoration.

From the perspective of our own age, Sigune is damaged, blighted, spiritually impoverished, able to catalyze compassion in others but unable to show it to herself. If the linden could have spoken, it would have asked her to move from her narrow self-centeredness to a wider reality-centeredness. It would have asked her to open her heart and embrace life.

Yet Sigune had genuine knowledge and deep connections to mystical realms. Not even Parzival knew his true name – but she did. She also knew the Grail question he would need to ask. Motherless, she was fed by the Grail's own motherly Messenger. She did not have to be a pathetic creature. Nevertheless, in the midst of vast, shimmering life, grief led her astray. We now need to call her back, for we need her strong. We need her knowledge and connections. We need her to conceive new children of hope.

Botany/History

Linden is famous for the warm honey-sweet fragrance of its creamy blossoms, which reach their peak around Summer Solstice. Bees love the abundant nectar and linden honey has long been prized. The flowers can be fermented into a light wine; as medicinal tea, the delicate flavor of dried blossoms soothes hysteria and stomach or gastric disturbances.[5]

Also known as limetree or basswood from its fibrous "bast," linden grows sixty to a hundred feet high. Since its wood burns with a foul smell, it is generally used artistically unless people are desperate. Its leaves are heart-shaped, its knotless wood is fine-grained, pliant, easily carved into holy ikons, oracle-tablets (used in divination), trumpets, tuning-pegs, musical sounding-boards, spoons, and children's toys. The tree's soft inner bark is moist, sticky, fibrous – ancient peoples used it to bind wounds; its antiseptic qualities greatly aided in healing. From Eurasia to the Americas, the strong bast-fibers were woven into baskets, mats, shoes, ropes, horse bridles. During famine, linden bark (as well as elm, beech, birch, and scotch pine – all of which are more flavorful than other barks) could be ground into meal, often with the addition of crushed nuts.[6] Some cultures took darker measures, sacrificing horses to the linden, dispatching these prized animals into other realms with desperate pleas for help.[7]

The linden is a vigorous tree, sending out countless new sprouts that hide the trunk unless grazed by cattle or cut back by humans. The parent trunk increases rapidly in diameter for the first fifty years, by which time it may be four feet thick. After that, growth slows. Four hundred years later, it may have added another three feet.[8]

Linden spread westward out of the Caucasus and European Russia, following in the wake of the elm, whose bark has similar properties and whose linguistic root in some regions is identical with linden's *(see Elm)*. Linden, in turn, was followed and often crowded out by forests of beech, fir, and spruce. Early peoples contributed to its depletion because of the economic value of its bark and easily carved wood. Its current range runs from southern England, east to central Siberia, and south to the Mediterranean. Related species are also found in the Americas as well as the Far East (jute comes from one such East Indian shrub).[9]

The Reading

Guided by linden, you are soothing, mellow, good for yourself. Recognize your gift for wrapping others in the soft bast-fibers of healing words. A life-long romance is favored. It is a honey-sweet time, fragrant as linden blossoms, light-bodied, like fine linden-wine. Your tall and spacious spirit can afford to be "lithe" (the word is cognate with "linden"), playful, unresisting because whatever is happening to and around you suits your creative purposes. The romance could be with a mate but could also involve work you love deeply. It may have a magical quality, a sense of galloping into parallel-universes and returning with gifts of healing and wisdom.

If you are asking about a child, issues of self-worth might be indicated (and the child in question might be your own inner-child). As with Chiron, whose mother thought him a monster, there may be values and needs that conflict with your own but which, if handled wisely, will enrich you both. Be pliant, yielding, yet crafty. Much is at stake – for every child has potential access to a whole world of civilizing wisdom. Take your own steps to insure your child's access to that wisdom because not all cultures value their young.

REVERSED:

In matters of romance and creativity, you may have misjudged the commitment. The situation may require more work (or less return) than you envision right now. The extra work may result in something wonderful – but you are wise not to expect rapid growth just yet.

Be careful of accidental injuries. As with Chiron, these might be more serious than they seem at first. Do not delay in seeking help. Also be careful of emotional injuries, yours or others. Do not let yourself get too tied up in your role as a "rescuer." You risk having your good intentions twisted, leaving you feeling abused and at the end of your (bast) rope.

Linden's medicinal use focuses upon the abdominal region and includes stomach and gastric disturbances as well as hysteria, which in ancient times was thought to originate in a woman's womb (Greek *hystera*, "uterus"). The abdominal region is the site of the second chakra and is highly charged with emotion. In Japan, this belly, or *hara*-center, was often stabbed when all hope was lost, but *hari-kari* is not the answer here. If this emotional center feels as if it is beginning to unravel, learn how to weave a safe cocoon around it in which new hope may be conceived.

In extreme cases, your emotional and economic survival may be threatened. Ours is a society that under-employs and wastes minds as recklessly as it wastes its environment. You do not deserve to be used as firewood, but this may not yet be a time to fight or resist. It is also not yet a time to attempt to create a splendid new art, cure, or song to speak to peoples' hearts. Those are strategies for reversed Corn, not reversed Linden *(see Corn)*. Instead, this is a time to stay flexible and to keep a low-profile. Go within, trust that the honeyed times will spring anew from another season's shoots – and never forget that linden, once its time comes, grows fast, mighty, and lives for many centuries.

Reversed Linden might be speaking to a root-issue underlying other reversals in your life. This involves long-standing grief. The specific cause is unimportant. It could be a significant death, rejection of your creativity, unrequited love, losing what you hold most dear. All these catalysts finally sink into a bottomless swamp of grief. You feel like Sigune, who lives within most of us, joyless, stern, blighted, too damaged to embrace life. When she is in control, there is no way to get on with your life.

LINDEN

Linden asks you to look at the situation from an entirely new perspective. Gently consider that the "reality" of your continuing anguish might be no more than the illusory pain of a phantom-limb. Climb higher into the tree. Perhaps your "bottomless swamp" is just a small pond clogged with grief, sadness, weariness. It needs a thorough cleaning so that clear waters can spill over the banks and bring new life to the wasteland.

Do not wonder what you need to let go of. This is not about something specific. Reversed Linden has to do with shapeless, formless, negative *emotion*. You have held onto it for so long that the initial "corpse" or cause has sunk into the mire instead. Life always seems a disappointment to you. That is why Sigune had to die once Parzival restored the Wasteland. She would be frowning and suspicious in a time of joy – so exit Sigune.

Do not be afraid to look back at your life without anger or pain. Then was then, now is now. Do not cling to whatever contaminated your wellsprings of hope, poisoned your Chiron, or struck down your youth. Regardless of what guilt, need, fear, abuse, pain, self-hate, or anguish exploded in your past, you survived or you would not be here now.

Tell your inner-Sigune that you want her with you. Do not let her lose her way in grief. Call her back. You need her wealth of knowledge and mystical connections. She needs you to trace a new path for her through the flowering linden wood. You need each other to be strong – and to go on.

Artist's Notes:

Chalice has Anglo-Saxon bird-brooch design: SE England, 600-650 C.E.

Endnotes

[1] Unpublished ballad, personal communication.
[2] H.J. Rose:47, 198; Graves, *WG*:128; 308; Graves, *GM*:151.g,
151.5; Stapleton:53-5.
[3] Grigson:107; Lehner:69.
[4] Weigand:184.
[5] Grigson: 107; Adrian & Dennis:17; Law:23; Hooker,
BF:214; Martin:pl.18; Brockman:228-9; Rose:77.
[6] Zim & Martin:81; Brockman:228; Grigson:107-8;
Ho"eg:118; Drury:58; Rose:77; Friedrich:88-9.
[7] Friedrich:89; Frazer:ii.365.
[8] Mitchell:104-5.
[9] Friedrich:88-89.

18
LOST FORESTS

Lost Forests

The greenness...is a vibration of consciousness itself...which is older than the frequency of our ego consciousness, a green consciousness which is always there, always present and throbbing at the core of our being....

...[W]e need to re-tune the frequency of our ego consciousness so that we might begin to respond to the other vibrations of consciousness which compose all creation.... What we call the unconscious is the many faceted consciousness of the world....

The unconscious needs to be re-imagined as the consciousness of animal and plants, of minerals and stars, of Angels, and atoms....

We need to see ourselves from the viewpoint of the star and the atom, the animal and the stone, the plant and the angel. We need to acknowledge with a sense of awe and humility these other frequencies of consciousness.

~ Robert Romanyshyn[1]

The Mythic World

In early Europe, there were 4 waxing-to-waning lunar cycles of 7 days each, making up the 28 days of the lunar month. There were 13 such months, totaling 364 days. The extra day was the time-between-the-worlds when angels, ghosts, and spirits roamed freely, whispering of ancient memories and truths. That day lay on the threshold of the New Year, which in some lands was All Hallows Eve, in others, Winter Solstice. In *The Green World Oracle*, this mysterious day belongs to the Lost Forests of Earth.

The light from this planet as she was 200 million years ago is only now just reaching far distant regions of the universe many light years from here. If there are advanced civilizations in those regions with the technology to see our planet's 200-million-year-old light, they would see a planet of oceans and great forests. No humans would yet have evolved. There would be no hint of the ravaging civilizations yet to come. From light years away, our primal Green World would still appear to flourish, covering the planet with abundance.

Those are the Lost Forests, the extinct ones, the ancient ghosts of a pollen-rich abundance. Mysteriously, however, they somehow still flourish in the etheric mists around the planet, even for us. At the Dark of the Moon, when our current forests are most shrouded in night, these extinct ones might make their presence known. Then they come as a whisper, a gift, a continuing presence of beauty, of vast grief. They speak to us of a Golden Age when earth was a garden of innocence and wonder. These forests are the cradle of mythology. Through them move gods of all colors in the shapes of birds, panthers, leopards, elephants, serpents, monkeys, owls, wolves. Here, a young goddess sings to her stag and this Lady of Wild Creatures walks with her consort who, once humans arrive, will include among his names: Rudra; Shiva; Dionysus; Pan; Cernunnos, the Horned One; Odin, the Green Man.

When those forests died, whether through natural or human causes, vast stretches of earth were made barren, like the Wasteland of Grail legend. Many forests vanished without a trace. Others left their time-rings, their cellular structures, their pollen, their resin, stilled in mid-breath, captured in mysterious rocks or resinous amber. These forests continue to be remembered in the myths of peoples everywhere, whether they be called Eden, Avalon, Fairyland, Arcadia, Hesperides, the Celts' Thierna na Oge, Persia's Pairidaeza, or India's Jambu Island, Land of the Rose-Apple Tree.

Amazingly, one tree still exists from that time: the ginkgo. This, earth's most primitive tree, survived during great deforestations in Asia because Buddhist monks and nuns, sensing its sacredness and valuing it for its beauty and curative qualities, protected it in their temple gardens – it might be remembered that the Buddha himself was a tree spirit in thirty of his earlier lives, so his followers tend to be sensitive to trees *(see Pipal)*.

Botany/History

Nearly 4 billion years ago, two-thirds of the earth was a warm, deep ocean.[2] Latest scientific evidence suggests that the remaining third was a single supercontinent of mostly flat, naked brown rock occasionally marked by hissing volcanic lava, deep fissures, and low mountain ranges. The sun spewed ultraviolet radiation over the planet's surface. There was no breathable oxygen. The humid, tropical atmosphere was filled with poisonous gases producing clouds, fog, rain, lightning, and fierce winds. Carried in rain, the gases dissolved in the sea, puddles, lakes, and began eroding the rock, slowly turning it to soil. Despite the toxicity, skies and seas nevertheless cradled the four elements basic to the organic building-blocks of life: hydrogen, oxygen, nitrogen, and carbon. These four combine into amino acids whenever they are exposed to volcanic heat, solar radiation, or stray flashes of lightning. Slowly, a few molecules at a time, the waters became a rich organic soup.

About 3.5 billion years ago, out of this mysterious ocean-womb, microscopic organisms (probably similar to modern fungi, viruses, and bacteria) emerged that were capable of reproducing. For the first time, the planet knew "life." Or perhaps it would be more correct to say that life "life-d" itself into a form complex enough to reproduce itself, a feat that would qualify it to be called "living" by humans a few billion years later. Since there was no oxygen to breath, for millions of years these new organisms handled energy needs by breaking down and feeding upon the organic soup. The process is called fermentation. Eventually, they came close to exhausting this source, which meant that the long process of replenishing the vital amino acid compounds and awaiting the next appearance of "life" might have to start all over again.

As complete depletion loomed half a billion years later, however, something new happened. When earliest "life" was breaking down what it needed, carbon dioxide bubbles were released as a byproduct. Now, in tidal pools along the supercontinent's shoreline of stark brown rock and black, crusty, hardened lava, a life form emerged which brought with it a spectacular new color – *green*. This new form of life, blue-green algae (*cyanobacteria*), possessed chlorophyll, capable of transforming carbon dioxide "waste," plus water and sunlight, into sugar – a process called photosynthesis. The blue-green algae did not need to drain the organic soup: it sustained itself on "waste" and ever-abundant water and light. It was strong, robust, and independent of an otherwise self-defeating cycle of consuming its own life-source.

The first life form used fermentation to meet its needs – and threw off carbon dioxide as waste. The second life form used that waste to develop photosynthesis, but this resulted in yet another kind of waste byproduct: oxygen. For a billion years, oxygen dissolved into the seas, killing many of the original fermenting organisms; 2 billion years ago, it began rising upwards into the atmosphere, critically altering the chemical balance of gasses. Then, a billion years ago, new life forms emerged that could use *that* "waste" and feed upon plants as well as upon each other. These were the remote ancestors of sponges, jellyfish, worms, coral. They had soft bodies, which decayed or dissolved back into the sea, leaving nothing from which to form fossils. We can only guess what they looked like.

The scale of time now shifts from billions to millions of years. The climate remains tropical, there are no seasons, there is still only a single continent, rocky, barren, devoid of the organic life with which the warm seas were teeming. But something new is again about to occur. At the end of the Silurian age some 400 million years ago, the first land plants, which had slowly evolved out of blue-green algae, related seaweeds, and gigantic slimy fronds, set down a few tentative roots along the vast shorelines of the single continent. They probably looked like ragged herbs and their chances of survival were bleak – except for one thing: the supercontinent was now undergoing a massive process of terra-forming. Its crust expanded, then buckled; mountains erupted out of the flatness; inland seas flooded outwards and then receded, leaving behind thick black mud that had been forming its own organic soup for millions of years. The oozing mud was now as fertile as the primal seas had been. Land plants began to survive in the shoreline muck and slime, in marshlands and estuaries. Unfortunately, most of these plants used spores, not seeds, for reproduction, and as the land dried over more millions of years, the spores' need for moisture-rich environments doomed many of them to extinction.

Yet some of these plants were able to develop larger leaves and take advantage of the sunlight, which energized the photosynthesis process. They learned to survive with less water; they grew taller and larger, which required deeper root systems for finding water and food, and tubular systems for delivering moisture to stems and leaves. Roots anchored them; interior systems let them stand tall; their spores gradually evolved into nutrient-rich seed-sacs.

In the Devonian period 350-400 million years ago, the first forests arose from these seed-bearing plants. They were entirely green, covering most of the supercontinent – there were no flowers and no seasonal changes, for there were no seasons. Some trees looked like gigantic fifty-foot-high ferns, others were mossy, or snaky, growing close to the ground. All were continually flooding the atmosphere with the oxygen that differently evolving species would eventually need to survive. The descendants of these plants are conifers – our evergreen pines, spruces, firs – which make up a third of our forests and occupy about 8% of earth's total surface.

LOST FORESTS

In the Carboniferous period 270-350 million years ago, land plants from the preceding period multiplied prodigiously. In the humid weather, conifers doubled their height to over a hundred feet; when they fell back into the marshes, they decomposed into peat and were compressed into coal. In the Triassic period 180-225 million years ago, the first dinosaurs and mammals appeared – and with them another primitive seed-bearing plant, the ginkgo, the only still-surviving member from the forests of that age.

Flowering plants first appeared near the end of the Cretaceous period about 70 million years ago. Instead of relying upon the wind to fertilize female seed with male pollen, as the ginkgo and other seed-bearing plants did, flowering plants held male and female elements within a single flower – insects, animals, or slight breezes were all that was needed to join the two. From them came fruits, vegetables, and grains. Although older conifers currently comprise about a third of our forests, these new flowering plants now make up, overall, 90% of all land plants.

More millions of years passed as the supercontinent began to split, drift apart, and form into the continents that are familiar to us today. Forests covered them – forests long lost to us as climate, floods, and numberless upheavals forced many into extinction. Humans appeared only a few million years ago and began playing their own role in altering the planet. Where forests once covered the deserts of Africa, the Middle East, and Eurasia, humans slowly depleted vast stretches. In China alone, the Yellow River's huge watershed once supported great oak forests filled with deer, elephants, rhinoceroses, wild ducks, and birds. By 3,500 years ago, these were gone, except for a few hunting enclaves for nobles. Trees were taken to build and furnish homes and to fuel fires for cooking or bronze-casting. With nothing to stop it, thick yellow dust blew in from Mongolia for centuries, creating a great dusty plain and a silted, sluggish river.[3]

Elsewhere in eastern China, south of the Yangtze, the ginkgo, that lone survivor from millions of years earlier, still thrived. It had once been abundant in Europe and North America but Ice Ages caused its extinction. China is its longest continuous home. At first, Chinese herbalists protected it for its curative properties. For 5,000 years, the tree has played an important role in Chinese medicine where it strengthens the *ch'i* (vital lifeforce) and is beneficial for heart and lungs. After processing, the seeds are edible and resemble dried almonds (dyed red, they are still eaten for good fortune at traditional Chinese weddings).

After Buddhism reached China, monks and nuns continued to protect the tree for its medicinal values but also for the beauty of its delicate fan-shaped leaves that turn a stunning gold in autumn; some trees in Chinese and Japanese Buddhist temples are more than 1,000 years old. In Japan, the spirit of the ginkgo (*icho*) is believed to be a loving old crone who guards mothers when they nurse their young.[4]

In our own time, tests have shown that ginkgo's abilities include improving circulation between brain and heart, slowing the aging process, boosting immune systems, lowering cholesterol, and improving short-term memory in the elderly.[5] Pests and diseases which developed to attack later species have no effect on the ginkgo. It is surprisingly tolerant of pollution – thus, the tree is widely planted along city streets all over the world, bringing echoes of long Lost Forests.[6]

The Reading

A major period of your life may have ended; its positive influence will always remain as a subtle presence in your life, but your growth cycles enter a new phase. This may be a long-awaited period of heightened activity and creativity. Despite many joyous aspects, however, it may include times of descent, remembering, renewed understanding, as if you are Persephone, torn from her flowered meadows to experience the chill of Pluto's underworld without ever forgetting the sweetness of her older memories. It is a time to meditate on wisdom and the ebb and flow of existence. Go deeply within, serene, compassionate. There is that in you that will always survive because your deepest memories are of the continuity of life.

Despite cataclysmic cycles, life survives. In grieving over what has been lost, there is also acceptance of what you cannot change, and knowledge that much can yet be transformed. You are one strand among billions in the web-of-life – each strand shimmers uniquely and is precious simply because it *is*. Remember that atoms, which once spiraled through tissues of extinct trees, now spiral through your own DNA.

REVERSED:

Your struggles may have narrowed your vision, making you feel as if it is you against the world. Do not be a fish angry with the ocean. Do not put your ego in charge of matters over which it has no control. Your ego functions wisely and well in the shallows of your life. In the depths, however, it might be time to surrender to processes hidden within your body's own cellular wisdom, a wisdom born of many levels of consciousness – mineral, vegetable, angelic. Something entirely new might await you. Trust that it will be good.

Artist's Notes:

"The Lady of Wild Things" Scythian necklace and staff are from c. 4th century B.C.E.; Ukraine. Small carved seal, lower right, is from 16th century B.C.E.: Knossos, Crete; next to it, gold-winged goddess with animals is from a hydria: Italy, 570 B.C.E. They stand on rock carved with the Goddess of Canaan: Israel or Lebanon, 1200 B.C.E.; deer to left of Canaan Goddess is Cro-Magnon cave drawing: Lascaux, France.

Endnotes

[1] Romanyshyn:1, 4, 6, 12.
[2] This survey was woven from TIME-LIFE, *The Emergence of Man: Life Before Man* (1972):25-36;40;43; and Roger Lewin, *Thread of Life* (Washington: Smithsonian Books, 1982):99-105; 138; 194-195.
[3] TIME-LIFE, *Great Ages of Man: Ancient China* (1967):11-12.
[4] Altman:62.
[5] Altman:148; also Steven Foster, "Ginkgo Leaves of Life," in *Better Nutrition,* August 1995, pp.46, 48, 50.
[6] Foster, op. cit.

19 LOTUS

Lotus

Om mani padme hum

...the lotus is a symbol of fertility and life that is rooted in and takes its strength from the primordial waters....As a symbol of the world, the lotus suggests a growing, expanding world imbued with vigorous fertile power. This power is revealed in [*the goddess Lakshmi*]. She is the nectar or essence of creation that lends to creation its distinctive flavor and beauty. Organic life, impelled as it is by this mysterious power, flowers richly and beautifully in the creative processes of the world.

~ David Kinsley
The Goddesses' Mirror[1]

The Mythic World

Because all life stages – bud, flower, seed-pod – exist simultaneously on the same plant,[2] the lotus is associated with birth, maturity, transitions, and past, present, future. Egypt's blue and India's pink lotus further symbolize the birth of creation out of primal waters. India's lotus also involves the awakening of the heart-*chakra*, for *padma* ("lotus") is another name for *chakra* ("wheel"). Thus, a lotus resides within each center. The "lotus of the heart" is itself a metaphor for the unfolding of blissful creation:

> The phrase "lotus of the Heart"...is fraught with symbolic meaning. The creative ocean in the Heart nourishes the growth of the plant, the cosmic tree that represents the entire manifest universe.[3]

The ancient mantra, *om mani padme hum*, reflects both layers, the personal and the cosmic. *Om* is the seed-sound, or *bija*, from which all creation sprang. *Mani*, "jewel," refers simultaneously to the seed in the womb, the awakened jewel-like awareness in the heart-chakra, and the deity resting in the heart of the *padma*. *Hum* is a sound-bridge leading to the next repetition of the mantra. In Hindu belief, the sacred sounds return one to that moment in time when nothing existed except a lotus containing pure sound itself, *OM*. Chanting this mantra raises one's vibrations, or sound-frequencies, which brings one closer to the heart's primal jewel-like awareness.

India's god Vishnu is often shown sleeping on a lotus in a cosmic sea, his wife Lakshmi seated at his side. She, wide awake, massages his feet. From his navel rises a long umbilical stalk with a lotus at its tip. Seated in the World Lotus, unaware of what lies below and thus assuming he is the sole cause of creation, is the god Brahma. It is a patriarchal fantasy of male born from male – but neither really grasps what is happening: one is asleep and the other confused. Only the goddess Lakshmi, patiently massaging her consort's feet, sees things as they are.

Lakshmi is also Padma, "Lotus," and it was actually from *her* body, not Vishnu's, that the universe emerged.[4] As a sign of her favor, Hindu and Buddhist deities are often associated with lotuses. Kuan Yin rides upon a giant lotus leaf.[5] A lotus sprang up to announce the birth of the Buddha. In China, the lotus is one of the symbols contained in the Buddha's footprint (which might be an echo of Vishnu's foot-massage). Chinese Buddhists speak of a Sacred Lake of Lotuses where the dead sleep in lotus buds until it is time for them to be admitted to paradise.

For Westerners exposed to tantric traditions from India and Tibet, "lotus" is the yoni or vulva and "jewel" is the phallus – but this is an oversimplification. As Indologist Paul Muller-Ortega reminds us:

> ...we have to remember that this [sexual] ritual was often only to be internally visualized....The process of human reproduction can then be celebrated as being itself but a specific instance...of the larger and much more important process by which the entire universe manifests from the absolute reality. This grand overflowing of the absolute reality into specific, finite realities is not in itself a sexual process....[T]here is an important sense in which sexuality simply repeats and continues the overflowing of the absolute reality as it emerges from...the womb of the Goddess....In this sense, human sexuality becomes a physical metaphor for this blissful, cosmic, creative wave that continuously surges at the core of all things and that may be experienced within the body as the bliss resulting from the awakened *kundalini*....The psychological sophistication of tantric groups was that they had recognized that the *sources* and *origins* of sexuality and spirituality are identical. It grossly distorts the Tantra to represent it as teaching that sexuality and spirituality are themselves identical.[6]

As noted, Egypt's lotus mythology lacks India's heart-dimension but shares the cosmogonic. In an Egyptian solar creation myth, for example, a closed blue lotus floats in primordial darkness *(see Seaweed)*. Light suddenly surges within this lotus-womb and the closed petals begin to open, allowing an infant sun to emerge. The lotus symbolizes fertility and eternal youth. It is also a metaphor for resurrection because it closes its petals each night, sinking down into the waters, only to rise anew with the dawn.[7]

Botany/History

The lotus is an elegant plant found in ponds and slow-moving streams. In the eastern United States and West Indies, the yellow lotus rises on a stalk above the water. The pink lotus of the Far East usually also lifts its round leaves and blossoms above the water's surface on a slender stalk.[8] In Hindu art and myth, this stalk is portrayed as an umbilical cord rising out of the navel of a sleeping deity – the imagery symbolizes the emergence of creation from a realm of formless, unconscious ("sleeping") primordial waters.

Egypt has two species of lotus, the narrow-petalled, exquisitely fragrant blue lotus, cradle of the sun-god; and the lush but unpleasant-smelling white lotus. Unlike their relatives elsewhere, these blossoms repose languidly on leaves floating directly on the water's surface instead of rising above it. Rooted in muddy depths, these open with the sun and close again at dusk. Egyptian temples, designed as replicas of creation, often had their columns carved with clusters of lotus-buds.[9]

In Egypt as well as southeast Asia, it is likely that lotuses were originally cultivated for food, not beauty, for the tuberous roots (rhizomes) and nutlike seeds could be ground into a fine, sweet flour and baked.[10] In China, the lotus is used medicinally to keep the complexion fresh, limbs supple, and bowels functioning properly; seed pods dissolve coagulated blood, leaf stalks are used for hemorrhages, and raw seeds are a soporific; overall, the plant strengthens and refreshes.[11] This plant, native to many tropical regions of the world, is now only rarely used as food, but its calm beauty remains to quiet the mind and stir the imagination of those who behold it.

The Reading

You are invited to live with kindness and without undue criticism or stress. Lotus reminds you not to judge by appearances: roots may be in slime, but from them come glorious flowers. This speaks to nurturing a compassionate heart. The organic life of the lotus, ever-expanding and contracting, is a metaphor for the spiritually mature heart. The East's lotus is often considered the equivalent to the West's rose, for both are symbols of cosmic wholeness and universal love. Yet as one writer wisely observes, linking the two flowers in this way is deceptive:

> The lotus, symbol of growth and maturation throughout Asia, grows out of the mud to open and blossom in the light of day. This creation is seen as a joyful, painless unfolding to the world in love. The West's rose, with its painful thorns, symbolizes love through pain and suffering.[12]

Lotus marks a time of new beginnings, new creation, without the drama of "pain and suffering." Do not worry if you are not given full credit for your work. Your contribution is crucial, even if unsung. Let the glory go to those whose stubborn pride drives them to demand it. Float calmly, serenely, above the turmoil. Enjoy the process without being attached to fruits or rewards. Do not forget that mud is not other than blossom: it is the "primal soup," expressing its wonders in the form of shimmering, tissue-fine blossoms. The lotus, in a sense, is the "thought," the "idea," the "creation" of the mud. Mud needs no reward – it is enough that its creation is seen and admired.

As soon as it finishes one project, it lets the universe handle the details, and turns to the next project.

If you are asking about health issues, you might wish to look into the art of reflexology (foot-massage). Nerve endings in the feet connect with major nerve-centers throughout the body – by massaging them, you send a flood of well-being through yourself. You might also bring your sleep-patterns more in line with natural circadian rhythms. Some form of meditation, perhaps combined with chanting and deep breathing, should prove helpful.

REVERSED:

The joy and freshness of the new bloom has faded, the time of new beginnings is over, the flower wilts and returns to the primal soup to add its nutrients and experiences to yet other new beginnings in the future. Accept that this one is over, let it go; it is decaying and you cannot stop it. Stay clear, patient. Do not give way to heavy emotions, neediness or anything that might create further stress. You can afford to be light and calm. Trust that yet more fertility, richness, and abundant blooms lie ahead. The reserves from which you drew this now fading "new beginning" have yet countless more seeds for you to germinate in many ways. You will continually birth new and fertile projects, relationships, plans, ideas, strategies.

Sometimes reversed lotus suggests that you have allowed emotional issues to coagulate like old, stale blood. Now is the time to dissolve them. Some form of calming meditation would be helpful here. Your mind needs to stay fresh and supple. Reactivate your sense of compassion, for yourself, for the world. Again, as with the upright reading, lotus reminds you that your nature is to be like it – unsullied, vigorous, unattached to blame or reward. Let the universe handle the details of what has already passed. Move on.

LOTUS

Artist's Notes:

Lower right hand in *abhaya mudra* (gesture), giving blessings and protection. Padma carving from stupa at Bharhut, 2nd-1st century B.C.E.; bracelet on right upper arm and bottom necklace: 16th-18th century India; Kronos earrings: 1st century B.C.E., India. The cosmic lotus, as door to the womb of the universe, was referred to as "The Goddess Moisture" or "The Goddess Earth." The lotus-leaf symbolizes the fertile earth; the flower represents the mother's lap and eternal renewal. Elephants, cousins of clouds, attract rain.

Endnotes

[1] Kinsley, *GM*:56.
[2] Lehner:39-40.
[3] Muller-Ortega:157.
[4] Campbell, *Masks/Occidental*:157; Kinsley, *HG*:21.
[5] Blofeld:plate 1.
[6] Muller-Ortega:53; 54.
[7] *EEC*:54b; Lehner:35; 37.
[8] Cowles:107a.
[9] *EEC*:152-153.
[10] *NG*:July 1947, pp.40-41.
[11] Georges Beau:132-133.
[12] Smith, Albert L., "The Silk Drum: A Re-Telling of a Japanese Fairy Tale." Winter 1998, unpublished paper.

20
MYRRH

A bundle of myrrh is my wellbeloved unto me;
he shall lie all night betwixt my breasts.
~ The Song of Solomon i.13

...your robes are all fragrant with myrrh...
~ Psalm 45:8

The Mythic World

The tree's name comes from the Arabic *mur*, "bitter," for myrrh has long been associated with bitterness and death. When Joseph died in Egypt, myrrh and other aromatic spices were strewn along his funeral procession for his grieving brothers to walk upon.[1] Along with frankincense and gold, myrrh was one of the precious gifts brought by the three Magi to the Christ-child – myrrh spoke to his death, not his birth, for barely three decades later his corpse would be anointed with the fragrant ointment by another triad, the three Marys.

In Greek mythology, a young princess of Cyprus named Myrrha was raped by her drunken father. She fled into the wilderness where the gods turned her into a myrrh tree to prevent further abuse; gum-resins exuded by the tree came from her tears,[2] for she was pregnant with her father's child, the tragic Adonis (Semitic, *Adon*, "Lord"), who would eventually be the beloved of Aphrodite-Mari, sea-goddess of love. The child grew within his myrrh-tree mother/sister for ten months, until her bark swelled, burst, and he emerged. Alternate versions claim a mother-boar gored the tree with her tusks, thereby opening a passageway through which the infant was born.[3]

To conceal him from the king's spies, Aphrodite hid him in a chest and asked Persephone, goddess of the Underworld, to care for him. When Persephone saw his beauty, she refused to relinquish him even when Aphrodite offered herself as ransom. Zeus settled the dispute by giving Adonis for half a year to each of his foster-mothers, a solution mirroring Persephone's own girlhood when, after being raped by Hades, she was forced to spend the dark months with Hades and the bright months with her mother, grain-goddess Demeter.

Upon reaching manhood, Adonis was castrated and killed by a wild boar in a hunting accident and poor Aphrodite grieved bitterly over his mangled body. That boar has been interpreted as a disguise of war-god Ares, a rival for Aphrodite's love, but such an explanation ignores the presence of the boar-"midwife" at Adonis' birth. The boar, one of the earliest known sacrificial animals, was viewed as the "alter-ego" of Adonis and other Near Eastern "dying gods," who were often sacrificed either in boar-form or by someone dressed as a boar.[4] Adonis, moving between the twin-poles of birth and death, came to both, equally, in violence.

For Aphrodite's worshippers, Adonis died each spring in Lebanon's mountains, where the Adonis River ran red with his blood, staining anemones along its banks. Each year he would be born anew, only to be slain once more at the end.[5] The myth echoes the death/rebirth, or dying/rising cycles of Attis *(see Pine)*; of Italy's beechen groves where the Old King is killed by the New

King *(see Beech)*; and of Egypt's papyrus swamps, where Osiris is castrated and slain by his brother Set (whose animal-guise is a boar) and later resurrected by his two magician-sisters *(see Papyrus)*.

These myths are mirrored in the life of yet another "dying god," Jesus, born of Mary or Miriam, a name cognate with Myrrha. In fact, early Christians called the Virgin Mary "Myrrh of the Sea."[6] Like Myrrha and Aphrodite, she is both birth-mother and death-mother, myrrh at his birth, myrrh at his death. She, with the other two Marys present at the Crucifixion, were called the *myrrhophores*, "myrrh-bearers," a title also given to ancient death-priestesses.[7]

Botany/History

Myrrh is native to lands bordering the Red Sea (Arabia, Ethiopia, and Somaliland). It is a low, spreading tree with pale gray bark which exudes drops of a reddish-brown juice. This liquid slowly hardens into gum-resin lumps, or "tear-drops," some as large as eggs. They are easily powdered, fragrant to the nose, somewhat astringent and bitter to the tongue. The lumps were prized by the ancients as medicine, perfume, and aphrodisiacal temple-incense. In addition, over 6,000 years ago, Egyptians discovered myrrh's essential role in the art of mummification, believed to preserve the body for an afterlife spent in joyful gardens.

In Israel, tabernacle, ark, and altar vessels were anointed with oil of myrrh. For half of the year-of-purification required of a Jewish woman after childbearing, she too, like a sacred vessel, was washed and anointed with myrrh. Although the reasons for such purification were religious, myrrh also happens to treat sore nipples and rheumatic illnesses, to which new mothers are prone.

Medicinally, gum-resin is used as a tonic, either dissolved in liquid (or syrup) or taken in minute doses of powder. As an antiseptic, it is used as a douche and on fresh wounds, sprains, bruises, sores, and ulcers. It improves circulation and increases white blood cell count.[8]

The Reading

Drawing Myrrh suggests that you have just emerged from a difficult, painful, perhaps even dangerous period. You may have given birth, physically or symbolically. Or you may have experienced the "death" of releasing a person, plan, or situation that you greatly valued. Myrrh invites you to let yourself simply relax and be pampered. Release troubling thoughts and feelings. Sink deeply into the goodness and wonder of your body. Treat yourself to a massage, pleasing fragrances, soft clothing. Blissfully squander as much time as you wish. Put your anxieties on hold and let the Myrrh-deva whisper over your body, running across your skin like the finest balm, soothing every joint and aching muscle.

REVERSED:

This could be a signal that it is time to take physical health matters more seriously. In the name of practical short-term goals, you might be ignoring your body, forcing it to pay the price of your climb towards success. Myrrh-balm is priceless in value, but so is your health.

Emotional or spiritual areas of your life might be in need of "purification." Explore your underlying motives in trying either to "birth," or to conclude ("mummify"), a relationship or project. Take time to honor your interior life.

On a psychological level, this exotic tree, "menstruating" precious balm along the southern shores of the Red Sea, came to represent not only a sea-goddess, but also a victim of incest. The fragrance of myrrh is an aphrodisiac, but since Myrrha *is* myrrh, it makes an aphrodisiac of her as well. From a patriarchal perspective, this is a cunning way to shift blame from the rapist to her. But from a more compassionate perspective, it might offer a self-healing aphrodisiac balm to other rape victims so that they can begin to appreciate their own bodies again.

Myrrha's newborn will be as beloved and precious as myrrh. The boundaries between mother, child, and tree are continuously blurring and shifting. The mother is myrrh but so is the beloved, held all night between the breasts of the woman in the "Song of Solomon." The confusion in identity between a too-young mother and her child is common in cases of incest. The boar-mother is angry because she sees all too clearly what is going on: the girl's powerful father has perverted the sacred nature of sexuality. In ripping the newborn child from the tree, the boar is offering both mother and child a chance to recognize their own unique boundaries and individuality.

From an interpretive standpoint, given the widespread nature of incest and abuse in modern societies, drawing the myrrh tree may point to a literal reality. This is not, however, an open invitation to probe into areas which are not already conscious. The mythic level may point towards a metaphoric, not literal, reality. Whether or not your body suffered physical, sexual, or emotional abuse, whether in childhood or adulthood, from a specific person or from institutions empowered by abusive hierarchies, your body nevertheless needs attention, needs to have its sense of its own beauty and worth restored. Like myrrh, it is precious.

If you are female, consider winding back through all the levels of abuse to your own essential nature: you are able to birth wonders from your mind, your womb, your heart, your soul; you are wise, a healer with an understanding of ongoing cycles of cosmic birth and death.

If you are male, a similar principle applies: you are sacred, beloved, powerful, confident, and you have been sacrificed enough. It is time to enjoy your youth – choose life – honor your body with love and respect, and give yourself a chance to grow into wisdom, to become one of the Magi, a sage or seer.

Neither gender should be afraid to seek professional help in dealing with emotions and needs: therapy is costly, but might be the soothing and purifying form of "myrrh" you need. Regardless of your gender, be clear about who you are. Do not let your identity shift into that of the victimizer. The pattern must be broken, which may require professional help as well as courage and insight on your part.

You have within you a wellspring of ancient strength and you will be able to succeed if you draw that into your life. Honor what has passed, grieve for the *you* who might have been, had you not been abused, limited, bound. But then go past that and find a new spaciousness and compassion for yourself. The worst is over. You cannot be hurt anymore. The three Marys anoint your body with tenderness. You are being transformed, enabled to explore a whole new, rich, aromatic dimension of wholeness. Myrrh is an essence of wholeness at a deep-down cellular level – a bundle of life-force, a creativity to hold between your breasts as you begin life anew.

Artist's Notes:

Figures of Madonnas in the myrrh tree in the background are, clockwise from upper left, La Moraneta of Monserrat, which arrived in Barcelona in the late 7th century; Mesopotamian Madonna from around 2000 B.C.E.; Madonna from Rhodes, late 6th to early 5th century B.C.E.; a blue faience amulet of Isis and Horus from Egypt, c. 945 B.C.E.

Endnotes

[1] Ginzberg:II.153.
[2] Lehner:72.
[3] Frazer/Gaster:347-8, 358-9.
[4] Walker, *WD*:365; Stapleton:10.
[5] Walker, *WEMS*:10.
[6] Walker, *WEMS*:10;702-3; *WD*:374; 423; 219; 351;
[7] Graves, *WG*:438-9.
[7] Walker, *WD*:467.
[8] Lucas:79-83; Rose:87.

21
NUT TREES

(ALMOND, WALNUT, HAZEL)

And on the morrow Moses went into the tent of the testimony; and behold, the rod of Aaron for the house of Levi had sprouted and put forth buds, and produced blossoms, and it bore ripe almonds.

~ Numbers 17:8

And he showed me more, a little thing, the size of a hazel-nut, on the palm of my hand, round like a ball. I looked at it thoughtfully and wondered, "What is this?" And the answer came, "It is all that is made....It exists, both now and for ever, because God loves it."

~ Lady Julian of Norwich[1]

...[F]rom the walnut "came a golden tambour and a maiden embroidering with pure gold."

~ Italian Folktale[2]

The Mythic World

ALMOND

Myths associated with nut trees, whose nuts are viewed as vulva symbols, are rich and varied. In ancient Phrygia (west-central Turkey), virgin-mother Nana magically conceived by placing a sweet, ripe almond as a catalyst between her breasts. Nine months later she bore Attis, the shepherd-lover of Cybele, fertile Mother of the Gods. Attis was western Asia's counterpart to Syria's Adonis, beloved of Aphrodite *(see Myrrh)*.[3] The narratives and rites of both Adonis and Attis are similar: each bleeds to death after being castrated, Adonis by a boar, Attis by his own hand *(see Pine)*; the blood of each turns into flowers, Adonis' red anemones, Attis' wild violets; both are mourned and annually resurrected with joy. Both are involved in cults in which the goddess' frenzied male followers feel called upon to become eunuchs, castrating themselves, dancing with tinkling bells, even dressing in female garments and jewelry to emulate her.[4] Making literal what was better left symbolic, they offered their genitals as sacred generative catalysts, akin to Nana's almond, to aid in resurrecting their goddess' beloved.

In ancient Israel the almond (Hebrew *sākēd*, "the waker") was also closely linked with the divine feminine, although the nature of the link was more subtle. Like exquisitely feathered male birds, priests dressed with a feminine sense of finery, which seemed designed, not to emulate, but to please the divine feminine. Theological disclaimers notwithstanding, she was the hidden Goddess within the Godhead. The element of priestly "castration" remains, although more prudently limited to the foreskin. In death, Jewish tradition recognizes the catalytic role of the "almond-bone," a tiny indestructible bone said to survive the corpse's decomposition. Like Nana's almond, this bone is the genetic nucleus from which the entire body will one day be reconstituted and resurrected at the coming of the Messiah.[5]

Also from Israel is Aaron's rod, a mysterious branch of flowering almond that Yahweh created at twilight – the realm of the divine feminine – between sunset on the sixth day and the Sabbath, when Yahweh rested. Along with the almond rod were created the rainbow (invisible until Noah's time when it restrains Yahweh's wrath), several sacred caves, manna, the underground springs from which the people would drink on the Exodus, and the invisible writing which would later appear on stone tablets in the Sinai.[6] Flowering almond, water, food, womb/tomb caves, invisible language, and a rainbow to restrain male wrath – all these are the purview of the divine feminine.

When Aaron's almond-rod transforms into a serpent and devours the rods of Egyptian priests (Exodus 7.12), it betrays an intrinsic connection to the Serpent

Lady, a pre-patriarchal form of the divine feminine worshipped by Semites (including Moses' in-laws) in the Sinai and Midian. When that same rod parts the waters of the Red Sea, we find a heightened resonance between rod and water, for lying just ahead are those underground watersprings, created along with the almond-rod in the same primal female-twilight.

Among ancient Tree of Life choices, the almond, first to flower out of barrenness in spring, was highly regarded. Thus, when the design for the sanctuary's golden seven-branched Menorah is divinely revealed, the female symbol of the almond plays a primary role (Exodus 25:31-40; 37:17-24). The main central shaft, dedicated to Wisdom (the *Shekinah*, or female presence of God), has four cups shaped like almonds and carved with almond blossoms. On either side are three branches, each with another three almond cups and golden almond blossoms. The central shaft with its six branching arms holds burning lamps, illuminating the sanctuary, creating on the etheric plane an entire almond grove "spiritualized" into pure light.

The divine feminine is present again when Aaron's role as high priest is challenged in the desert (Numbers 17). Yahweh tells each jealous tribe to cut a rod and place it overnight in front of the ark containing the *Shekinah*. The rod of his favored tribe will sprout by morning; the others will remain barren. Aaron deliberately places his rod at some distance from the in-dwelling presence of the *Shekinah* lest others claim that proximity caused his to sprout. Yet in the morning, not only has his rod sprouted blossoms and almonds, but the ineffable name of God also appears along its length. His priesthood, and that of his Levite tribe, had been confirmed.[7]

Shortly thereafter, Miriam, prophetess, dancer, and older sister of Moses and Aaron, dies. While she lived, those watersprings originally created in holy twilight, accompanied the people's wanderings. When she died, the waters vanished:

...that all Israel might know that only owing to the merits of the pious prophetess had they been spared a lack of water during the forty years of the march.[8]

Here again is that link between woman, almond-rod, and water. Without Miriam's grounding presence, the situation soon gets out of hand and the frantic, thirst-driven people go to Moses for help. Yahweh tells him to speak to a rock of the people's choosing, asking it for water. Speaking will suffice, he is told, there is no need for more. Moses nevertheless takes the rod from the tabernacle and sets off.

His nerves are frayed over Miriam's death. He needs time to grieve but the people deny him this. They follow, grumbling, breaking into smaller groups, each clamoring for a different rock as a good site for the promised miracle. Infuriated,

Moses selects a rock of his own and yells at it, demanding water. When the rock complies too slowly, Moses pounds it twice with the rod and a torrent gushes forth, so great that some of the horrified people are drowned. For such a severe loss of balance, although his people will eventually enter the Promised Land, Moses himself will be denied entry.⁹

In ancient Greece, the almond tree is connected with Phyllis ("green leaf"), a Thracian princess in love with Acamas, a Greek warrior who fought in the Trojan War. When the war ended, she watched for the return of his ship at a lookout point called Enneodos, "nine journeys." Other ships arrived, but not his. She went back again and again, each time losing more hope. What she did not know was that Acamas' ship had sprung a leak, was unavoidably delayed, but not lost. After her ninth futile visit to Enneodos, the heartbroken princess died of grief. The sympathetic goddess Athena transformed her into an almond tree, with branches bare of leaf or flower out of respect for the woman's pain. Acamas arrived the very next day. When he learned what had happened, he embraced the tree's rough bark and wept. Responding to his dear presence with all her heart, the tree's leafless branches suddenly burst into flower. In honor of the two lovers, Athenians annually performed round-dances in their almond groves.¹⁰

WALNUT

The walnut, like the almond, involves a woman in love: Princess Carya, from Laconia in the Greek Peloponnese – her beloved is Dionysus, god of wine and joy. When she dies away from home, Dionysus transforms her into a walnut tree. Moon-goddess Artemis goes to Laconia with the news. Out of gratitude that their princess has been so favored, the Laconians build a temple to *Artemis Caryatis,* Artemis of the Walnut, its roof held up by caryatids, "pillars of wisdom" made in the form of Artemis' dancing nut-maiden priestesses.

In nearby Arcadia, there was another walnut-grove, where Artemis' nut-maidens danced near a stream filled with spotted singing fish. In such nut-groves, throughout natural cycles of loving, dying, and returning to trees, there is an underlying and supremely confident sense of joy, dance, and music.¹¹

HAZEL

The connection of the nut-world with a tiny compact universe emerges in medieval England when the mystic, Mother Julian of Norwich (1342-1416), is shown a hazelnut in a vision. "It is all that is made," Christ tells her. He adds that "it," which is to say creation, owes its very existence to God's love.¹² This mirrors the procreative parenting and loving relationships intrinsic to both

almond and walnut myths. Christ goes on to reassure Mother Julian about the fate of this creation:

I may make everything all right; I am able to; I intend to, and I shall. You will see for yourself that every sort of thing will be all right."[13]

In European fairytales, hazelnuts, and other nuts appear as hidden realms of wisdom and wealth. Garments of silk so fine they can be folded into a nutshell are found, or magical nuts containing golden tambours, looms, silver swords, garments of gold.[14] An empty hazelnut-shell even becomes the chariot of the fairy queen, Mab herself:

Her chariot is an empty hazel-nut,
Made by the joiner squirrel or old grub,
Time out o' mind the fairies' coach-makers.
And in this state she gallops night by night
Through lovers' brains, and then they dream of love...

~ *Romeo and Juliet*
iv.53

Queen Mab is the last remnant of an ancient and powerful goddess, now reduced to riding through dreamscapes. Yet even here, the lover-motif in conjunction with nuts persists, for hazelnuts were used in marriage divination, especially on All Hallows Eve. Two nuts would be thrown on the hearth together. If they burned quietly, brightly, side by side, all was well. If they crackled, spit, and leaped apart, the union was doomed.[15]

In Celtic myth, hazel is connected with sacred language, inspiration from intuitive female realms, and the mystic number "nine." Irish *coll,* "hazel," means "nine," for hazel does not bear nuts until its ninth year.[16] Like walnut, hazel is connected with "spotted fish which sang." In the River Boyne near Tipperary, these speckled salmon inhabited a deep pool overhung by nine hazel trees – these were trees of goddess-wisdom, repositories of all knowledge of human arts and sciences. When their nuts fell, bards ate them (or ate the fish that ate them) and found in them the source of all their poetry and magical tales.[17] Only hazel and apple trees were so sacred in the Celtic world that the reckless felling of either was punishable by death.[18]

The connection between language skills and hazel also emerges in Greek myth. Sun-god Apollo gave his younger brother Hermes a winged hazel-wand around which coiled two serpents. Whomever Hermes touched with his wand was given the gift of eloquence and harmonious speech. The serpent-twined rod still remains a symbol of communication and reconciliation.[19]

NUT TREES

Hazel wands, like Aaron's almond-rod, could communicate with water and were used by dowsers when seeking underground springs.[20] In light of the startling amount of water (40%) found in hazelnuts, this is intriguing. In Nordic and Teutonic myth, this water-connection might explain why hazel belonged to Thor, god of rain and thunder. In Celtic myth, hazel belonged to Manannan, god of the sea. In later times, these connections led to "wishing caps" woven from hazel twigs and worn by shipmasters to ensure safety in the midst of storms.[21]

Nuts, in general, are a tiny world unto themselves, meaty and rich with wonder. So it is not surprising that a medieval mystic would see a hazelnut as a symbol of creation. Nor that the almond would come to symbolize the Virgin Mary:

...this birth-bringing nut was Womb of the World.[22]

Botany/History

Nuts were highly prized as a rich source of food in the ancient Near East. When Jacob sent a ransom to an Egyptian minister, unaware that the official was his own son Joseph, he included nuts among the most precious gifts he could offer.

Take some of the choice fruits of the land in your bags, and carry down to the man a gift, a little balm and a little honey, gum, myrrh, pistachio nuts, and almonds.

~ Genesis 43:11

Because the kernel is protected inside hard, woody shells, fresh nuts travel well. In addition to being a rich source of oil, carbohydrates, and protein (thirty walnuts provide as much as twenty-eight grams of beef), nuts are also rich in iron, lime, and other minerals. Their only disadvantage is that they turn rancid after several months, no matter how carefully they are stored.[23]

ALMOND

Almond, a member of the Rose family, is one of the best known nut trees. Almond, in Hebrew, is *sāk̄ēd*, "the waker," for the tree wakes early, late January or early February, and sets forth its delicate flowers even before it leafs. Although the tree is native to central Asia, it spread west and was found growing wild to a height of sixteen feet in early Palestine.[24] Despite rich traditions involving the almond east of Egypt, the tree did not reach there until it was introduced in Greco-Roman times.[25] Today, it is cultivated all around the Mediterranean as well as in California. The almond is about 20% protein and 50% fat; the bland oil has the good nutritional value of olive oil. Almonds are eaten fresh or ground into flour. Fragrant blossoms resemble those of other Rose family relatives, the peach and cherry.[26]

WALNUT

The common walnut is native to western Asia from India to Persia. There are some fifteen species, handsome trees ranging in height from 70 to 150 feet and native to both the Old and New Worlds. The nuts are about 60% fat and 18% protein. Many species yield hard timber wood, which is especially prized because it rarely warps. The tree's pale gray bark, leaves, and green hulls have many medicinal uses (bowel-astringents, gargles, and remedies for ulcers and sores). The tree belongs to the Walnut family, other members of which include butternuts, hickory nuts, and pecans.[27]

HAZEL

Hazel, a species with eight different shrubby trees, including both hazelnuts and filberts, is a member of the Birch family.[28] Hazel trees were pioneers, spreading through eastern and central Europe after the last Ice Age, co-existing with pine and birch forests during their long domination. Then about 9,000 years ago, the hazel began a spectacular and vigorous spread on its own, moving north to the Baltic and east into central Russia, sometimes creating entire forests of hazel trees growing more than thirty feet tall. There is good reason to suspect that prehistoric peoples, relying upon hazelnuts as an important food source, cut down other shrubs to aid in this rapid expansion. Pioneering trees like the hazel, birch, pine, and willow have high light needs and relatively short lifespans. Thus, about 7,000 to 8,000 years ago, tenacious oaks intruded into the "hazel time," forming mixed hazel-oak forests for several thousand years. By some 5,000 years ago, oaks finally predominated, leaving smaller stands of hazel scattered across northern Europe.[29]

Hazelnuts are only 9% protein, which is considerably less than either the almond or walnut, although its fat content of 36% is good. Of all the nuts, hazel has the highest percentage of water – more than 40% (compared with almond's 4.8% and walnut's 3.4%).[30] Although small amounts of almonds and walnuts have been found at Neolithic sites from Turkey to central Europe, far more hazelnut shells have been found at northern European sites, some dating back into the Mesolithic, indicating that hazelnuts were a major food source longer than any other nut.[31]

There are many other nuts: hickory, chestnuts, pistachios, pecans, cashews, macadamias, and countless more. Regardless of where they are found, as Robert Graves writes, nuts represent:

...concentrated wisdom: something sweet, compact and sustaining enclosed in a small hard shell – as we say: "this is the matter in a nut-shell."[32]

The Reading

Nut trees invite you into realms of intuition, poetic inspiration, dance, and magical language. These vulva-energies birth entire universes of lore and wisdom. They welcome you among priestesses who perform round-dances in nut-groves and support Greek temples as the original "pillars of wisdom." Here, language flows like music and even fish sing. It is a female realm – yet one in which the male is not only welcomed, but embraced as the beloved. Gender boundaries, both intra- and interpersonal, should remain unblurred and clear here, each honored for itself, each half of a whole, co-creators of the universe.

Just as prehistoric peoples cut away unneeded shrubs so that their hazel trees could flourish in light, airy forests, so too you may need to prune away whatever hinders what is most nutritious in you. It is your "hazel time." Enjoy it. You need this pioneering time/space of fertile growth.

At first glance, the joy of nut trees seems similar to the pipal *(see Pipal)*. The pipal, however, belongs to joy's primal first-stage – it speaks more to those workaholics who have little experience with playfulness. Nut trees are more purposeful. They address that stratum of creativity in you which is mature and supremely confident. Unlike the pipal, nut trees do not nurture play for play's sake. Rather, the nut-maidens ask you to trust your intuition in bringing a sense of play to every task, allowing yourself to join all other "pillars of wisdom," steadfastly holding up the world with a light heart. You have been at this game for a long time and you know that even when you play, something tangible and good for yourself and others will come from it.

You already know what you need to know – and you also know how to motivate or catalyze yourself with simple things around you, like Nana's almond, nurtured at her heart-center, between her breasts. From that comes the beloved and spiritual delight.

Drawing Nut Trees may indicate that what you are asking about is undergoing a process of transformation, as Phyllis was transformed into an almond tree, or Carya into a walnut tree. Despite initial setbacks, your project will eventually be turned into something nourishing and grounded. Trust the process – let it happen.

The transition of a beloved's death is also possible here. If so, you are being gently reassured that your relationship, however changed, will survive. Unlike myths in which lovers are changed into distant stars, far from human touch and longing, your relationship with the beloved will be "as if" that one has become a comforting tree – not a literal tree, physically present (although many peoples plant a tree to honor death as well as birth), but rather an energy-field surrounding you with a richly loving, earthy aura, stable and serene, like a tree's presence. This is a beloved to be kept near, not reassigned to the chilly heavens.

Despite changes and transitions, you are cautioned to remain wakeful (almond in Hebrew is *sākēd*, "waker"). Do not let strong emotions unbalance you. When Phyllis did that, she lost her chance to be with her beloved, who arrived the very next day. When Moses did that, he lost the chance to enter the Promised Land. Give yourself time to feel negative emotions and to cleanse, as with walnut leaves and hulls, their "ulcers and sores." Also trust your underground waters, your intuition, that part of you that is connected with time, space, and Beyond, that part of you that dates from a primal twilight when rainbows, watersprings, caves, and almond-wands were created, just before the first Sabbath of rest. As the rainbow restrained God's rage when he would have destroyed the world in a flood, so let the rainbow restrain your own black moods when you too feel tempted to obliterate your world.

Retreat to a sanctuary filled with soft almond-light and allow a wise period of transition away from the niggling demands of others. You might wish to weave yourself a ritual "wishing cap" from the twigs of whatever nut trees grow locally. Then return to life's call at your own pace – with your light heart restored.

> **MEDITATION:** sit comfortably and let your mind roam among various nut trees, real or imaginary. Ask that one of them reveal itself as the "birth-bringing nut" symbolizing the creative womb of your inner world. Whatever you sense about it will have deep personal relevance. Dialogue with it: What color is it? Is it thin-shelled or a "hard nut to crack?" What is its shape, taste, texture? Draw or sculpt the tree from which it fell. From what kind of place does it grow? Does it get what it needs from its soil? What kind of weather does it prefer? If it grows in a garden, who takes care of it? Dance, sing to it, dress in its colors. If your tree is "real," eat its nuts in communion with its energy, include its nuts and twigs on your meditation altar. If a spiritual being were to give you a "magical" nutshell from your tree, and you opened it, what would you find inside? Again, trust your intuition.

REVERSED:

The trees respect what you are asking about. They wish you to know that it was well-conceived and you have brought a good heart and immense skills to it. The outcome, however, is still unclear and subject to forces beyond your control. Something may be unavoidably delayed. The trees remind you that important as this is to you, even more important is your attitude. Guard against letting your emotions, like old nuts, grow rancid. Regardless of what develops, do joyfully whatever is required by this task. If the outcome is not what you had hoped, do not lose sight of your project's original underlying joyfulness, wholeness, beauty, and richness. Do not lose the spirit of joy.

Remember that from bleak, barren branches, almond blossoms sprout overnight. It is never too late. Remember too that even if everything seems to die and decay, the indestructible "almond-bone" remains as a kernel of hope around which new life will one day be constellated. Finally, take for yourself the words spoken to Mother Julian of Norwich:

I may make everything all right; I am able to; I intend to, and I shall. You will see for yourself that every sort of thing will be all right.[33]

Artist's Notes:

The ancient Near East's divine feminine is known by many names, including Asherah (associated with sacred groves), *Shekinah*, and Tree of Life. Asherah was often flanked by lion and ibex, as seen here in the tree's Canaanite ritual stand in bottom register; a Tree of Life with three pairs of branches flanked by ibex and lion can also be seen two registers above: Taanach, late 10th century B.C.E. Roman gold-glass base in tree branches depicts Menorah flanked by lions: 4th century C.E. Necklace from Deir el-Balah: 14th-13th century B.C.E; its ibex-headed pendant: Ashod, 4th century B.C.E.

Endnotes

[1] Julian of Norwich:68.
[2] Cited in Peter Bishop:140.
[3] Frazer:v.5, 263-4; Graves, *WG*:342.
[4] Frazer:v.5, 264-276.
[5] Ginzberg:v.5, 184,363.
[6] Ginzberg:v.1, 83.
[7] Ginzberg:v.3, 306-7; v.6, 106.
[8] Ginzberg:v.3, 308.
[9] Ginzberg:v.3, 308-14.
[10] Graves, *GM*:86.a, 1, 2.
[11] Graves, *GM*:86.b, 1, 2; Stapleton:50; Walker, *WD*:86.
[12] Julian of Norwich:68.
[13] Julian of Norwich:107.
[14] Bishop:139-149.
[15] Frazer:v.10, 237, 239, 241, 242, 245.
[16] Graves, *WG*:188.
[17] Graves, *GM*:86.1; Walker, *D*:465; Graves, *WG*:68; 187-188.
[18] Graves *WG*:271.
[19] Lehner:60-62.
[20] Frazer:v.11, 68.
[21] Lehner:62; Walker, *D*:465.
[22] Walker, *D*:490.
[23] Renfrew:194.
[24] McKenzie:21.
[25] *DEC*:94b-c.
[26] Cowles:78c; Renfrew:157, 194.
[27] Friedrich: 79; Jeanne Rose:113; Cowles:128c-129a, 101c-102a; Renfrew:194.
[28] Cowles:101a.
[29] Friedrich:75-76; 19-21.
[30] Renfrew:194.
[31] Renfrew:156-159.
[32] Graves, *WG*:187.
[33] Julian of Norwich:107.

22
OAK

Oak

In the elm-woods and the oaken,
There where Orpheus harped of old,
And the trees awoke and knew him,
And the wild things gathered to him,
As he sang....

~ Euripides
The Bacchae

The Mythic World

Arcadia is a wild, mountainous land. Europeans would later romanticize it as a pastoral paradise but that is a distortion of the facts. It was a world of eerie beauty where great waterfalls, including the headwaters of the river Styx, named for the death-goddess, thundered down out of craggy heights. It was a world of dark oak forests where Hermes was born, Orpheus sang, and Pan played his pipes. Outcasts took refuge there, especially in Arcadia's forbidding Peloponnese Mountains, a place too backward and inaccessible to tempt pursuers.[1]

Arcadia's oak forests, sacred to mother-goddess Rhea, represent a pre-agricultural epoch. The earliest inhabitants were said to have lived there even before the moon existed. The mountainous land was unsuitable for farming, so these "pre-moon" peoples lived on nutritious boiled acorns from Rhea's oaks. Other Greeks disdainfully contrasted the unrefined existence of these "acorn-eaters" with their own civilized existence "fed by milled grain."[2] Rhea's ancient realm and the younger realm of her daughter, Demeter, goddess of cultivated grain, were world's apart.

Ancient Arcadia was not impoverished, however – it was rich in sheep, goats, and horses. To compensate for the harsh environment, music played a significant role in educating young boys, more than anywhere else in Greece. Festivals were frequent, as were banquets, at which slave and free ate together, drank wine from a single vessel and, as skilled musicians with no need of hirelings, gladly entertained themselves.[3]

Oaks belonged to Rhea long before her son Zeus claimed them. Rhea's father, sky-god Uranus, disgusted at having sired three single-eyed Cyclopes and three Hecatoncheires (hundred-handed giants), coldly hurled the misfits from his sky *(see Laurel)*. Gaia, his outraged wife, turned to her bravest son, Cronus, and asked for help. Equally coldly, Cronus castrated his sire with a flint sickle and hurled the bloody genitals into the sea. Here their gender-polarity was mysteriously reversed, transforming them into Aphrodite, beautiful goddess of loving relationships. She, like her half-sister Rhea, would later be honored among Greece's oracular oaks.

Meanwhile, Cronus married Rhea, proving himself no better than their father because he swallowed their first five children, fearing they would otherwise overthrow him. When Rhea birthed her sixth child, Zeus, she was determined to save him. She handed Cronus a stone disguised as a swaddled newborn and he, unsuspecting, swallowed it. Then she slipped away in the dead of night and brought the boy to Crete, where Amalthea, a wise she-goat, became his foster-mother. Local smiths, herders, and beekeepers volunteered as bodyguards – Rhea taught them to dance with clattering weapons to mask the infant's cries lest Cronus discover her ruse and seek him out.[4]

Zeus grew in secret. Once fully grown, Rhea tricked Cronus into vomiting out their older five children: Hestia, Demeter, Hera, Hades, and Poseidon. None of these had a childhood. Unparented, unsocialized, they defeated Cronus and began the Olympian dynasty of classical Greece under the erratic leadership of their youngest brother, Zeus. The five are like science fiction's "in vitros," awakened full-grown out of a technological matrix without knowledge of relationship or compassion.

Afterwards, Rhea's majestic oaks gradually became Zeus' – not only because of their immense power, but also because Zeus' lightning-bolts were so irrepressibly drawn to them. The roots of oaks also make their way into the ground more deeply than other trees and, since it was believed knowledge of the future lay buried in the earth, oaks were preeminent among oracular trees. Thus, Zeus eventually claimed Arcadia's oak forests as well as those at Dodona, a famous oracular center in the mountains of Epirus, north of Arcadia. At Dodona, even to eat "the acorns of Zeus" bestowed wisdom, a curious reversal of the scorn reserved for rustic "acorn-eaters" in Arcadia.[5]

It was said that a dove, Aphrodite's "familiar" but also Rhea's, once flew from Egypt to Dodona and commanded Dodona's founding.[6] It would thereafter be sacred to Dione, sometimes considered Aphrodite's mother, sometimes Aphrodite herself,[7] sometimes equated with Rhea.[8] Regardless, oaks originally grew in a powerful realm of female earth-connections and relational energies. Only much later, incorporating shadowy memories of violence and horror, does Zeus, young leader of the new Olympian dynasty, claim oaks as his own.

At Dodona, oracles revealed themselves in three primary ways: rustling of oak leaves ("phyllomancy"); Zeusian-thunder from bronze gongs hung in trees; and flight-patterns of temple doves who nested in oaks and were sacred both to Aphrodite and Rhea. Wood itself could also speak – in the story of Jason and the Argonauts, for example, Athena, who favored Jason, inlaid a piece of Dodona oakwood in the ship's bow to speak words of guidance to the sailors.[9]

For many generations, commoners loved Dodona. From lead tablets inscribed with petitioners' questions, we know the oracle resonated to personal, private matters; in contrast, wealthier Delphi specialized in high-profile statecraft. As Dodona's fame grew and increasing numbers of people sought guidance, three priestesses known as the Peliades ("Doves") served the oracle by channeling Zeus' voice – rustling oak leaves confirmed their authenticity.[10]

In addition to oracular dimensions, Oak is inextricably linked to the "golden bough," formed when clusters of creamy mistletoe-berries attach themselves to oak and turn golden as they dry. Although its berries are poisonous, mistletoe healed so many ailments that it was called "All Heal."[11] The parasitical plant prefers ash, hawthorn, apple, or linden; thus, its rare appearances on oak were especially meaningful. Mistletoe symbolizes male genitalia – its pale berries, semen. When the moon was full, ancient priests harvested mistletoe with a sickle-shaped knife, reminiscent of the sickle with which Cronus castrated his father. This is yet one more echo of ritualized injury to male organs which, historically, reflects a time when royal succession demanded the castration and death of a weakened leader at the hands of a younger, stronger male.

Going back still earlier, when the religion of Orphism, (based on poems attributed to Orpheus) originated in the 7th or 6th century B.C.E., Orphic mystics envisioned Rhea eternally playing a drum before the cave of black-winged Night, the cosmic goddess who mates with the Wind and conceives a milky-silver egg. From this is born Eros, a winged, double-sexed being who then spins his mother's Universe into motion. Thus, Night and Eros exist as a beautifully balanced syzygy, or partnership. In the midst of their wondrous unfoldings, Rhea, seated attentively in the womb of Darkness, plays her drum, "compelling man's attention to the oracles of the goddess," summoning all who respond to the rhythms of her instrument.[12]

Night's power would later pass to Uranus, who retroactively becomes Rhea's father. Because he abuses his offspring, he will be castrated by Rhea's brother-consort, Cronus. Thus, Rhea is the daughter of a *castratus*, sister-wife to the castrator, and eventually the mother of Zeus, infamous for taking any female he desires, whether mortal or sacred. Despite Rhea's being at ground-zero among these self-absorbed males, Orphism understands her as being *elsewhere*, ecstatically beating her drum, summoning mortals to the oracles of Night because, for Rhea, oracles born of a *genuine* balance between female and male are woven into the very structure, or DNA, of the universe.

Botany/History

As glaciers receded from Eurasia, alder and aspen seemed already to be growing through the melting ice. Juniper arrived directly afterwards, accompanied by water-loving willow. These early migrants, called "pioneers," were relatively short-lived and unable to survive much shade – thus, when birch and pine arrived next, many pioneer trees were crowded out. Around 7200 B.C.E., the climate became drier and cooler: optimal conditions for the dramatically increasing hazel – birch retreated quickly while pine struggled to hold on. During what is called the "hazel time," oak finally entered, then elm and possibly ash. These are known as climax species, tolerant of deep shade and very long-lived. Around 5500 B.C.E., the climate again warmed and moisture increased – conditions favoring elm and linden, which crowded out all but slow-growing oak to form new climax forests from the Caucasus to Germany. When moisture and warmth declined, elm and linden retreated and the now mature oak became dominant, mixed with spruce, fir, hazel, maple, and beech. From the fifth into the fourth millennium, all of Germany and the Ukraine were covered with these mixed oak-dominant forests. Oaks survived succeeding climate changes but were much reduced by human deforestation during the following millennia.[13]

There are some 300 kinds of oak, some majestic, soaring up to 170 feet, others small and gnarled. These strong-hearted, generous trees have a lifespan of two to three centuries. They are powerful enough to draw up hundreds of liters of water from the soil on a daily basis; further, where most trees angle their branches upwards from their main limbs to lessen their weight, oaks defy gravity, sending their branches out horizontally.

They bear their fruit as cup-held acorns; a tree needs 40-80 years of growth before producing its first good crop; full production after that amounts to 700-1,000 liters annually, which is the equivalent of 90,000 acorns per season. Acorns were an important source of nourishment for many ancient peoples; to remove their bitter tannin, they could simply be roasted; boiled, dried, and dipped in honey; or ground into a coarse meal and baked into bread or porridge. A few varieties were sweet enough to be eaten raw. In forests, under the watchful eye of a swineherd, acorns also served as pig-fodder.[14]

Besides food, acorns were valued for tanning leather and making red dye. Oak tannin is not produced uniformly: as a defense against insects, especially caterpillars, its use diminishes vital resources required for leaf-production. If there is no threat, or if an attack is small-scale, oak directs its energies elsewhere. If there is a major onslaught, oak will produce tannin only in leaves being attacked. The chemical does not kill, but its bitter taste drives caterpillars elsewhere, which increases their exposure to birds, whose hunting reduces the number of caterpillars. If an infestation is severe, a tree may alert its neighbors by releasing "messenger" chemicals, warning them to start producing tannin even before caterpillars reach them.[15]

Glans is the Latin word for "acorn" or anything with an acorn-form, such as the glans of a penis; related to this is Sanskrit *gulah*, which means "acorn" as well as "penis" and "clitoris." Ancient words for "oak" involve meaning-clusters of thunder, life, soul, spirit, thunder god, and Thor's Mother. As one scholar comments, to many ancient Indo-European peoples, who developed during the period of mixed oak-dominant forests in their ancestral homelands, oak was "one of the underlying themes" in their cultures, "a basic life symbol...and a root of myth and of sacrament."[16]

In medieval Europe, the sense of oak's numinous mystery was responsible for its widespread appearance in cathedrals, where oak leaves and acorns were a common motif on the undersides of misericords and in roof bosses; foliated masks of Green Men, their mouths "speaking" oak leaves, are also found sculpted on soaring pillars in many cathedrals *(see Hawthorn)*.[17]

The Reading

As we have seen, Rhea had a far older claim to oaks than Zeus, but in allowing a connection to young masculine power, perhaps deeper purposes are ultimately served. Rhea's idea of the masculine is certainly not the aggressive phallic dimension of Uranus, Cronus, and Zeus. Her sacred oaks are of Orpheus' songs, Pan's pipes, double-sexed Eros spinning his mother's universe into being, and all males who patiently and respectfully tend seeds of on-going life. To that end, Rhea plays her drum, drawing attention to oracles speaking of a forgotten metaphor, that of the "testicular male," a concept recently brought into clearer focus and beautifully elucidated by Genia Pauli Haddon's *Body Metaphors*:

> To be masculine traditionally has been defined as to be like the penis, or phallus: potent, penetrating, outward thrusting, initiating, probing, forging ahead into virgin territory, opening the way, swordlike, able to cut through, able to cleave or differentiate, having powers of discrimination, goal oriented, to the point, focused, directive, effective, aimed, hitting the mark, strong, firm, erect....
>
> Such a view does not take into account that along with a penis, a man's physical genitals include testicles. The testicular component of a man's sexuality has very different qualities than the penis or phallus. Physiologically, the testicle is a reservoir, a holding place, where seed is nurtured to maturation. Unlike the penis, whose power manifests itself through intermittent erection and ejaculation, the testicle is stable and abiding. It quietly and steadily undergirds the man's sexuality. It "hangs in there." The testicle is the germinal source, the vessel from which is poured forth the sap or water of life.
>
> If our cultural and psychological definitions of masculinity were based solely on the qualities evident in the testicles, we would conclude that the archetypal Great Masculine has a yin nature. We would describe it as the eternal Source, vessel-like, containing, patient, steadfast, nurturing. And we would expect men to embody in their personalities concomitant qualities.[18]

In the fascinating development of sperm in the testicles, Sertoli, or "nurse" cells, tend sperm in delicately precise sixteen-day cycles; when sperm cells are ready to leave, they travel through a *tubule lumen* ("tunnel of light"), bathed in honeyed liquors (i.e., "milky, liquid fructose") within the testicles.[19] In this sensitive process, Grail-like testicles become a metaphor just as valuable and intrinsically masculine as the phallic.

One immediate benefit is to shift the advice often given males: "get in touch with your feminine" to the more accurate "get in touch with your testicular." Restoring this lost dimension would provide a far more balanced and satisfying interpretation of masculinity. We have countless worldwide myths celebrating phallic, heroic beings, but almost none celebrating the testicular – except for a few wizards and healers like Merlin, some of the Grail-cycle knights, the Green Man, and shamans of indigenous lore.

Regardless of your gender, the oracle asks you to recognize and re-activate, not the injured, aggressive, phallic dimension, but the nurturing, gentle, seed-bearing testicular function. Take time with your life, your relationships, and your projects. From small beginnings emerge Rhea's majestic, rustling oaks. "Hang in there."

REVERSED:

Oaks know well how to husband their energies. Both genders could learn from them how not to squander tannin. Not everything requires a full-scale attack. Males have long been defined by phallic metaphors. When women have been free to make choices, many have helped disseminate this narrow perspective by scorning sensitive males, marrying "he-men" instead, and raising their sons to be the same. Our violent, warring cultures demonstrate how destructive this has been.

Maleness should no longer be limited to false heroics and trigger-happy decisions. It is time for both parents to nurture more depth in their offspring, female and male. It is time for heroes and heroines to grow up and become wise, earthy, caring sages.

Artist's Notes:

Rhea stands near a frieze of herself seated on a lion: Pergamon Altar, Greek, 165-156 B.C.E., found in Bergama, Turkey; necklace with acorn pendant from Tharros, c. 7th-6th century B.C.E.; gold oak-leaf diadem from Tarento, c. 4th-2nd century B.C.E.; bee earring from a pendant: Crete, 1700-1550 B.C.E.

Endnotes

[1] Borgeaud:6-7;193, fn.36;14; Zimmerman:90.
[2] Borgeaud.:15.
[3] Ibid.:20; 195, fn.74.
[4] Ibid.:251, fn.118; Graves, *GM*:vol.1, 7b, c.
[5] Altman:167.
[6] Montet:162; Stapleton:70.
[7] Stapleton:29,70; Zimmerman:87; Rose:53.
[8] Graves, *GM*:vol.1, 7.1.
[9] Frazer, vol.ii:356-357; Stapleton:70; Altman:166; Goelitz:120; Rose:198.
[10] Stapleton:70; Goelitz:120; for dove and Rhea:Graves, *GM*:vol.1, 7.8.
[11] Graves, *GM*:vol.1, 7.1; Walker, *Ency.*:661-663; Altman:152; Sylvia Woods:82; Hadfield:124.
[12] Friedrich:19-23.
[13] *Cowles*:112; Lehane:52, 54; Penistan:103;
Frazer, vol.ii:355-356; Renfrew:154-155.
[14] Attenborough:77.
[15] Friedrich:137; 139.
[16] Hadfield.:127.
[17] Graves, *GM*:vol.1, 2b.
[18] Haddon:10-11.
[19] Jenks, *Zygote/ Syzygy:*112-116; 122-126.

23
OLIVE

Olive

[Olive] has this remarkable interest, in the first place, that its foliage is the earliest that is mentioned by name, when the waters of the flood began to retire (Gen.viii.11).
~ William Smith[1]

The Mythic World

Long associated with peace, the olive was sacred to Mediterranean goddesses. Olive trees were especially abundant in Palestine, which is why the flood story in Genesis, but not in older Mesopotamian sources, mentions the olive as the only tree to survive the deluge. Noah, his relatives, and all their animals had been living in severely confined quarters in the midst of vast stretches of storm-tossed waters for a very long time. The ark, which had once been a means of escape, had become a prison. There was no land, no harbor, nowhere to anchor. They were drifting endlessly without direction or hope, humans and animals multiplying dangerously in the ark's fixed space. It was a bleak, desolate, frustrating time. Pairs of doves were sent out in search of land, but they returned without success.

Finally, one dove found land and the other returned with an olive branch. Something besides the overburdened ark had survived the flood and was already pushing forth new leaves. This epiphany of new life was experienced as a profound miracle.

Robert Graves identifies Libya as the original home of the cultivated olive. He argues that Libya is also the point of origin for Athena, who eventually brings the olive to Athens.[2] The Libyan precursors of Athena, however, would have been among the region's Great Mother Goddesses of pre-patriarchal times, bearing little resemblance to Greece's Athena. This war-goddess, fully armed when she emerges from her father Zeus' head, is motherless, often scornful of women, fiercely loyal to male comrades, and famous for her cunning military strategies. Yet she has the same piercing eyes, wise and all-seeing, of older, staring, owl-eyed goddesses of the Near East. As if to emphasize this dimension of sight, she is usually accompanied by her owl, whose oracular vision looks deep into secret places.[3]

Athena's gift of the olive occurs when she and sea-god Poseidon compete in a contest sponsored by a proud new city in Attica, which desires to adopt as its titular deity whoever provides the greater gift. Unlike Athena, Poseidon prefers drama and does not think strategically. He boldly thrusts his trident deep into the earth and a geyser of seawater shoots upwards. Impressive as this spectacle is, however, the salty water is undrinkable. More sensibly, Athena manifests a tree, which provides abundant olives as well as shade.

Furious, Poseidon challenges her to single combat. Athena is battle-ready and eager, but Zeus forbids it. Instead, he asks the other Olympian deities to determine the winner. Gods vote for Poseidon, but goddesses choose Athena and she wins by one vote. Thus, she becomes the city's patroness and bestows her name upon it: *Athens*.

Just as with Noah, a flood now enters this story because the enraged Poseidon summons a tidal wave to inundate a nearby plain. Anxious to appease his anger, Athenian males deprive their wives of all voting rights and decree that male children will henceforth bear only their fathers' names, not their mothers'.[4]

The olive plays a role in yet another Greek myth, one about the birth of moon and sun. It shows, as in Noah's story, the olive's ability to give hope in a time of crisis and to participate in the emergence of new life. Here, the Greek Titan-goddess Leto is in labor for the first time, alone on a tiny island in a vast sea, as isolated as Noah's ark. She is frightened, screaming in agony, unsure what to do. Racked with pain, she reaches out to a female olive tree with her left hand and a male palm (a Near Eastern "Tree of Life") with her right, desperately clinging to that yin/yang partnership as her daughter Artemis, goddess of the moon, emerges.[5] No sooner has Artemis been born than Leto's labor pains begin for Artemis' twin brother, Apollo, god of the sun – and the tree-world bears witness to yet another divine epiphany.

Botany/History

The wild olive, native to warm, semi-arid Eurasian regions, especially around the Mediterranean, was probably first cultivated in Libya in northern Africa. It is an evergreen tree, gnarled, knotted, its willowy leaves silvery, especially beautiful when they ripple in a wind. The tree grows slowly but lives for many centuries. It has a wide-ranging root system – thus, to allow space for these roots, cultivated trees need to be over thirty-five feet apart. The flowers bloom in pale yellow clusters; later, the fruits, shaped like small eggs, begin green and darken to black as they ripen.

This is not a tree that invites you to reach up, pick a handful of fruits, and eat them as you wander through the grove. These bitter fruits are inedible unless they are properly treated. This requires effort, care, and a good deal of time. To avoid bruising the fruits or injuring the gnarled boughs, the fruits must either be handpicked or gently shaken off with a light reed. Those destined as food are then soaked in a lye solution to leach out the bitterness; after that, they are washed and pickled in brine under carefully controlled conditions. To harvest the oil, in ancient times fully ripe fruits were either trodden underfoot or bruised in a mortar; it was not until Hellenistic times that technology had advanced sufficiently to allow the fruits to be crushed in a press or ground in a mill. The oil-producing process required cooperation and an unusual degree of efficiency because oil left in bruised olives swiftly turned rancid.[6]

As food, cooking oil, and lamp oil, the olive had enormous economic value in the ancient world. But it also had other uses: after bathing for a festive occasion, olive oil was rubbed into the hair and body, giving a smooth, shining appearance. Medicinally, it was used as an ointment on wounds. It was also crucial in ritual, required, for example, to consecrate a king, priest, or prophet. In Israel, mixed with flour or used alone, it was presented to Yahweh as a first-fruit offering. The presence of olive oil spoke of gladness. Its absence, on the other hand, spoke of sorrow or shame, which is why sin-offerings (*Lev.v.11*) or offerings of jealousy (*Num.v.15*), were never accompanied by it.[7]

The olive is the only fruit with high fat content in its oil – from 20% to 60%. In our own time, olive oil, especially in its Extra Virgin form, which keeps the oil closest to its original source, is drawing great attention because of its ability to lower cholesterol, thin the blood, protect the heart, and retard aging through its antioxidant properties. Where olive oil is the main source of fat, death rates from heart disease and many illnesses associated with aging decline dramatically.[8]

The Reading

Olive is a tree of peace, harmony, wisdom – and also hard work. Whatever area of your life has brought you to seek the trees' advice, know that you are promised rich rewards, but the path may be gnarled, not smooth, and you must be prepared to invest quality time in this endeavor. The work will require attention to details and the results may seem bitter at first, but that bitterness, like the olive's, is amenable to transformation. From the olive comes the oil of gladness – trust that the harvest will bring you satisfaction.

Your attitude towards this work is significant. Although the olive originally symbolized peace, not war, the olive's symbolism was eventually so warped that wreaths fashioned from its leaves were awarded to Roman soldiers for excellence in battle. Stay alert and avoid seeing your work as a "war" requiring unrelenting bravery and heroism. That attitude bruises the olive's vibration of graciousness and peace. Be a patient gardener, not a warrior-"hero," and the fruits of your work will ripen fully and gladly.

Familiarity with Noah's Ark has eroded the stark drama of that event, yet if you have drawn Olive, the tree asks you to consider it anew, especially in relationship to your own life. You may currently be living, emotionally or physically, in cramped quarters. You may feel your potential is being stifled, the duration of your imprisonment unknown, the future hopeless. Like the olive, you need more space for the extensive root-system that is yours by nature. Olive asks you to keep sending out gentle doves. Do not despair. Keep probing beyond your confines. One day the olive branch will come to you as a promise of new life, one that will require the best of your skills and give you a solid future at last.

If you are female, take care not to let the male world swallow you up, steal your vote (metaphorically or otherwise), and disenfranchise you. Refuse to be subjugated to a realm of cold intellect without compassion. If you are male, avoid getting caught up in pointless power games with women – find an inner balance or bitterness may leave both of you the poorer. Leto's divine-labor *needs* the trees' yin-yang balance. Poseidon's briny spring is *necessary* to make the olive edible – without it, each would be of little value. It is not about *either/or* solutions – find the *both/and*.

Olive further suggests that both genders need to be aware of the emotional ecosystems inhabited by their parents so that they may work towards more loving partnerships. Athena, for example, unmothered, never managed it. Despite her many gifts of peace, she remained an unyielding warrior-maiden. Trapped in Zeus' head, trapped in her own, this goddess reveals much of vengeance but little of love. Male or female, you deserve better. Work towards that.

REVERSED:

This may indicate that you are hoping for an easy way out, an easy answer, overnight success. If so, Olive reminds you that your current situation needs to be taken more seriously. Olive gives no oil of gladness unless you are willing to invest your own hard work in the process. It is time to commit yourself more fully or you may drift, like Noah's ark, without direction. You may also need to take health and diet issues more seriously or they may undermine whatever else you may be inquiring about.

When this card is reversed, it might also be a signal that your attitude could be your own worst enemy – thus, like an angry, defeated Poseidon, your emotions threaten your balance. Although war-goddess Athena never managed a loving relationship of her own, it should be remembered that in addition to the olive tree, she gave her *people* such crucial arts as music, metallurgy, spinning, and pottery. You might consider looking to such arts as alternate channels for your own creative energies. You might also look for wisdom from her alter-ego, the clear-eyed owl.

Olive reversed might also indicate that you are already doing everything wisely and well but that there may be further delays in obtaining the peace and gladness you seek. It may be that more sorrows lie ahead and must be patiently endured to the best of your ability. Trust that the dove will finally come flying towards you through the bleakness, an olive branch in her mouth. Remember that when all seems lost, that branch is already on its way to you as a promise of renewed joy.

Artist's Notes:

Athena wears a snake bracelet after a ring from Madytos, 330-300 B.C.E., and wears an earring and holds a coin with her portrait from Athens, 450-20 B.C.E. On the left, in the trunk of the olive tree, is a representation of Athena as the Goddess of Wisdom, with living snakes entwined around her, c. 6th century B.C.E. In the background is a statue of Athena flying her owl, c. 460 B.C.E.

Endnotes

[1] William Smith, L.L.D.:468.
[2] Graves, G.M. I,62.
[3] E.g., see where she makes her appearance in Homer: Iliad 1.206. A few lines earlier, I.200, Achilles immediately recognizes her by "the terrible eyes shining" (tr., Lattimore), which also suggests some of the fearsomeness of the Gorgon/Graiae eye. On the owl, Walker, E754-755.
[4] Graves, G.M.:I, 59-60; 62.
[5] Walker, E533; the twins were fathered by Zeus – for more, although there's no mention of olive, Rose:114 flg.
[6] Cowles:112/c; Smith's Bible Dictionary:464; 468; McKenzie:625; Renfrew:131-134; National Geographic, September 1951, p.348.
[7] Smith's Bible Dictionary:464; McKenzie:625-626.
[8] Carper:242-245; National Geographic, op.cit.

24
PAPYRUS

Papyrus

...The tall, straight stems, the young plants, and the old, drooping umbels were entangled in shady groves where Isis and her son hid themselves...

~ Jean Yoyotte[1]

The Mythic World

To predynastic inhabitants of papyrus marshes in northern Egypt over 5,000 years ago, the Mother of Creation was cobra-goddess, Wadjyt. Her name derives from *wadj*, "papyrus," "green," "joy," and "youth," reflecting the essence of her own exuberant creativity.[2] By dynastic times, Wadjyt was depicted on royal crowns as a rearing cobra (*uraeus*), protecting the "third-eye" brow-center. Each Egyptian queen was regarded as Wadjyt-incarnate. Only by marrying her was a pharaoh legitimized as sun-god Horus-incarnate.[3]

The Greeks called her Buto, a manifestation of their own goddess Leto, mother of sun and moon *(see Olive)*. The "Swamps of Buto" (*Per-Wadjyt*), one of Egypt's oldest-known oracular sites, were hidden within vast northern marshes. Mythically, this was a floating island with no specific location – as marsh-womb of the sun, its position changed daily. Falcon-headed Horus rose out of Buto's dense swamps at dawn – at dusk, he returned as if to a tomb, for Buto was dual mother of life and death.[4] Hours later, with the aid of gods carrying magical papyrus-wands, Horus fought his way back out through her uterus, struggling against dark swamp-creatures, before again being reborn.

After inhabitants of the swamps were united politically with aggressive peoples of the arid south (First Dynasty, c. 3000 B.C.), new cycles of myth and ritual arose, recombining over the centuries, then splitting and shifting into more complex patterns. Wadjyt's original functions were "borrowed" as other deities came to the forefront. Thus, Isis took on Wadjyt's birth-mother aspect and her sister, Nephthys, assimilated the transformative death/rebirth aspects (see *Apple*).[5] Their brother, Osiris, vegetation dying/rising god of barley, wine and beer, was Isis' mate. Their brother, Set, Nephthys' mate, was god of dry trackless deserts – the realm most alien to Wadjyt's swamps. Psychologically, perhaps the fratricidal theme set in motion by treacherous Set reveals how northern marsh-dwellers truly felt about unification.

Despite all the changes in this ancient cast of characters, however, the Swamps of Buto remained the ritual theatre in which Isis and Nephthys worked their greatest miracles. It began when the jealous, cunning Set tricked Osiris into a chest, sealed it, and threw it into the Nile, where it drifted to the sea. Devastated, Isis went in search of the body and, after many adventures, found it in Byblos and returned home with it *(see Pine)*. Set ruthlessly dismembered the corpse, scattering the remains along the Nile. The determined sisters, however, found all but the phallus and brought the pieces back to the marshes.

There, in that shadowy, mysterious realm, aided by moon-god Thoth, they reassembled the body while Wadjyt's fierce energy wound through the swamps, crackling and hissing like protective snakes around their heads as they worked.

Finally, lying upon Osiris' corpse, Isis took bird-form and magically conceived Horus. Then she, Nephthys, and Thoth resurrected Osiris, who withdrew to the Netherworld, over which he thereafter ruled.

Isis, meanwhile, had to protect the unborn child from Set. She fled further into the marshes, gave birth in secret, and hid there, guarded by Wadjyt, seven scorpions, and other friendly deities, until Horus grew old enough to defeat his uncle Set and claim his birthright.[6]

The oldest, most archaic sun-myth in northern Egypt involves only a young, solitary cobra-goddess, birthing the sun on her own each dawn. There were no hatreds at work, no treachery, no patterns of dominance and succession. All that came later. Yet even then, the cobra-goddess, two powerful goddess-sisters, and their loyal allies intervene and overcome malice. Wadjyt's swamps and ancient serpent-wisdom protect the vulnerable sun-child until he is strong enough to reverse Set's patterns of negativity. When Horus succeeds, the cycles resume their turnings.

Botany/History

Papyrus is a tall, vigorous plant, top-heavy with umbels that sway and rustle in the slightest breeze. After rooting themselves in rich mud, three-sided stalks easily grow more than twenty feet high, forming into dense, shadowy thickets teeming with birds, insects, crocodiles, hippopotami, reptiles.[7] For the ancients, the marshes were a place of fertility – lush, secret, mysterious. Hunters entered them to track exotic prey. Families of the nobility went picnicking or fowling, traveling on graceful skiffs along narrow streamlets covered with floating lotuses. The marshy interiors were the last refuge of outcasts, slaves, or women fleeing oppression (Moses hidden in the marshes is a familiar example). As sacred beech groves offered refuge in ancient Italy *(see Beech)*, papyrus swamps offered it in Egypt.

The Swamps of Buto lay in the Western Delta in the middle of a vast marsh that once spread across northern Egypt. Only a few miles from the Mediterranean, the nearby city of Buto was said to be Egypt's oldest oracular shrine.[8] The entire region was the domain of the cobra-goddess. Her uterine swamp had no specific location: it was a floating island of papyrus – the sun rose out of her womb and returned to it at dusk. In recognition of this power inherent in papyrus, Egyptian architects imitated the tall reeds in stone, sculpting them into columns to support temples, thereby making each temple into a microcosmic "marsh," a place wherein the rebirth of the sun was celebrated each dawn.

Egyptians also turned papyrus-pith into paper and inscribed the wisdom of their civilization upon it, sacred and secular, magical and mundane. Much of what we know of the ancient world's mythology, beliefs, medicine, math, and history would have been lost without Egypt's beautifully inscribed rolls of papyrus. Unfortunately, paper-making was not its only use – huge papyrus trunks were bound together to make fine skiffs and rafts; fibers were twisted into ropes or woven into sails, sandals, mats, baskets; roots were eaten as a delicacy. Papyrus was *too* serviceable and its lucrative, multiple uses doomed the great marshes. They were systematically dismembered by teams of well-organized workers and shipped as raw material to workshops all over Egypt. None remain.[9]

The Reading

Papyrus offers you encouragement over a project already well underway. You have placed much skill, hope, and energy in this work, yet it never seems to get off its feet. You may feel as if you should cut your losses and let it go. But Papyrus is a place of resurrection, healing, magic, bringing to life a project seemingly killed off by negative forces. It may be time to consider new approaches and allies. Trust your own deep serpent-wisdom and do not be afraid to try again.

In active imagination, let yourself enter that dreamlike realm. There in the moonlight with allies at your side, become aware of the fierce energy winding everywhere through the swamps, crackling and hissing like snakes around your head as you work. See what new options emerge.

On the simplest level, Papyrus gives you access to a realm of fertile creativity. It tells you not to give up hope. This is a time of renewal, of re-patterning your innate cycles of growth. Papyrus may be encouraging you to travel into a realm of new knowledge – anything that will take you out of your usual existence. This might mean exploring something you once dreamed of doing, learning, experiencing, but you let it go when you felt "swamped" by more pressing realities. This would be a good time to resurrect whatever it was.

REVERSED:

This might be a warning that you are hacking away at the roots of your own joy, demanding that they turn a profit, always looking for lucrative ways to exploit your creativity without ever giving yourself time to recover. Are you currently involved in a project that keeps draining your life-energies away? It might be time to let it go. Only you can protect your Swamps of Buto with all its teeming, dreamlike life. You need to keep that inner realm available to the "Isis and sun-child" within you. You and they may one day need to hide there and learn to feel safe again.

If you are in a relationship with parents, siblings, or friends where you are continually cast in the role either of rescuer (Isis) or monster (Set), here too it might be time to let go. While Isis had the power to resurrect Osiris, Papyrus *reversed* reminds you that you are not Isis. Your loved ones need to solve their own life problems. You may have reached a time when you cannot do anything except protect your own papyrus realm from further dismemberment.

If you are involved with allies, you are cautioned against too much trust. Pay attention to issues of power and popularity. If you find jealousy, explore ways of defusing it. Osiris loved his brother, but his naïve love blinded him to Set's trap. Do not let anyone box you in. There is too much at stake to let yourself be victimized.

On the other hand, if you are feeling like Set, frustrated and jealous over the success of another, go more deeply into the root-causes of your emotions. Look for repeating patterns, for this will not be the first time you have felt unappreciated. Even if you could hack your supposed enemy into a thousand pieces, you would still not find love or acceptance. Seek another path: first, before you can learn how to rebirth yourself each dawn, recruit trustworthy ancients to help you struggle past your dark, cunning swamp-creatures.

Set exists in each of us – he points the way to our weakest point, or what Carl Jung calls the "inferior fourth function." Of Jung's four basic psychological functions – thinking, "ethic-ing (i.e., "feeling" your way into the rightness or wrongness of something), intuition, and sensation (i.e., having practical skills in the sensate "real" world) – the "inferior fourth function" lies opposite your primary function and is the one over which you have least control. It is what seems most mysterious and alien to you.[10] When you are in balance, insights from that realm come shimmering with magic and delight. You cannot explain it. It is "other" – magnificent. But if you are not in balance, "evil" enters the same way and along the very same trajectory. Beauty, but also dangerous fault-lines, fissures, and alternate universes, tend to lie in what is most alien to you.

If you are an intuitive type, for example, at ease with dreams and mystical realms, your opposite pole lies in the sensate realm. Simple physical things will have the power to move you tremendously, like "magic." It might be the play of light in a tree, a special smile, wind chimes on a windy day. When the sensate realm turns ugly, however, then such stimuli as noise pollution, secondhand smoke, or broken appliances will be a special torment for you. People who accuse you of being melodramatic or too sensitive only make it worse. Set-like, you might hack away at your own self-esteem over issues where you feel least in control. To stay with the intuitive example, this might be an inability to be on time, make more money, get your prose or poetry published, keep a spotless home, or handle minor "real-world" emergencies with serenity. In Set-mode, you lose all perspective. The solution is not to deny Set's self-hate, but rather to deal with him as the unhappy child he is. Give him love, reassure him that imperfections are not fatal, let him play in the Swamps of Buto and learn anew to trust life in all its rich, juicy diversity.

Artist's Notes:

The relief on the left shows Wadjyt in a gesture of protection from the pyramid temple of King Neuserra, 5th Dynasty. To the right of that is a papyrus marsh from the Mastaba of Mereruka, Saqqara, 6th Dynasty c. 2300 B.C.E.; behind it, on the left, is a statue of an otter, an inhabitant of marshes, from the Ptolemaic Period c. 304-30 B.C.E. and, on the right, a copy of a previously existing mural of a papyrus marsh from the north palace of Akhenaton at Tell-el-Amarna, c. 1360 B.C.E. The relief on the right of Wadjyt in cobra form is from the funerary bed of Queen Hetephras, 4th Dynasty. Wadjyt is wearing an earring and an armband (design adapted from a pectoral) from Tutankhamen's Tomb, c. 1323 B.C.E.

Endnotes

[1] DEC:206.
[2] DEC:206; Gardiner:73; 560a (under alternate spelling, Edjo).
[3] Gardiner:32,n.1.
[4] Walker:WEMS:904.
[5] Walker:WEMS:904.
[6] Montet:185-186.
[7] DEC:206.
[8] Buffie Johnson:277.
[9] DEC:206; 208.
[10] For an excellent in-depth discussion, see Irene Claremont de Castillejo, Knowing Woman: A Feminine Psychology (New York: Harper & Row, 1973) – the work is useful for both genders.

25
PEONY

Peony

In the stillness,
Between the arrival of guests,
The peonies.
          ~ Buson[1]

So he spoke, and told Paian to heal him...
     ~ *Iliad,* Book Five: 899

The Mythic World

Paian was a renowned Greek physician. His father was Endymion, the male "Sleeping Beauty," a youth so handsome that moon-goddess Artemis fell in love when she saw him sleeping nude on a mountaintop. Since he feared growing old, she cast him into a perpetual sleep of eternal youth, which suited her own needs, for it allowed her to embrace him every night without the tumult of his immature, demanding passions. She bore fifty of his daughters. His wife, one of Artemis' priestesses, bore him four sons, Paian among them. Since their father slept day and night, the boys were raised by women.[2]

Paian, son of a moon-priestess and the moon-goddess' lover, became a master herbalist, privy to the secrets of every plant, for the moon was in his blood just as much as it was in the roots and sap of all plants. Paian's skills, according to Homer, gave him the reputation of being a god as far away as Egypt:

> ...where the rich plantations grow
> herbs of all kinds, maleficent and healthful;
> and no one else knows medicine as they do,
> Egyptian heirs of Paian, the healing god.[3]

Paian was official physician to the Olympians. During the Trojan War, he was summoned to heal Hades, whose shoulder had been pierced by an arrow. Hades was in agony for even the god of death could feel pain. Had he been mortal, not even Paian could have cured him, but Paian scattered pain-numbing medicines over him and soon healed his wound.[4] Hades later returned the favor by turning Paian into a beautiful and medicinally powerful peony when a jealous follower of Asclepius, or perhaps Asclepius himself, was about to take his life.[5]

In another Trojan War incident, Ares, violent and bloodthirsty god of war, lunged at horse-tamer Diomedes, one of the bravest Greek leaders and a favorite of Ares' half-sister, Athena, goddess of wisdom. Athena deflected Ares' blow, and instead, guided Diomedes' spear deep into Ares' belly. When she wrenched it out again, Ares bellowed in excruciating pain. He went to Zeus, bitterly complaining, even blaming Zeus for letting his "maniac daughter" get so out of hand. Zeus replied:

> Do not sit beside me and whine, you double-faced liar.
> To me you are the most hateful of all gods who hold Olympos.
> Forever quarrelling is dear to your heart, wars and battles....
> And yet I will not long endure to see you in pain, since you are my child, and it

was to me that your mother bore you.
But were you born of some other god and proved so ruinous long since you would have been dropped beneath the gods of the bright sky.

Zeus then calls Paian to heal this "most hateful of all gods."

> So he spoke, and told Paian to heal him; and scattering medicines to still pain upon him Paian rendered him well again, since he was not made to be one of the mortals.
> As when the juice of the fig in white milk rapidly fixes that which was fluid before and curdles quickly for one who stirs it;
> in such speed as this he healed violent Ares;
> and Hebe washed him clean and put delicate clothing upon him.[6]

For a time at least, Paian and Ares' sister Hebe (the gods' cupbearer) had "stopped the murderous work of manslaughtering Ares."[7]

Ancient physicians and botanists who were trained in Paian's healing arts established at least one hospital, called a *paioneion,* at the site of a natural hot spring.[8] In later times, Paian's skills would be confused with those of sun-god Apollo (brother of Artemis and thus Paian's uncle). Even Paian's songs of thanksgiving, "paeans," were usurped by Apollo. In Homer's time, however, Apollo was neither herbalist nor healer. It was only later when his priesthood gained political power that Paian's name and functions were assimilated by Apollo, making him *Apollo Paian*, but that title was more honorary than functional, for any healing was actually done by Apollo's son Asclepius, fosterling of the centaur Chiron, son of the linden tree *(see Linden).*[9]

Originally, Asclepius, like Paian, was linked to chthonic realms of moon, oracles, and serpents. But as Greek civilization shifted away from "dark" mother-realms of wisdom and towards male solar-realms of "light" and logic, the cult of Asclepius was adopted by Apollo's priests.[10] Paian's cult was swallowed up entirely – only the flower itself, the peony, remains to remind us of a simpler age of wisdom.

Botany/History

The word "peony" comes from a Greek root meaning "to strike." Paian's name has been interpreted as *he who cures maladies by his magic blow,*[11] reflecting the fact that in healing rituals a patient is often therapeutically "struck" with an empowering staff, wand, caduceus, sprigs of evergreen, bunches of leaves or flowers, which transfer the vitality and harmony of nature, via the patient's subconscious, to the body's deep-level cellular structures.

"Peony" is also cognate with "paean" – a song of thanksgiving chanted by Paian's followers, the *paeoni*, after a healing. In classical times, paeans were offered to sun-god Apollo, who by then had appropriated Paian's role. Since the Mediterranean wild peony, *paeonia*, blooms only for summer solstice and drops its petals soon afterwards, this is a further connection with the sun-god.[12]

The peony is a hardy perennial and exists both as flower or shrubby three- to six-foot tree. Blossoms range in color from white to deep wine. There is a wild peony native to the American Pacific coastal mountains but all other varieties are indigenous to Eurasia.[13] The flowers may be single (five to ten petals) or double. The term "double" does not mean a doubling of the simpler form – the effect, as a double bud opens, is of thousands of petals unfolding out of an inner universe. Time seems to stand still; everything steps back, awed.[14]

China has been cultivating peonies for thousands of years – royal gardens frequently had vast double-flowered collections. Since the flower's beauty and medicinal usefulness were considered sacred, its exportation was generally forbidden.[15] Chinese medicine uses the root of the white peony (*P'ai shao*) for treating complications in pregnancy and childbirth;[16] it is also used for general female disorders and gonorrhea.[17] A tree peony species, *suffructicosa*, is used to encourage metabolism and improve the endocrine system; applied as a styptic or astringent, it stops bleeding by contracting the blood vessels or tissues.[18]

Hundreds of cultivated varieties of peony now exist worldwide. They generally start blooming in early spring and continue for nearly two months. The plants are easy to grow as long as they are given enough sun, uncrowded space, clean soil, and good drainage – they may die if they get wet feet. They are heavy feeders and if they are not given enough space from the roots of other plants, their essential nutrients may be stolen. They should never be planted where another peony has grown unless a depth of three feet of nutrient-exhausted soil has been removed and replaced with new soil. If stimulants are used to force plants into spectacular but abnormal growth, they will burn out after a few years. With reasonable care, many peonies last fifty years or more and it is not unusual to find plants older than a century. This gives the peony a touchingly human-sized time frame. You plant a peony to last your lifetime.[19]

In medieval Europe, it was believed peonies could protect a home from violent storms and demons; further, its ground-up seeds were taken morning and night to prevent another kind of "storm" – nightmares.[20] Medicinally, powdered peony root-extracts have been used for thousands of years as a tonic to soothe nerves.[21] Early American colonists continued this practice[22] – and as they spread west, they stored peony roots in their covered wagons for eventual planting around their new homes. American Indians used peony root-tea for lung problems. The plant has also been used to cleanse the uterus and to relieve headaches, convulsions, and liver obstructions.[23] Its magnificent beauty and the wide range of its medicinal uses have made the peony highly valued wherever it is found.

The Reading

This is a plant of healing on many levels. Allow the healing to unfold without indulging in drastic actions. Your soaring spirit and that in you which is "immortal" cannot help you here – you need what is human, mortal, of the earth. You may be looking for a major healing, forgetting the little ones, the small graces, the commonplace blessings that are always around you – a smile, a kind word, a special song, the fall of light through the leaves, the taste of fresh water, the fragrance of a flower. Make more space in your life for these. Like the peony, these things seem frail, but they have an inner spaciousness that makes them the hardy "stuff" of life. When the big dramas fade, these little things remain, standing the test of time.

Paian, a mortal, could heal the immortals because he had something they did not. His was no "heroic" medicine. Like him, look to your mortal side. Explore something simple, usually overlooked, in yourself – see what ancient, clean, still vital wisdom is hidden there. See an herbalist, make healthier changes in your diet, make space in your life and environment. You and your body still have a long time together. Do not attack it for being too much this or too little that. When you surround your body with love, you give its cells permission to draw deeply from the healing energies in its nutrients, water, sun, space.

From "peony" comes *paean,* a song of thanksgiving for healings, offered anciently to Paian and Apollo but, by extension, to all life unfolding under the sun. *Nobody is truly sane,* Oscar Ichazo wrote, *until he feels gratitude to the whole universe.* Paeans improve the emotional drainage of your soil for, like the peony, your roots cannot tolerate stagnant, standing water. The peony reminds you that living in a "climate" of thanksgiving is what life is all about.

REVERSED:

You may be feeling like Paian at the moment when a jealous student is about to kill him. Hades, god of death, intervenes and transforms Paian into a medicinally powerful peony instead. But in that moment of transformation, you are still caught between the confusion of being betrayed and the too-abrupt shift to a new life that feels weak, out of control, paradoxically dependent upon the forces of *death* (Hades) for its continued *life.* You remain caught in that freeze-frame, neither here nor there. The ego's frustration feeds from twin-sources: an awareness of your inner worth and a strong sense that you have already suffered enough and deserve better.

Understandably, you want to fight back. Psychologically, you have mistakenly let yourself shift from healer to warrior. In this impossible situation, your expectations are outpacing your current reality and you are fretting and pacing your cage like a captive warrior. You scarcely recognize yourself. Your turbulent feelings seem too intense to belong to you. They should belong to cold, non-human Ares, Paian's one-time patient, not you. They surge with superhuman, titanic power, working against you, threatening the clarity of your inner wisdom. Yet these feelings are yours – and they need to be humanized. You cannot drop them out of your bright sky, as Zeus yearns to do with his quarrelsome son. You have equally fathered and mothered your rage and neither indulgence nor denial will help you now.

You need to calm these feelings for awhile, cleanse and dress them in the "delicate clothing" with which Hebe garbed her brother, Ares. This might mean going on a weekend retreat for spiritual renewal, or staying home to meditate on your soul's rainbow "garment of light." Make time for the soft colors and "delicate clothing" of journaling, drawing, silence. Silence, to use one of Thomas Merton's insights, is not broken by speech but by the anxiety to be heard. And the Sufi poet Rumi wrote, "In your depression, there is insolence in that you refuse to praise." Find a way to move your ego back into praise, into paeans. To persist in feeling like an angry victim only feeds the negative cycle. It drains your power and gives it to the very situation or relationship that failed you in the first place. Whatever that was, it no longer deserves your quality attention.

Reclaim your power by learning to tame those intense, furiously charged emotional centers within you, before they lead to serious problems. Ares' rage caused him to be disemboweled. Such rage could also lead to stomach ulcers, liver or colon problems, a feeling of being tied in knots, or of being confined in a cage too small and dirty to support you. At this point, the cage is of your own making. The key to your release is already there but you have overlooked it. This is about attitude. It is about paeans, not power. Let your life be enriched by your inner convictions, not impoverished and weakened by your discomforts. Walk the "little way," the peony-path, the Beautyway, and experience being brimful with the richness of life on its *own* terms. As the medieval mystic Meister Eckhardt wrote: "If the only prayer you said in your entire life is 'thank you' – that would suffice."

Artist's Notes:

Originally, Paian and Hebe just heal Ares, but here they also heal *earth* by melting the implements of war with their hands. Hebe feeding Zeus' eagle symbolized overcoming death. Earrings are after a pair from Kalymnos, 450-400 B.C.E.; her necklace from Kourion, 400-300 B.C.E. Her cup is after an Attic black figure dinos, c. 580 B.C.E. and Attic red figure pyxis, c. 350 B.C.E. The relief behind her is after Epidauros, Sanctuary of Asklepios (who displaced Paian), 400-350 B.C.E. Weapons are after some found in Peloponnesian tombs, 8th century B.C.E.; helmet is after one from Corinth, c. early 5th century B.C.E.

Endnotes

[1] Blyth, *Haiku*, vol.3:287.
[2] Zimmerman:94; 188; Graves, *GM*:64; Rose:258; 293.
[3] *Odyssey*, iv, 232 (tr. Fitzgerald).
[4] *Iliad*, v, 401-2 (tr. Lattimore).
[5] APS:3.
[6] *Iliad*, v, 899-905.
[7] *Iliad*, v, 909.
[8] Jayne:232.
[9] Jayne:224-225.
[10] Jayne:242-242.
[11] Jayne:341.
[12] Graves, *WG*:491.
[13] Cowles:115b; *APS*:17.
[14] Blyth, *Haiku*, vol.3:285-295.
[15] *NG*, July 1947:42-43; *APS*:18.
[16] Wallnöfer and von Rottauscher:62.
[17] Beau:133.
[18] Palos:186-188.
[19] *APS*:9-10; 35; 46; 54.
[20] J. Rose:95; *APS*:3.
[21] Law:30.
[22] Cowles:115b.
[23] J. Rose:95; *APS*:3.

26
PINE

Pine

The something in the pine seed, let us say, the soul of it, built a trunk that stood erect....Pine trees always stand up straight....Do you know why? The pine soul built soft white wood with pitch in it....The pine soul clothed itself with spears, five in a sheaf....The pine soul dotes on helical curves....

~ Henry Turner Bailey[1]

Pine knots...[on a] stormy winter evening...burn with a bright distinctive light that is a playback of summer Suns.

~ Frank Rowsome, Jr.[2]

The main purpose of the rites was to secure the union of the votary with the Great Mother in one or other of her forms, not infrequently by the aid of frenzied dancing, wild music, and sexual symbolism, in the hope of attaining communion with the source of life and vitality in a condition of ecstatic abandonment and mystical communion.

~ E.O. James[3]

...Freed from the dichotomies which oppose earth to sky, flesh to spirit, the feminine appears here clothed in light and space, as that pregnant zero point where the illusion of ego is lost and the world, no longer feared or fled, is re-entered with compassion.

~ Joanna Macy[4]

The Mythic World

There was a pine-clad mountain, Mount Ida, in Phrygia (west central Anatolia, modern Turkey). In ancient times, a meteorite blazed through the skies and fell among the pines, setting many of the resin-rich trees aflame, germinating the heat-resistant pinecones, and re-seeding the forest. All that was left in the crater was a great black meteoric cube which was worshipped by the ancient peoples of the region as a manifestation of Kybele, the Anatolian "Magna Mater," the Great Mother of the Gods. The earliest form of her name may have been *Kubaba*, whose likely root is *kube* or *kuba*, "cube."[5] On Mount Ida, Kybele sometimes appeared on the highest pine:

> ...hidden thickly in the fir-boughs, in the likeness of the clearvoiced bird...that the gods call *chalkis*...[a nightbird, probably a species of owl].[6]

To her followers, this pine was the cosmic tree, connecting the misty earth to the skies beyond. The pine, the nightbird, the meteor were all manifestations of the goddess' ability to bridge earth and sky. Her worship, whose origins went back into Neolithic times, later spread throughout the Graeco-Roman world. Her massive chief temple, to which the dark meteoric cube was brought in 204 B.C.E., occupied the site of what is now the Vatican in Rome.

Kybele was originally androgynous. When her male genitals were severed, a lilac-flowered almond tree sprang up where they fell.[7] Her shepherd-lover Attis was born from one of the tree's almonds. In some myths, he was the son of the virgin Nana, who conceived him by holding the sacred almond to her breast *(see Nut Trees)*. In other variants, Nana is one of Kybele's own earthly incarnations.[8]

The drama of Attis' life resembles that of Adonis, son of the myrrh tree and beloved of Aphrodite *(see Myrrh)*: both are young savior/vegetation gods identified with grain and wine, dying under a tree, their blood transformed into living flowers. For Attis, death followed the love-madness to which he was driven by being torn between Kybele and his betrothed, a princess named Ia. He fled to a pine tree, fastened himself to it, castrated himself, and bled to death as violets sprang up from his dark blood. Kybele, her followers, and Ia found him there. Ia, broken-hearted, took her own life while the others uprooted the pine to which Attis' body was still bound and hid this makeshift bier in Kybele's sacred cave, where she bitterly mourned his death. His corpse never decayed. After three days, he returned from the dead amidst much rejoicing.[9]

In the annual March 22nd re-enactment of these ancient Mysteries, a phallic pine, bandaged like a mummy and hung with violets and ribbons, was carried into the Goddess' temple. On March 25th, after three days of mourning, Kybele's followers greeted the risen Attis: "Hail, Bridegroom, Hail, new Light."[10] Then began a feast of joy known as Carnival or *Hilaria*. While the populace outside, often masked and disguised, indulged their sexual desires, Kybele's initiates in the temple shared in an ecstatic communion by celebrating a sacred marriage between goddess and consort. They danced, ate grain-cakes from a timbrel, and drank wine from a concave cymbal – both instruments, along with Phrygian double-pipes, flutes and tambourines, figured significantly in Kybele's other festivals, her *ludi*, or "games."[11] The element of ecstatic communion-trance through dance is still found among the Sufi dervishes of Turkey.[12]

It is customary to refer to such goddess-rituals as "fertility rituals." This implies that the ritual was primarily product-oriented, designed for maximum cause-and-effect: in other words, the goddess' human surrogate would sleep with the consort's human surrogate in order to ensure a fertile harvest. To reduce ritual to a form of farmers' insurance, however, is to trivialize it and miss its central significance. The ecstatic sense of communion underlying these mysteries was a recognition of the union and harmony, or "music," lying at the heart of life, whether human, divine, or vegetative, for all are connected in the cosmic web. These rituals were a sacred *process* in which joy was drawn forth from grief, new life from death, and all was transformed, transfigured.

The myth of another of Kybele's Phrygian lovers, the satyr (goat-man) Marsyas, also unfolds against the backdrop of a pine. Marsyas was a flute-master who loved Kybele, in whose rituals music was always present. The two traveled with their followers to a mountain site where Marsyas accepted a challenge from Apollo, whose musical skills on the lyre were renowned. The Muses would judge the contest and the winner could do as he wished with the loser. Marsyas was the better player but cunning Apollo won through a ruse. Vindictive in victory, he tied the poor satyr to a pine and flayed him alive. From the satyr's tears, as well as those of the satyrs, fauns, and nymphs who mourned for him, came a river which bore his name. Apollo hung the flayed skin in a cave at the river's source, where the skin shivers ecstatically whenever strains of Marsyas' native Phrygian music drift up to it.[13]

Attis dies under a pine because of rivalry in love, Marsyas because of rivalry in music. A pine-death – and Kybele, goddess of love *and* music – links them both.

In Egypt, we meet Osiris in myths in which the green-faced vegetation god is castrated, hacked into pieces by his brother, Set, and resurrected in the papyrus swamps of cobra-goddess Wadjyt *(see Papyrus)*. Other variants of Osiris' myth, however, claim that a coffin containing his body first washed ashore in Phoenicia, where a pine tree grew around it, preserving it until his sister-wife, Isis, was able to return it to Egypt, where she resurrected him. Before she finds Osiris, however, there is a period in which the grieving goddess becomes a nursemaid, caring for the young son of the Phoenician king and queen. Loving the child, wishing to gift him with immortality, Isis does a curious thing: she immerses the boy in a cauldron of flames. The child's horrified mother, unaware of the identity of her son's nurse, rushes frantically to stop her.

Myths of pine often include this fire motif. An ancient Egyptian ritual reflects the significance of both: a pine was felled, then carefully hollowed out; from the exposed heartwood, a statue of Osiris was carved and then "buried" in the hollowed-out tree, as if to indicate that the god himself was the pine's tree-spirit, or heart. After a year, both tree and image were burned, and a new pine felled in recognition of the on-going cycles of rebirth. Because the pine was a symbol of divine resurrection, pinecones were offered to Osiris by his followers.[14]

In a myth related to Isis' story, another mother-goddess, Demeter, whom the Greeks equated with Kybele, also comes to Phoenicia, grieving for her lost daughter Persephone. Here it is the daughter, not a male consort, who is the dying/rising vegetation deity. This hints at a very ancient mythic strata involving a double goddess, mother and maid. The introduction of the consort seems to be a much later development, one which betrays its uneasiness in the theme of castration connecting Osiris, Adonis, and Attis. It is as if these male figures, interjected into a far older drama, could not quite hold their own maleness and too easily slipped into an ambiguous gender. The mysterious princess Ia, who kills herself after she sees Attis dead, his blood turned to violets, seems to echo that earlier strata, as if she may have been the original focus, not him, for her very name, *ia,* refers to blue-purple violets. Persephone and Demeter are also associated with that same deep kyanean purple color.[15]

In Phoenicia, Demeter, unable to find Persephone, also cared for the young son of a royal couple. Like Isis, she tried to give the child the gift of immortality by plunging him into a raging fire until the child's mother tore him from the goddess' arms. Like Kybele, Demeter is associated with the pine: pinecones were thrown into her underworld temple clefts along with other sacrifices for quickening the earth.

Finally, there is the myth of Dionysus, god of the vine. His father was Zeus, disguised as a mortal; his mother was Semele, a Phoenician princess. This time, the love-rivalry is between Zeus' jealous wife Hera and Semele. When Semele was six months pregnant, Hera, pretending to be an old woman, befriended Semele and deftly aroused the young woman's suspicions about her lover. The next time Zeus visited, Semele asked one favor. When he promised this, she demanded to see him as he truly was. Zeus knew that if she saw him in his full, blazing glory, it would kill her, but he was bound by his word. Semele had only one glimpse before his divine fire consumed her, turning her to ash. That same divine fire, however, rendered the tiny fetus immortal. Zeus rescued the boy and hid him in his own thigh for the last trimester. After he was born, Zeus found nurses to raise the child. In gratitude, the young god would one day restore their youth when they aged. Later, Dionysus would also go into the underworld to rescue his mother Semele and transform her into a goddess.[16]

As a vegetation deity of life-force, Dionysus was hung from a pine and torn into pieces as a sacrifice, akin to Attis, Marsyas, and Osiris.[17] The pine was sacred to Dionysus: a wine could be brewed from the nut-like seeds of some species (resin is still used to flavor Greek wines); the god's image was often carved out of pine and handpainted red and gold; Greek vineyards were often planted around a pine hung with masks of long-haired Dionysus – as the wind blew through the boughs, the masks moved, scaring away birds, fructifying the vines, protecting the harvest;[18] Dionysus and the women who followed him frequently carried the *thyrsus*, a pinecone atop a wand.[19]

Dionysus' followers, or *maenads*, are notorious for tearing voyeurs into pieces during their frenzied dances. From one perspective, since Dionysian rites were one of the few emotional outlets grudgingly allowed Greek women, such violent imbalances, if indeed they ever happened, need to be seen in that context. At the same time, such lurid tales reflect a patriarchal culture's fear of the full depth of a woman's emotional life. It should be mentioned that some scholars link the origins of Greek drama to archaic Dionysian rites, which suggests that *maenads*, who would have overseen all production details, possessed more presence of mind than their reputation indicates, and that stories of their dismembering male victims owe more to theatrical legerdemain than reality.

Dionysus was an ecstatic god who represented the surge of life in all living things – that "surge" was given physical form as wine, but wine, at its best, remains only a symbol of his deeper, transformative "fire." Fire runs like an undercurrent through these myths. Kybele descends into mountain pines as a fiery meteorite; evergreen, undying pines have the ability to be fire-germinated; both Isis and Demeter attempt to "germinate" immortality in a boy-child by immersing him in flames – as if these children were human phoenixes, able to rise, as does the pine, from that fire; divine fire renders Dionysus immortal even in his dying mother's womb; at the Great Mother's sacred sanctuary at Delphi, navel of the world, a perpetual sacred fire was kept burning – and while some say it was oak or laurel that fed it, others say it was pine.[20]

In northern lands, pines stand tall and green on mountain slopes, while trees in valleys below turn to fiery colors and shed their leaves. The *greenness* of pines – fragrant, stable, serene – has long made them symbols of eternal life. While all else appears to die in the dark-half of the year, pines remain fresh and untouched. They played a special role among far northern European peoples on Winter Solstice, the longest night of the year: amidst much merry-making, festive pine boughs, often with companion evergreens – holly and ivy – festooned caves, cottages, and candlelit halls.

Around the Mediterranean region, where seasonal boundaries are far less dramatic and well-defined, compensatory human dramas emerged, and yet pine remained as the archetypal substrate. In the far north, pine stood immortal while other trees appeared to die around it. In the south, it stood just as immortal but now, not leaf-dropping trees, but sacrificial "savior" gods appeared to die around it. In either place, the drama revolved around the great cycles of birth, death, and rebirth. Pine remained as the grounding, stabilizing force while the players undergoing death and resurrection shifted from a simple tree-plane to an intensely dramatic god-plane. Both north and south, dramas surrounding the pine stir human hope, a motivation which may lie at the heart of each of these myths:

> ...and the world, no longer feared or fled, is re-entered with compassion.[22]

Botany/History

We do not distinguish here among pine, fir, or spruce, since today, as well as in ancient times, these terms are often interchangeable and applied to any of these three fragrant, resinous trees. The Scotch pine, for example, is called "fir" by many British and a cognate, *fura*, by the Vikings; one species of fir (*Picea abies*) is called the "spruce fir." Latin *pīnus* refers to both the pine and the fir. Albanian *pišė* refers equally to all three. In Greek, Lithuanian, Middle Irish, German, and in many Eastern European tongues, similar words apply to two or more of these trees, their most ancient root probably being a word for pitch, tar, or resin. None of these languages include other evergreens (such as larch, yew, juniper, cedar, cypress) in words for the pine-fir-spruce cluster – these three seemed always to comprise their own grouping.[23]

The pine is a tough, yet graceful, survivor, an ecological pioneer capable of competing well with the large hardwoods that followed it. Pine grows swiftly, producing huge amounts of pollen. Since its high resin content increases the chances of forest fires when hit by lightning, one would think the species might soon die out. But this is a "phoenix" among trees: its pulpy bark scorches but rarely burns, thus it deflects heat away from the delicate tissues lying just below it. Further, some pines have cones coated with resinous tars that actually require the intense heat of a raging firestorm before the cones can fully open. When they do, they release an abundance of viable seed, enough to completely re-seed a forest. Fire is also helpful to pine in other ways: the smoke kills harmful fungi, the flames eliminate competing plants, and they also allow fallen needles (which would otherwise not decay for many years) to release valuable nutrients into the soil.[24]

Pine burns too rapidly to be a good fuel for humans; pine knots, however, added to an already robust fire on the hearth, provide moments of colorful drama, for they are "densely packed with channels of resin," causing them to burn with a brief, intense radiance, creating on stormy winter nights "a playback of summer Suns."[25] A more lasting form of the resin's beauty is amber, which preserves more ancient summers, rich with insects, once busily humming through the pines as golden pollen drifted down around them.

The pinecone itself is an amazing example of bioengineering, although it was long thought to be passive, fixed in place:

> Consider the pinecone. For the past 200 million years, this intricate, scaly creation has sat out on a limb and dumped or received pollen, depending on the sex of the cone. The standard textbook line on female cones is that they are catcher's mitts, haphazardly snagging whatever pollen happens to be on the breezes.[26]

Recent work, however, has revealed something very different:

> Here was no baseball glove, succeeding by simply being in the way. Rather...[it is] a coniferous air-traffic controller deliberately bending the flight paths of the pollen grains to its aerodynamic will.

> The pollen grains flew over the top of the cone, and once on the lee side, a secondary, corkscrew current carried the fliers in a spiral around the scales. These set up eddy currents of their own that swept the pollen between the scales where it would eventually complete fertilization.[27]

This is a beautiful example of bio-intelligence at work among these lovely trees, ancient symbols of everlasting life and, now, contemporary symbols of the deep wisdom at work in our own life-structuring.

The Reading

Pine comes with a sense of reassurance: you are deeply in harmony with your true path. There are many complex details associated with pine's myths but the Oracle sees these as so many pollen-grains being swept towards the central core of your life. Pine is a tree of destiny, *dharma*. Whatever dramas you are drawing to yourself are meant for you – they are necessary for your germination. Fire glows warm within your heart. Even if firestorms approach from without, you can meet them with grace and let them help you to re-seed your life anew.

Pine stands at the ever-green and silent turning-point of many mysteries. This is a realm in which wholeness is expressed through a spiraling cone – the cone's bio-engineering guides even the wind's pollen-path through the Higher Self's structuring of your life. Accept this gracefully, mindfully. Everything is unfolding exactly as it is meant to – there are no mistakes here, no karmic "accidents." Trust the process. This has to do with your destiny and cannot be changed.

REVERSED:

It may seem as if movement is hidden, blocked, or not flowing as you wish. Deep down, however, everything is on course. Remember that the pine's period of greatest growth is during the winter, when to all appearances, it seems nothing is happening – cones remain closed and pollen is quiet, its destined journey still lying ahead. Everything seems at a standstill yet powerful forces remain at work in hidden ways. What is happening in your life is simply outside the ego's range of awareness, unfolding beyond conscious monitoring. Be patient. You cannot force cones to open untimely, nor can you blow the pollen towards them on your own.

If reversed Pine is drawn in answer to your beginning a new project or relationship, this may not be the appropriate time or path for you. Pines stand tall and forbidding, unmoving. Something is wrong – and they sense it. Perhaps the wind is wrong or the pollen has been weakened by factors beyond your control.

Regardless of your question, go more deeply into your own spirit, seeking what the *I Ching* calls "clarity within and strength without."[28] Do not forget that you, like the pines, are strong, beautiful, graceful. If you choose to act, do so from this awareness. Above all, do not despair. As Joanna Macy writes about seemingly hopeless situations:

> "What do you substitute for hope?" I asked. He looked at me and smiled. "Possibilities," he said. "Possibilities...you can't predict, just make space for them. There are so many." That, too, is waiting, active waiting – moving out on the fog-bound trail, though you cannot see the way ahead.[29]

Artist's Notes:

Roman statue of Kybele, 2nd century C.E., on an Altar to Kybele showing a frame drum and cymbals hanging from a pine tree, c. 2nd-3rd century C.E.; necklace from Capua, Italy, 4th-3rd century B.C.E.

Endnotes

[1] Bailey:3-4.
[2] Rowsome:125.
[3] James:299.
[4] Macy:106.
[5] Baring and Cashford:395-6; 400.
[6] Lindsay:47-49.
[7] Baring & Cashford:408; Frazer, V:264.
[8] Walker, WEMS:77.
[9] James:98.
[10] Baring & Cashford:409;
Walker, WEMS:77.
[11] Walker, WEMS:201; Baring & Cashford:406.
[12] Baring & Cashford:400; 408.
[13] Zimmerman:160; Stapleton:132-133; Rose:111-112; 145; Lindsay:277; Graves, GM:77; Frazer, V:289.
[14] Frazer, VI:107-108; 110.
[15] Lindsay:56-57; 51.
[16] Stapleton:68-69; Rose:152; 149-150.
[17] Frazer, VI:98-99, n.5.
[18] Graves, GM:79.2.
[19] Frazer, V:278; I:4.
[20] Frazer, II:91, n.7.
[21] Baring & Cashford:414.
[22] See 4.
[23] Friedrich:31, 34-35.
[24] Friedrich:38; Attenborough:83.
[25] Rowsome:125.
[26] Bruce Fellman, "An engineer's eye helps biologists understand nature," in Smithsonian, July 1989; pp.98-99.
[27] Ibid.
[28] Wilhelm & Baynes, The I Ching or Book of Changes:91n.
[29] Macy:27-28.

27
PIPAL FIG

(BODHI TREE)

Pipal Fig

In early Buddhist art, as is well known, the Buddha is constantly represented by a simple seat or throne situated at the foot of a Mahabodhi-tree *[pipal-fig]*, the Prince of Trees.
~ Ananda K. Coomaraswamy[1]

Figs were...female genital symbols.... This may account for the common use of the fig tree as a symbol of man's enlightenment, which was formerly supposed to come through his connection with the female principle.
~ Barbara Walker[2]

The Mythic World

The most famous pipal, or "Holy Fig," is the majestic, sheltering tree under which the Buddha, seated on a grass-throne, attained enlightenment. It is with strong justification that India's ancient Tree of Wisdom (*bodhi*), came to represent the Enlightened One. One might even speculate that the tree aided him during his pre-enlightenment hours, for he was one of the trees' own. His mother, Queen Maia, was the incarnation of the May-tree guise of one of India's many mother-goddesses. According to the *Jataka Tales*, the Buddha himself was a female tree spirit in twenty-nine of his earlier incarnations and the King of tree spirits in a thirtieth life.[3] The trees must have been very proud that he was accomplishing so much as a human.

Pipal's sacredness goes back thousands of years to the Indus Valley of pre-Aryan times. The great cities of Harappa and Mohenjo-Daro were flourishing c. 2500-2000 B.C.E., trading with Mesopotamia via the Persian Gulf, exporting ivory, carnelians, sisu-wood, lapis lazuli from Afghanistan, and Himalayan jade. According to Mesopotamian records, such goods came from *Meluhha*, their name for this Indus Valley civilization.[4] Such trade ended abruptly c. 1800 B.C.E. for unknown reasons, although it was likely due to invading Aryans.

Excavations at Mohenjo-Daro reveal a peace-loving people with few weapons.[5] In addition to valuing cleanliness (they had indoor plumbing), large numbers of ingenious terra-cotta toys suggest a playful people whose children were precious to them.[6] Homemade clay votive statues were also found, most of them depicting nude mother-goddesses, their hourglass-figures bedecked with intricate necklaces, bracelets, hip belts.[7] They were made from flattened lumps of clay – prodded, poked, patted, and coiled into some semblance of the divine. They were fashioned by loving hands, but not very skillful ones. Yet these crude little statues bespeak an ancient, earthy sense of devotion to the mother-goddesses. The not-very-talented artists seem never to have doubted that the work of their hands, done with loving care, would be perfectly acceptable to their deities.

Exquisite art was also found here. One tiny three-inch masterpiece, a seal carved of soft stone, reveals a very energetic sacred dimension.[8] A tree-goddess wearing an elaborate crescent-crown stands in profile between a pair of pipal branches; her hair hangs in a long braid; her feet are placed in such a way as to suggest that she is about to shift her balance from one branch to another. A masked male worshipper, kneeling on the ground, is accompanied by a large horned bull-goat. Across the bottom are seven priestesses, their faces also in profile, their hair braided, their feet carrying them off to the viewer's right. Unlike Aryan dance, which is thought to have involved vigorous leaping, foot-stomping, and hand-clapping, Indus Valley art suggests a sinuous, intricate, erotic dance –

qualities echoed much later in Shiva's dance. The seven dancers moving across the tiny seal hint at the sexual boldness and grace inherent in such dancing.

To the stiffness of the kneeling male, the pipal goddess and her seven priestesses bring a complimentary element of movement. This is coupled with an ascent/descent theme associated with cosmic trees worldwide. Indus Valley writings have not been deciphered, so we do not know this goddess' identity, yet Buddhist legends many centuries later speak of an aboriginal chemist-goddess, protectress of the sacred pipal tree, who was adored for twelve years by the Buddhist sage, Nagarjuna, before she found him worthy of being entrusted with her primordial secrets of science.[9] If the goddess of the kneeling male in the ancient seal is not the same as Nagarjuna's, they are surely kin.

For comparison purposes, there is a Mesopotamian carving from the same period. It shows a female deity known as "Mistress of Animals."[10] She is full of confident power (known in India as *shakti,* the active polarity, which quickens passive male gods). With the agility of an acrobat, she is taming a pair of enormous reptiles while balancing on the backs of a pair of panther-like beasts. Curiously, her feet are not firmly planted. She seems to have been caught in a freeze-frame, about to shift her weight, comfortable in responding to changing dynamics. The feet of the Indus Valley pipal-goddess show a nearly identical placement. This is not to suggest there was necessarily any direct religious influence between the two regions but, as we have seen, sea routes connected them and the region was also located along a traditional land route to India.

We do not know either goddess' identity with certainty – but their message is clear. Balancing the more masculine-attuned spiritual technique of withdrawal and interiority, which the Buddha developed to its fullest extent, these anciently youthful goddesses offer another spiritual method – one of active, even playful engagement with the natural world. They demonstrate a celebration of the female-principle as a powerful force equally involved in life and death, opening out, folding in, inhalation, exhalation. These functions had not yet been split: there was a totality, a sense of flow and wholeness, a bold sense of trust in the processes of nature rather than an often anxious attempt to escape from them.

Botany/History

The "holy fig" (*ficus religiosa*), native to Hindustan and Ceylon, is one of 800 varieties of fig trees. It is very long lived – a still-living Ceylonese tree dates from 288 B.C.E.[11] Although pipal fruit is inedible, it produces a milky lac, prized as a remedy for agonizing toothaches, which often plagued the ancients.[12]

The pipal has been sacred for thousands of years. A pre-Aryan carving of 4,000 years ago shows a nude tree-goddess, her hair in a long braid, standing between the curving limbs of a pipal. Below her, a male worships her. Centuries later, the Buddha attained enlightenment while seated under an ancient pipal. The tree is frequently found outside Buddhist shrines, where it provides medicinal lac as well as dense, welcome shade from the tropical heat.

Most fig trees are remarkable for the balanced degree of gender/species cooperation essential for their female-to-female cross-pollination. A wasp-like female insect, after brushing through male flower pollen, is the only means of pollinating a female flower. Each species of tree is adapted to its own species of insect – if the tree species dies out, so will the insects; if the insects die out, their tree-mates will die as well.[13]

All fig flowers are internal, found on the *inside* of cup or flask-like vessels which later develop into figs. The flask has an overlapping opening, preventing easy access. After working her way inside, a female insect (of whatever species is bonded to that specific fig-species) lays her eggs inside specialized bladder-like gall-flowers, which are neither male nor female. As she enters and exits these flasks, she brushes through male flowers, transferring their pollen and fertilizing nearby female flowers. The insect is uninterested in gendered flowers: she wants only to get her eggs safely to neuter gall-flowers.

After the insect lays her eggs, they mature into larvae and hatch into male and female insects. Mating takes place within the developing fig. Within a few hours, males die, blind and wingless, having left their fertilized females rich with eggs. Females exit, flying to another flask, depositing their loads. In exchange for using the fig as nursery/nuptial/death chamber, insects insure both species' survival through this strangely balanced, unerringly timed choreography, each species playing its own role perfectly.[14]

In some fig trees, gendered flowers are inside the same flask as neuter gall-flowers, which simplifies pollination. Other species create obstacle courses: for example, the same tree will have "decoy" flasks holding only female flowers and other flasks holding both gall-flowers and male flowers. Inevitably, the insect will enter a female-only flask, hoping to find gall-flowers; unsuccessful, she will leave, but only after first inadvertently pollinating the female flowers.

Still other species, especially Smyrna figs, have female flasks on one tree and combination gall-flower/male flasks on another, which creates unique pollinating problems. From ancient times, humans have helped by facilitating a "marriage of the trees," hanging strings of wild male figs (caprifigs, or "he-goat-figs") in domesticated female trees.[15]

The Reading

You are invited to know that you are Nature's beloved child. Play, move freely as the wind in the branches, run, dance, draw, paint, make toys. This is not a time to relax – you are being drawn into energetic, exhilarating playfulness. Pipal refreshes and restores. She returns you to a full heart and light spirit, especially during periods of delay in your life. Just let go. The pipal's flowing lightness lessens rigidity and obstinacy in or around you. Think of the goddess' dance with life – or fertile "playgrounds" created by figs and insects. Despite obstacle-courses, all participants apparently enjoy themselves – hopefully, after brief nuptials, even male insects die happy.

Especially if you are a workaholic, this is your time to focus on your active playful *shakti* element. Yes, balance male and female – and *maybe* your male-side needs to meditate and sort things out, but the usefulness of that is better indicated by other trees. Pipal invites you to go to an earlier, simpler, playful time – just sing and leap and claim a greater spaciousness around yourself, even if only for a few hours.

REVERSED:

Lighten up. You may be feeling heavy, taking yourself too seriously, squandering your energies. Everything is going to work out just fine. The pipal, as an ancient "Tree of Life," serves as a metaphor for the Akashic Record – its leaves covered with sacred writings and images recording past events, wisdom, discoveries, and insights.[16] You are being told that you too have access to that realm – your ideas are born and nurtured from there. Trust this and do not allow self-doubt and worry to constrict that flow.

Artist's Notes:

Already described in the text above, the seal in the tree branches in the upper left is from Mohenjo-daro, c. 2500-1750 B.C.E. Thought to be worn for protection, the original bangles on the goddess's arms were made from shell and found at Harappa, the widest ones dating earliest, c. 2600 B.C.E.; the thinnest from c. 2000 B.C.E. Her necklaces and earring are all from Mohenjo-daro, 2600-1900 B.C.E.

Endnotes

[1] Coomaraswamy:39.
[2] Walker, *WD*:484-485.
[3] Compiled from the Jataka Tales.
[4] Bibby:57; T/L:*TF3000*:135, 138, 141, 164, 166.
[5] Eliade, *YIF*:357; T/L:*TF3000*:134.
[6] T/L:*TFC*:125-126, 149, 131; T/L:*TF3000*:135.
[7] T/L:*TFC*:128-129.
[8] T/L:*TFC*:136.
[9] Eliade, *YIF*:344-345.
[10] *Larousse World Mythology*:57.
[11] Lehner:24.
[12] Lucas:23.
[13] Bor:133-134.
[14] Bor:134; Frazer:ii. 313-316; *NG* 9/51:346-347.
[15] Bor:134.
[16] Walker, *D*:474

28
RAIN FORESTS

Rain Forests

I wanted to be by myself...I knew what the challenge was, for to be alone was as though you were daring to look on the face of the great God of the Forest himself, so overpowering was the goodness and beauty of the world all around. Every trembling leaf, every weathered stone, every cry of an animal or chirp of a cricket tells you that the forest is alive with some presence.

~ Colin Turnbull[1]

Yakshas often play the part of fertility symbols in Indian art and are associated iconographically with trees, vines, and vegetative growth. They are often shown embracing trees, leaning against trees, or pouring forth vegetation from their mouths or navels. To identify Śrī-Lakshmī, the goddess who embodies the potent power of growth, with the Yakshas is natural. She, like them, involves herself and reveals herself in the irrepressible fecundity of plant life.

~ David Kinsley[2]

The Mythic World

Among the Yoruba of Africa, an ancient deity named Osanyin is the guardian of the medicines and rituals which are dependent upon the leaves of the rain forests. No ritual can occur without his help, for in the plants he keeps the *ashè*, the primordial force or power which sustains all the other gods. A story is told of Osanyin's relationship with the healer and prophet, Ifa, who asked his followers for a slave to till his fields. They purchased one at the slave market, not knowing that it was Osanyin himself. Ifa told his slave to go out and clear the ground by uprooting wild herbs that had strayed from the jungle. As soon as Osanyin began his work, he realized the first herb was one that cured fevers. "Impossible to cut that one!" he shouted. "It's too useful." The second cured headaches and he also refused to harm that one. The third cured stomach aches and he saved it, too. The other slaves hurried back to Ifa and reported that the rebellious slave was shouting, "I cannot dig up such vital herbs!" Ifa went out to see for himself and realized how valuable this slave was. After that, Ifa kept him by his side whenever he was healing people.[3]

With simple, dramatic wisdom, this Yoruba story shows the foolhardiness of destroying ancient plants and lore for short term gain. For these people, the jungles are precious, for –

> Each deity has its own leaves. Each leaf is endowed with a certain virtue. There are leaves of fortune, happiness, glory, fertility, joy, luck, coolness, and courage, but there are also leaves of misery, indiscreet chatter, and others still more undesirable. While making the various preparations using these plants, one must utter incantations in order to awaken and activate their power, their *ashè*.[4]

To many Africans who farm cleared land or graze herds upon it, jungles are evil places of ghosts, witchcraft, and death. Storms are especially terrifying:

> When [the jungle] whips itself into a fury, conjuring up rain and thunder and lightning, it turns small streams into raging torrents and sends heavy branches or even whole trees crashing down, some of them with trunks as thick as houses, destroying the living trees that stand in their way.[5]

To a people who have lived in Africa's friendly, nurturing rain forests since ancient times, however, even storms are good, for the forest is good. These are the Pygmies of Africa's Zaire, or Congo, a race that so fascinated Egyptian pharaohs that they sent expeditions to capture them as exotic additions to their royal courts. Before they were driven into the depths of the jungle in more recent times, these small people ranged over a large area. Widespread stories of mysterious sprites and gnomes may reflect glimpses of Pygmies from afar.

Africa's towering trees meet far overhead to form a dense canopy, shutting out the sun and creating a mysterious sense of twilight below. Humans walking on the soft leaves of the forest floor feel dwarfed. Growth in areas once cleared comes back tangled, almost impenetrable, but the oldest regions of the jungle retain a spacious, awe-inspiring quality.[6] For the Pygmies, these damp, cool forests provide water, small game, roots, tubers, mushrooms, fruits, nuts, honey, and leaves for the roofs of their conical huts.

Pygmy women and men usually share tasks jointly and women are not discriminated against as they sometimes are elsewhere in Africa.[7] This cooperation, coupled with the forest's bounty, means Pygmies only have to work a few hours a day to provide for their needs, which gives this fun-loving people a great deal of time for communal events, celebrations, music, dance, story-telling, and rituals.

The most sacred ritual is the *molimo,* a word both for the ritual and for the fifteen foot wooden-tube "trumpet" that creates the ritual's eerie music. The instrument originally belonged to women, but men stole it and created exaggerated protocols to prevent women from ever seeing it again. This is more in the nature of a game, however, and there are occasions when women participate fully.[8] The instrument has a –

> ....wistful sound, hollow and ghostly, answering the men with snatches of their own song, sometimes singing its own variations, sometimes breaking off into low, growling animal noises....[Then the] sound was gentler and a little sad....[9]

Most of the songs have one underlying theme: "The Forest is Good."[10] The songs are performed when there is a crisis: poor hunting, illness, death. These crises are a disruption of the forest's underlying goodness, a goodness restored when they sing with the molimo. The people trust the forest to be like their father and mother – it gives them food, shelter, clothes, warmth, and affection. When things go wrong, it is not because of evil spirits or a sorcerer's curse, as it would be among many other peoples. As Colin Turnbull, who lived among them, writes, Pygmies' "logic is simpler and their faith stronger, because their world is kinder."[11] When they are asleep, for example, they cannot prevent ants from invading the camp or a leopard from stealing a dog. It is the same with the forest – when things go wrong, they reason, it is because the forest is sleeping and not being attentive to its children:

> So what do we do? We wake it up. We wake it up by singing to it, and we do this because we want it to awaken happy. Then everything will be well and good

again. So when our world is going well then also we sing to the forest because we want it to share our happiness....*[God]* must be good to give us so many things. He must be of the forest. So when we sing, we sing to the forest.[12]

Thus the molimo became a means of "an intimate communion between a people and their god, the forest." They never ask for something to be done – for the hunt to improve or health to be restored. Their faith is such that it is enough simply to waken the forest with their singing. Then the forest will do whatever is needed.[13]

Only in times of death do they sing one of their greatest songs in its entirety. It is this song that perhaps best expresses their complete faith. Here is its core:

> There is darkness all around us;
> but if darkness *is*,
> and the darkness is of the forest,
> then the darkness must be good.[14]

When wealthy landowners in the American South, Haiti, and other Caribbean islands began importing slaves in the 18th century, most came from the West African Yoruba and Fon peoples. After horrific sea-journeys, new slaves saw tropical rain forests similar to what they had known but everything else was brutally altered. Their masters broke up families on a whim, tearing husbands from wives and both from their children. Women were routinely raped as a cheap and satisfying way of obtaining more slaves. In this time of dark horror, slaves were even denied any open expression of their traditional worship. Christianity – Catholicism, for the most part – was forced upon them. Like many indigenous peoples who were enslaved and Christianized in the New World, West Africans had to disguise their deities behind names of archangels, saints, and the Virgin Mary.

A major goddess, or *Loa,* developed in this period – Erzulie, goddess of love, sexuality, health, good fortune, jewelry, dancing, flowers, wealth, dreams, art, language, beauty, creativity, hopes, and aspirations. Her peaceful, carefree Rain Forest roots were in Africa (Dahomean) but the tragic circumstances of her people in the New World changed her. She added vengeance, discord, jealousy, and wrenching sorrow to her roles as she entered the altered New World pantheon of the ancient nature-based African religion known as Vodoun (from an African word for "spirit" – variant spellings include Vodun, Voodoo, Vodou, Voudou). Erzulie's "dark" side caused her to be immensely fierce and vengeful when offended, arousing fear in her followers. But because she also gave her desperate people solace and taught them to hope, dream, and aspire, she was the most beloved goddess of all.

At a tragic time, when slave-women were torn from their husbands, Erzulie wore three wedding bands, one for each of three husbands – sky-god Damballah, sea-god Agwe, and fire-god Ogoun (patron of warriors and ironsmiths). Three husbands are sometimes seen as suggesting that Erzulie is a "Triple Goddess," but since that concept has a strong Eurocentric tradition, it may not reflect genuine African beliefs. Her three wedding bands seem more like a promise to other women that their anguish will not last forever and that a time will come when they will again enjoy an abundance of love – *threefold*. Her love for fine things like perfumes and clothes – and *sweet* things, like bananas fried in raw sugar – also seem to promise that her followers' lives will once again contain such sweetness.

Despite her role as giver of life's pleasures, there is a profound sense of dark tragedy in Erzulie that causes her to break down and sob uncontrollably. Her moods shift abruptly – from the heights of joyful passion to complete misery – as if the roots of her people's trauma lie too deep to be absent for long from her consciousness. Then she curls up into a ball like a terrified child, weeping inconsolably until she is red-eyed and haggard. If a human exhibited such a seemingly mismatched range of emotions, they would be viewed as suffering from Post-Traumatic Stress Disorder (PTSD). They would probably also be labeled bi-polar (manic-depressive). But Erzulie is a goddess and not subject to human labels. The traumas coursing through her are collective, not individual. She knows that life comes with pain, but the devastating, ruthless treatment of humans from cultures built upon slavery to the contemporary enslavement of women and children in the sweatshops and brothels of the world are a perversion of anything "natural" in humanity. So is unending warfare fought for greed and power. When grief wracks Erzulie, she loses her boundaries and tries to carry all those millennia of collective agony. Like the Virgin Mary, who shares that same burden, and with whom Erzulie is associated, Erzulie is symbolized by a heart broken with an arrow.

If the goddess Erzulie, generous, strong, fierce and immensely powerful, is also bi-polar and afflicted with PTSD, would that more of the world's deities were as well. Together, they might influence a new age of deepening compassion and common sense. It is to her credit – and, one might suggest, to the shame of the others – that she has the courage to remain on the cutting-edge of such suffering.

Erzulie's strongest connection to the rain forests of Haiti is at Saut d'Eau, where a magnificent waterfall descends over one hundred feet. Alfred Metraux writes:

> ...The Tombe river, having crossed a green and laughing plain, hurls itself in one leap into the void. All the mysterious charm of tropical forests which have

today disappeared survives in that dense grove where the falls gleam like jewels, darkly cased. An iridescent mist crossed by tiny rainbows rises from the foaming water, bedews the ferns and blurs the luxuriant foliage of the giant trees whose roots break the moist ground into humps and valleys....[15]

Wade Davis further explains her bond with this place – and the devotion with which pilgrims approach it every mid-July:

...The most revered site is a waterfall named Saut d'Eau, where years ago Erzulie Freda, the goddess of love, escaped the wrath of the Catholic priests by turning into a pigeon and disappearing into the iridescent mist....

One need only touch the water to feel its grace, and for some it is enough to dip into the shallow silvery pools, leaving their offerings of corn and rice in small piles. But most go directly to the cascades, women and men, old and young, baring their breasts and scrambling up the wet slippery bedrock that rises in a series of steps toward the base of the falls. At the lip of the escarpment the river forks twice, sending not one but three waterfalls plunging more than 100 feet. What is not lost in mist strikes the rocks with tremendous force, dividing again into many smaller chutes, each one becoming a sanctuary....Everything is in flux, with no edge and no separation-the sounds and sights, the passions, the lush soaring vegetation, primeval and rare....The ease with which the Haitians walk in and out of their spirit world is a consequence of the remarkable dialogue that exists between human beings and the spirits....[16]

In the rain forests of India, the god Kubera is the leader of female forest-spirits, the Yakshas. Kubera and these spirits are in charge of the earth's treasures, especially jewels hidden in the rich earth of tropical jungles. Kubera is also linked with the goddess of good fortune, Lakshmi, for she too is guardian of wealth and fertility. Together, they dispense the riches of mysterious forests – jewels may symbolize that wealth, but the real treasure lies in the "irrepressible fecundity of plant life."[17] The Yaksha-like benevolent elephant god, Ganesha, another jungle-dweller, is also associated with good fortune and wealth and is also depicted with Lakshmi.[18] From this it is clear that ancient Hindus viewed the great rain forests, with their powerful elephants and tree-spirits, as places of wealth, good luck, and unexpected treasure.

The Hindu and Buddhist religions, unlike the desert-born monotheisms of the Middle East, are forest-bred. The greatest sages found spiritual enlightenment by retreating to the forests and living in harmony with animals and trees. As Shantideva, an 8th century Buddhist poet-sage wrote:

> When shall I come to dwell in forests
> Amongst the deer, the birds and the trees,
> That say nothing unpleasant
> And are delightful to associate with?[19]

India also knows an earlier, more archaic forest goddess named Aranyāṇī. Although only one hymn to her exists in the *Rig Veda*, its conclusion gives a deep sense of her nature:

> [She] never slays
> unless one approaches in fury.
> One may eat at will of her luscious fruits
> and rest in her shade at one's pleasure.
>
> Adorned with fragrant perfumes and balms,
> she needs not to toil for her food.
> Mother of untamed forest beasts,
> Sprite of the wood, I salute you![20]

Rarely seen except at night, she "speaks" through the sounds of birds and insects, even tinkling bells. She provides food without the need to till or cultivate it. This quiet, elusive goddess may well be a very early version of the later Yakshis.[21] Even in ancient times however, she would kill if violently provoked. The destruction of forests in our own time might be seen as sufficient provocation for incurable diseases erupting unexpectedly out of rain forests as civilizations recklessly transgress their boundaries.

Botany/History

African rain forests were the cradle of that strand of mammalian life that evolved into the earliest humans. Those equatorial jungles remain a cradle of *flora*, offering vast medicinal resources for humankind. In addition, they provide a major source of the oxygen necessary to sustain countless species; they also absorb toxic carbon dioxide, which thus slows global warming and is critical in stabilizing the world's climate. Yet, scorning such gifts in favor of short term logging, farming, and cattle-grazing profits, humans are in the process of forcing rain forests to join long-extinct primeval forests, creating an etheric-plane band of grief and vanished beauty all around the planet *(see Lost Forests of Earth's Dawning)*. The balance may have been broken beyond healing.

We focus on what still remains, however – those frail yet tenacious pockets of loveliness, power, mystery, and balance growing around earth's equatorial zone, the moist Tropic of Cancer. In rain forests, life comes in greater abundance than anywhere else on earth. Here the monkeys, big cats, elephants, serpents, lizards, and millions of brilliantly colored birds and insects still hold out, roaming, climbing, swinging, slithering, jumping, leaping, crawling, lumbering, walking, spinning, diving, plummeting, and flying – living fully in each passing moment, tasting the richness of each moment under the dense green canopies of hundred-foot trees.

There are still a few pristine rain forests left on earth, in Papua New Guinea, for example, stretching from the equator south, the forests cover an area about the size of Texas. About 200 species of mammals live there, including the recently discovered tree-climbing kangaroos. The lush forests hold more than 700 bird species, among them the world's largest parrots, bird species threatened elsewhere, and most of the world's birds of paradise. Gigantic butterflies fly among the flowers of 1,500 different tree species and 11,000 varieties of plants, some found nowhere else on this planet.[22]

These forests deserve to live in their own right, not simply because they are "useful" to humans. Yet they *are* useful, especially in pharmacology. Many of our prescription drugs and countless over-the-counter medications originally came from plants, mainly from the tropics. Our current plant-derived drugs make use of only about 90 species, yet there are perhaps 250,000 plant species on earth, many of which have never been studied. In the Amazon alone, it has been estimated that 90% of the plants have not even superficially been analyzed – and knowledge of their uses is rapidly dying out among indigenous peoples.

These plants are potentially priceless because, since plants cannot flee from insects, viruses, bacteria, fungi, and solar radiation, they have evolved sophisticated biochemical defenses in their roots, bark, stems and leaves against such enemies. Some of these biologically active compounds can also help mammals fight infections and protect against cancers and immune disorders. A plant from Peru, for example, is a hundred times better at reducing inflammation than aspirin. Just as jungle-born malaria has now been largely eradicated by jungle-born quinine, so too it may be that AIDS, which originated among monkeys in African jungles, may eventually be eradicated by cures from the jungle, such as *Homalanthus nutans,* a tree used by Samoan healers to treat hepatitis, but whose wood-extracts also stop the AIDS virus.

Examples could be multiplied endlessly. Unfortunately, many native plants are being destroyed faster than they can be studied. In the words of one of the world's leading researchers, Norman Farnsworth, professor of pharmacology at the University of Illinois in Chicago:

It's not enough to go tearing around the globe grabbing up unusual plant species and rushing back to the lab with them. To protect the medicinal plants that nature has evolved, we're going to have to protect the world of nature that created them.[23]

That "world of nature that created them" may be as much as a hundred million years old, a green belt of endless summer, the lungs of the planet, filtering out poisonous gases, and the womb of the planet, containing the wildest, most abundant forms of life anywhere on the planet. The largest surviving forests are in only three countries: Africa's Zaire, Indonesia in Southeast Asia, and Brazil. The average temperature in these jungles is 80 degrees Fahrenheit; the average rainfall can amount to 400 inches a year. An acre of temperate forest holds an average of 3 or 4 different tree species; an acre of tropical forest often holds an average of 80.[24]

Such an enormous diversity in life suggests that the soil of these jungles must be the richest on earth. The opposite is true. This is very old soil, most of its biochemicals leached away by eons of rain. The trees get most of their needs from the sky's sun and rain. Because of this, their bark and leaves are usually thin to enable them to soak up their nutrients from rainwater; roots too are shallow, close to the surface. If the great trees were not supported by the close proximity of branches all around them, and by thick lianas woven from tree to tree, many would topple. When dead leaves, twigs, flowers and other debris fall, specialized forms of bacteria, plants, and insects rapidly recycle the precious and scarce biochemicals; this means the forest floor is generally cleaner than in temperate forests, but it also means that the soil is never replenished by rotting vegetation. When local people resort to "slash and burn" farming, the ashes stirred into the soil only remain viably fertile for a year or two. Then, without expensive and sophisticated aid, including massive irrigation, the soil is worthless and the slash and burners have to move on.[25] Unfortunately, the sensitive ecosystem cannot bounce back to what it was:

> Most of [the rain forest's] plants and animals are specialists; they are adapted to the misty, shadowy, tangled world of the forest itself. They cannot tolerate the strong sunlight and the rain in clearings. The trees depend upon soil fungi called mycorrhizae to help their roots ingest minerals....Mycorrhizae often are killed by the heat of burning forest. The survivors may be killed by chemical fertilizers. It is then difficult for either tree or fungus to return to the burned place....It is a terrible waste of the biosphere's resources.[26]

Many of these plants and animals of the rain forests are so specialized that they grow only on one mountainside, or in one valley, along one stream, or on one jungle island; clearing enough land for only one farm could wipe out these species forever.[27]

During the ice ages from between 1.8 million to some 11,000 years ago, those rain forests that survived served as "ice age sanctuaries" for countless forms of life. When the ice retreated, the forests, these "islands of ancient genes," recovered and expanded outwards, and new genetic diversity came forth from this womb. Such a recovery is unlikely to happen ever again. In the eloquent words of science writer Jonathan Weiner:[28]

> We are razing the forests much faster than the ice ages ever did [...] – too rapidly and completely to give the forest much chance of coming back. We are burning one of the wonders of the world, the greatest library of life on Planet Earth.[29]

The Reading

Earth's rain forests are her lungs and womb. Take time to breathe deeply. Enjoy fragrances, scented oils, exotic blossoms, brightly colored fabrics, birdsongs, music from the indigenous peoples of the rain forests. Go within – this is not a time for action. Let good fortune, whether material or spiritual, come to *you*. It is a time to stand still and *be,* living as fully as possible in the moment, detached from those forces trying to wear you down from the outside. You are your own rain forest – trust that the forest is good. Sing to it, awaken it to happiness, and trust that ways will be found where, to human sense, there are no ways. Eat some of the food products from rain forests, consciously aligning with that primordial energy called *ashè* by the Yoruba, an energy akin to the Greeks' ambrosia or India's *amrita*. Play vibrant music from the Caribbean and follow the pleasure-loving example of Erzulie, goddess of love, dance and music, as you dance to the intoxicating rhythms.

If you are inquiring about a relationship, find new ways of cooperating and sharing tasks so that you will have more time to enjoy each other. Do happy, playful things with one another, but also explore dimensions of the sacred that you can celebrate together. Be generous and great-hearted with one another.

If you are asking about health issues, consider combining Western medical techniques with alternate approaches using herbs, roots, leaves, flowers, seeds, and nuts. Breathing exercises and forms of breathing-meditations will be useful. Instead of writing off an illness or physical weakness as an "evil curse," which is how many people also see the jungles, try to shift your attitude so that it can include deeper levels of insight and trust.

If you are inquiring about another person, someone considered "different" or strange, especially if Post-Traumatic Stress Disorder or bi-polar issues are involved, know that it is important to help this person, for this is someone with unusual healing gifts – one who is a hidden source of beauty.

In India, jungles are considered realms of good fortune, abundance, and treasure. Drawing Rain Forest might be an indication that wealth is about to enter your life. If so, drawing this card suggests that you then have a special opportunity to help support some of the foundations struggling to protect earth's fast dwindling rain forests. As those forests have gifted all humanity with medicines and foods like wild maize, avocados, wild rice, brazil nuts, wild yams, cashews, so it is now humanity's turn to shelter the forests and their indigenous peoples in networks of aid. "When the Forest dies, we shall die," as Moke, one of the Pygmies, told Colin Turnbull. His words now apply to all of us.[30]

REVERSED:

In Chinese tradition, problems with the lungs relate to old unexplored grief that needs your attention. When it is time to leave that grief behind, move into the future with stronger, wiser values. Be willing to rescue beauty against great odds. This may include rescuing your own health. Do not let anyone write you off. Your "unconscious jungles" have access to a whole rich pharmacopoeia of healing powers. Relax, banish fear, trust your intuition to find the way.

The Rain Forests ask that you not let your life get too fragmented. You are a rich ecosystem just as you are. Do not try to make your "soil" support a way of life that is alien to your sensitively balanced strengths, or you will not be able to last for long. Do not let your resources be wasted. Even the Rain Forests, although threatened and seemingly doomed, have some hope of reprieve and new life, but only if their interior integrity is maintained against those who would "slash and burn" them. In meditation, stay centered in the depths of these forests and envision their robust health spiraling out to heal whatever is happening around the periphery, in you as well as in the world.

If you are asking about a relationship, it may hold a potential for abuse that you need to explore. Erzulie, the Haitian Goddess of Love from the Caribbean rain forests, is a special protector of women who are caught up in cycles of domestic violence. She is fierce and has seen too much brutality. Be like her and refuse to tolerate being enslaved by anyone who cannot stop harming you, either physically or emotionally. Find a way to claim your power, disguise yourself if you must (as slaves once disguised their deities and as Erzulie disguised herself as a pigeon), and escape into wherever the "Rain Forests" are for you.

Artist's Notes:

Erzulie is seen here holding one of her symbols, a mirror, with her "veve" detailed on it.

Endnotes

[1] Turnbull:291.
[2] Kinsley, *GM*:60-61.
[3] Verger:149.
[4] Verger:149.
[5] Turnbull:54.
[6] Larousse:520; Turnbull:49; 50; 54.
[7] Turnbull:37-38; 47; 52-53; 145; 96; 156-157.
[8] Turnbull:297; 91; 156.
[9] Turnbull:37-38.
[10] Turnbull:80.
[11] Turnbull:89.
[12] Turnbull:90.
[13] Turnbull:90.
[14] Turnbull:91.
[15] Metraux:329.
[16] Wade Davis, *Shadows in the Sun: Travels to Landscapes of Spirit and Desire* (published in the U.S. by Island Press and in Canada as *The Clouded Leopard* by Douglas & McIntyre. See Bibliography for further data.)
[17] Kinsley, *GM*:60-61.
[18] Kinsley, *HG*:34.
[19] Cited in Batchelor:unnumbered pages.
[20] RV 10.146: Panikkar, tr.
[21] Kinsley, *HG*:16.
[22] Statistics from the World Wildlife Fund, 1250 Twenty-fourth Street, NW, Washington, DC 20037.
[23] Cited in Jaret:78-80; data in this paragraph is from the same source.
[24] Weiner:331-332.
[25] Weiner:333-334.
[26] Weiner:334.
[27] Weiner:335;336.
[28] Weiner:337.
[29] Weiner:337.
[30] Turnbull:292.

29
ROWAN

Rowan

In Icelandic myth rowan is particularly strong at the Winter Solstice, the beginning of the new solar year. At this time the tree is bare of foliage and when covered in frost appears as though covered in stars, powerfully expressing the outpouring light of the spirit in the darkest part of the year. It also shows the reflection of the moon's light and the myth of the star-dressed rowan possibly evolved from an ancient tradition of erecting "moon-trees," an early representation of the sky-goddess energy.... Irish legend is full of accounts of serpents and dragons guarding rowans, yet it goes unnoticed that the rowans themselves guard the earth dragons which express the life-force of the land. The later Christians, in suppressing the old traditions, created saints to "kill" such dragons as they claimed the traditional sacred spaces as their own.... [Planting new rowan saplings] is especially relevant at sacred sites that have suffered from disuse, misuse and ignorance. It is a time-honoured method of ecology which positively affects all.

~ Jacqueline Memory Paterson
Tree Wisdom[1]

The Mythic World

Among the ancient Finns, the powerful fertility/harvest goddess, Rauni ("Rowan"), was married to Ukko, oak god of thunder. Their wedding, held directly after the spring sowing, was celebrated annually with dancing, music, and drinking. Some say the nuptial union of Rauni and Ukko produced the first humans: Rauni provided their strong physical forms and Ukko their invisible spirits; others add that their union also brought forth all plants.

Rauni's name comes from the Icelandic *reynir* and the Swedish *rönn*, both of which are names for the rowan, a tree associated with the Thundergod, as well as with protection against evil spirits.[2] An Estonian-Swedish riddle connects the rowan to yet another meaning-cluster: *Iwe wärde rauntrā* – "What is 'the rowan-tree-over-the-world'?" The answer is *rainbow* because its predominant color, like that of clusters of rowan berries, is perceived as red (other hues lack red's magical powers). Finnish folklorist Uno Harva argued in 1948 that the rowan-tree was a euphemism for the rainbow and that *rauni* originally meant both rowan and rainbow. Only later, since the rainbow has long been associated in folklore with protective powers against thunder, was the rainbow personified as the actual wife of the Thundergod. There is an Old Norse word for "red": *rauda* (Icelandic *raudr*, Lithuanian *raũdas*, Sanskrit *rudhir*). Harva suggested that Rauni's name might originally have been derived from this Old Norse *rauda*, especially given the connection between red and rainbow in Balto-Finnic folk songs. Thus, the goddess of the rowan, like her tree, seems to have rich associations with rainbows and the magical color of red.[3]

In Finland's great epic, the *Kalevala*, the rowan is emphasized when a new bride is being instructed in the ways of being a wife:

> Be very careful about those rowans in the yard.
> The rowans in the yard are sacred, sacred the branches on the rowans,
> Sacred the leaves on the branches, more sacred still their berries
> By which a girl is counseled [i.e., through divination]....[4]

Again in the *Kalevala*, when the Mistress of North Farm senses strangers approaching, she has her hired girl perform a rowan-divination lest there be danger afoot:

> The mistress of North Farm said: "Where may an omen be got
> About the strangers who are arriving? O my little girl,
> Put rowan sticks in the fire, choice wood into the flame.
> If perchance blood streams, then war is coming;

If perchance water streams, we will continue to live in peace."
The little hired girl of North Farm, humble maiden, the servant,
Thrust rowan sticks into the fire, choice wood into the flame.
No blood streams at all, neither blood nor water;
Honey started to stream, honey to ooze....[5]

Honey streaming out of the oracular sticks was a surprise, but an old woman sitting in the corner, wrapped in a rough blanket, understood the significance: a fine suitor with many followers was coming to ask for the hand of the daughter of the house. And so it was.

Rowan is richly connected with oracular language. The very word is cognate with Norse *runa*, or rune, because spells and oracular runes were so often carved from rowan's soft wood. This association with oracles and runes explains why rowan groves found on Baltic islands were revered as oracular shrines.[6] The tree's name is also related to a Sanskrit word for magician, also *runa*, a word whose root is *vr*, to hide, conceal, cover. The same root appears in the name of ancient India's great pattern-maker, *Varuna*, the shaman-god of the Netherworld, in whose depths lived Voice-goddess Vak (see *Amrita*). Whether as *runa*-stave or *runa*-magician, the tree is intimately connected to the realm of shamanic language, especially when used to protect someone. The rowan's dark red berries also manifest this theme, for opposite the stalk-end is a tiny five-pointed star – an ancient mystical sign of protection.

In Greek mythology, the origins of the rowan go back to a little known myth involving the goddess of youth, Hebe (see *Peony*), daughter of Zeus and Hera. Hebe was cup-bearer to the gods, charged with guarding a vessel of ambrosia that kept the gods eternally young. When she was distracted one day, enemies snatched the precious cup and fled. The gods were appalled – without their elixir, they would swiftly age and die. Zeus immediately sent his great eagle after the thieves and a ferocious battle ensued. Drops of blood poured from the eagle's wounds, feathers were torn from his flesh – and a rowan tree sprang up wherever they landed on earth. Since both feathers and blood shared the same mythic "DNA," each rowan had feathered leaves as well as berries that looked like drops of blood. Despite grave wounds, the eagle recovered the cup and returned safely to Mount Olympus.[7]

The basic elements in the myth are familiar – a cup of immortality, a goddess who guards the cup, and a conflict between godly "haves" and demonic "have-nots." There is a shifting of focus and sequences but this is still a recognizable variant of India's "Churning of the Ocean" myth as well as medieval Grail legends concerning a war between angels and devils (see *Amrita*). A major difference between India and Greece is that where India's vessel is at first hidden between the roots of an underwater tree, guarded by the goddess Vak, Greece's vessel is already highly visible, stolen from its guardian, and only in being retrieved does a tree appear. *That* tree, born from the winged feathers and blood of Zeus' cosmic eagle, is the rowan.

Zeus, like Finland's Ukko, as well as the Germano-Nordic god Thor, with whom Ukko is often compared, are thunder deities – all three are also connected with the oak, a tree struck by lightning more than any other tree because of its low electrical resistance.[8] Ukko's wife and co-creator of humanity is the rowan. The rowan appears in Greece after a successful quest for the Cup of Life by Zeus' eagle. Red-bearded Thor has his own fortuitous experience with the rowan when the trusting and rather simple-minded god is lured by Loki into going to a vengeful giant's abode without any weapons. En route, he attempts to cross a raging, treacherous river that has been bewitched by the angry giant's hag-daughter. Thor would have been swept to his death except that a rowan growing on the riverbank sees what is happening and swiftly bends low, extending her branches to Thor – he grabs hold and pulls himself onto the bank.[9]

Wife to one, spawn of another's red blood and feathers, and rescuer of a third – the rowan holds strong energy and is present as a protective force at times of high drama. It is no wonder that this tree is viewed as so potent.

We have seen Rowan in a cluster of myths relating to conflicts between have's and have-not's over a cup of a precious liquid that bestows immortality – these themes come from ancient India, Greece, and medieval European Grail lore. Rowan is also part of another mythic trajectory, again connected with immortality, which involves eating its berries. In the Celtic "Legend of Fraoth" a handful of magical red rowan berries guarded by a dragon provides the equivalent of nine nourishing meals – these berries also heal and add a year to one's life. In Ireland's County Sligo it is said that rowans originally existed only in the Otherworlds until a single berry from the Fey Realms accidentally fell in the Forest of Dubhous, took root, and swiftly matured into a huge tree. Its berries tasted like honey and eating only three of them had the power to turn a hundred year old man back to the age of thirty.[10] There is also a Celtic myth about a rowan tree "in the north" whose berries conferred immortality – to prevent the theft of those berries, a one-eyed giant guarded them.[11]

Botany/History

WARNING: the seeds of rowan berries can be poisonous to children.

The rowan (*Sorbus aucuparia*) belongs to the Rose family. Despite being called mountain ash due to similar feathery, fernlike leaves, the two are unrelated: the rowan's leaves are more delicate and easily distinguished; furthermore, the rowan produces berries, not winged seeds.[12] Other folk names include quick-beam ("tree of life," or "quickening"), "delight of the eye" (for its ability to open psychic vision), sorb apple, Thor's helper, wicken-tree, and witch wood.

The rowan's creamy, fragrant flowers attract bees in May. By late June, the ground around the tree is carpeted with falling blossoms that have left behind dense clusters of tiny green berries. Birds arrive in late summer when the berries have ripened into orange-scarlet splendor – songbirds will sing for hours after feasting on them. At the first touch of autumn's frost, the leaves turn into gorgeous colors until winter's winds finally strip them from the tree.

Rowans do not usually cluster together in their own woods. Baltic island groves are an exception – thickets of rowan were also found near ancient stone circles in the British Isles, for these were sites of great power and planting rowans helped ground the energies. Generally, however, rowans grow in mixed forests, shading new saplings of other species until they eventually tower over the rowans, cutting them off from their need for plenty of light and air. Rowans will grow even in poor soil but they prefer high altitudes where they do not have to worry about getting sufficient light. In Scotland, the tree is known as Lady of the Mountain because it grows in altitudes as high as 2,500 feet.[13] Elsewhere, rowans rarely grow taller than 30 feet and thrive best in cool climates where they are protected from the winds. A rowan can live over two centuries –since its branches rarely die, it keeps its grace and shape throughout.[14] The tree's range includes all of Europe, western Russia, the Caucasus, and the mountains of Morocco. The tree was introduced into the New World during Colonial times and now grows from Canada as far south as California and Georgia.

The tree's wood is easily carved. Reflecting this, its name, *rowan*, is related to Norse *runa*, a talisman carved with magic runes. Tough rowan wood was also used to make walking sticks (especially favored for protection at night), spindles and spinning wheels,[15] ship masts, poles, staffs, hoops for baskets and barrels, and tool handles. Anything made of rowan wood is protected in a special way. Rowan berries and bark are used to dye wool black – the druids prized the dye for ceremonial garments. Even its smoke has unusual powers – incense made from ground leaves and berries can be used to smudge one's house, banishing negative energies and cleansing and restoring the wholesome ones.

The rowan figures in many spells and other magical practices wherever it is found. Druids had a ritual known as *Tarbh Fheis* involving interwoven rowan twigs – these were constructed into a platform called the "Wattles of Knowledge" where druids would go into trance, seeking secret knowledge. Druids used rowan smoke to invoke spirit guides and other magical spirits; before battles, they used the smoke of rowan fires to summon spirits to fight on their side against evil. Today, the smoke has been used to scry into the future to see one's destined mate.[16]

 ROWAN

In medieval times, witches' wands and amulets were frequently cut from rowan. In Wales, rowans, known as "witchen" or "wiggen" trees, were planted in church graveyards (like the yew elsewhere), where they created an aura of peace for the dead and kept them from growing discontented.[17] As a protective force, rowan was also used for stakes designed to be driven through vampire hearts; people wore rowan sprigs to protect them from the "evil eye;" when fastened to one's front door, the sprig also protected against storms and lightning (the sky's "evil eye"); taken aboard ship, they protected against storms. As a tree of life, or "quickening," sprays of rowan flowers were hung on cattle sheds centuries ago to protect the herds inside; goats were driven through rowan hoops. In medieval Britain it was believed rowan would protect one against illness caused by anything unnatural – demons, witches, malicious spirits, and the like.[18] Wearing rowan beads or carrying a small pouch of rowan berries and bark was said to increase psychic "sight," bring good fortune, and aid in recuperating from illness.[19]

One of the most fascinating spells comes from Russia. If one wishes to help a sick relative or friend, one would go into the forest, locate a rowan tree, and perform various rituals. Then one would carefully write out a petition to the king of the forest spirits, *Tsar Musaila*, who was presumed to live in the rowan. The petition would say in effect, "Look, I want to know why you've allowed 'servant of God, Ivan' [or whomever] to get so ill. You'd better tell me what he needs or I'll hire archers from Moscow and Novgorod to come and shoot you! And then I'll get Cossacks from Azov who'll come and hack you down to a stump if you don't help us!"[20] The threats sound peculiar to modern ears but this was nevertheless an entirely serious tribute to the enormous healing powers perceived to lie within the rowan.

Rowan is used for a wide range of medicinal matters: it is an excellent astringent and antibiotic; the high vitamin C content of its bitter berries helped prevent scurvy in earlier times; ripe berries made into a gargle are a good remedy for sore throats and inflamed tonsils; a decoction of bark is useful in curbing diarrhea.[21]

The leaves of spring and early summer can be added to salads. In difficult times when food was scarce, the berries (separated from their seeds, which are toxic to children) were ground into a flour substitute. In better times, they are added to apples or crabapples and made into jellies and chutneys. The berries are made into fine wines in Wales and the Highlands. Scots also make a strong spirit from it, the Welsh an ale, and the Irish flavor their mead with it.

The Reading

The Rowan grows higher up the sides of mountains than any other native tree, often sprouting and growing from the tiniest of crevices and growing in the most inaccessible of spots. Its life-force energy is strong and determined. It reflects a power, a vitality and tenacity, with a clear message that harnessing this powerful life-force will make any manifestation possible. Its message is not to give up, but to hold on strong to what you believe in and to the power of the life-force....

~ Glennie Kindred
British herbalist[22]

The ancient Druids recognized that the power of the rowan was at its height when it was used for the well-being of the land. This is why they planted rowan groves near places of worship, especially at stone circles, where the rowan protected the leylines, or dragon-lines, linking them.[23] If you have drawn this card in answer to a question concerning your house or land, you might consider planting a rowan, if possible, or getting some of its leaves, bark, or berries and creating a small altar-space for them in your home.

It is a good time for scrying or protective spell-casting. If you are asking about a relationship, it may involve invigorating thunderstorms, like Ukko and Rauni's, but it will also be joyous, kind, and fertile on many levels as you enjoy your Cup of Life together. In health matters, early preventative medicine is suggested – thus, eat plenty of red fruits and vegetables. In questions concerning work or partnerships, be especially attentive to the dynamics of haves and have-nots – try to find ways out of conflict through creative cooperation.

REVERSED:

There may be a tendency to be carried away, as Thor was in the raging river, by every influence entering your life. As others ensnare you in their dramas, you merge first with one, then with the next, until your energies are scattered and you feel raw and exhausted. At such times, bring your common sense and intuition into play. Keep a "single eye" vigilantly guarding the rowan's bright berries. Do not let them be wasted upon those who lack the wisdom to appreciate their worth.

This is a time to protect your oracular gifts and quietly guard your healing knowledge, inner fire, poetry, and dreams. Conceal your awareness of the magic lying underfoot. Pull back. Mute your eager, even anxious, desire to share knowledge. Wait until your feet are firmly grounded and you can again walk your inner rowan grove with serene purpose.

Rowan can break negative enchantments and protect your psychic vision, helping you to know what is useful and what might undermine you. If you are feeling weakened, confused, or distressed for no reason, the cause might lie in psychic attacks, often sent unconsciously by the negative thoughts of angry or envious family or colleagues. Invoke the tree and let it create a powerful protective field to ward off such negativity. Within that rowan-field, you are then able to call back into yourself any true part of you that you have willingly or inadvertently given away or have had taken from you or compromised at any time, any place, by anyone, under any circumstances. Call that part back into you that you may be whole, fully healed and restored, fully harmonized and empowered.

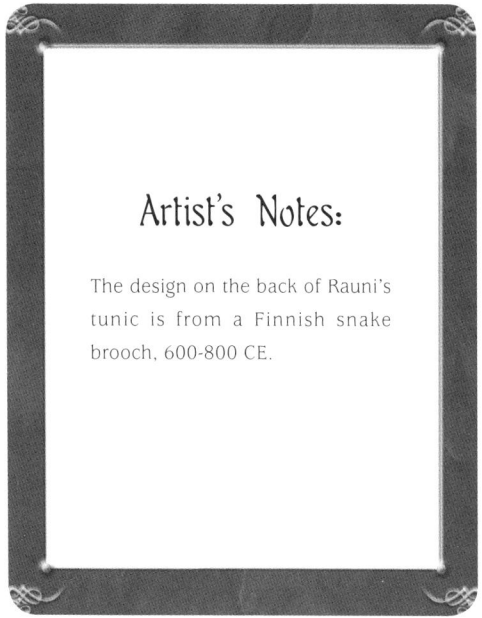

Artist's Notes:

The design on the back of Rauni's tunic is from a Finnish snake brooch, 600-800 CE.

Endnotes

[1] Paterson:228; 233-4.
[2] F&W:927.
[3] Sarapik, Virve. "Rainbow, Colours and Science Mythology" in Volume 6 of the English peer-reviewed journal Folklore: An electronic Journal of Folklore, published since 1996 by the Institute of the Estonian Language: http://haldjas.folklore.ee/folklore/vol6/rainbow.htm.
[4] Kalevala:157.
[5] Kalevala:120.
[6] Graves, WG:171.
[7] Paterson:228.
[8] Paterson:177.
[9] MacKenzie:132-134; Paterson:228
[10] Paterson:229 and related sources.
[11] Walker, D:470.
[12] Paterson:226.
[13] Paterson:226.
[14] Paterson:225.
[15] Paterson:230; 240.
[16] Paterson:232-233.
[17] Paterson:236.
[18] Altman:137.
[19] Paterson:236.
[20] Ryan:175.
[21] Altman:156.
[22] Glennie Kindred, "The Rowan Tree: Tree of Imbolc, Divine Inspiration and Seership," in White Dragon Journal, UK: White Dragon Publishing, 1998.
[23] Paterson:233.

30
SANDALWOOD

Sandalwood

[Sarasvati's] garments are said to be fiery in their purity, or they are described as white, and she is sometimes said to be smeared with sandalwood paste.

~ David Kinsley[1]

The Mythic World

In the earliest *Vedas*, Sarasvati, "besmeared with sandalwood paste," was the goddess of northwest India's mighty Sarasvati River, cleansing, fertilizing, and hallowing the dry lands around her. Because of her purifying power, she also became associated with medicine and healing. The most powerful of rituals were celebrated along her shores centuries before the Ganges became India's most sacred river.

In later Vedic literature, Sarasvati was equated with voice-goddess Vak who, during the "Churning of the Ocean," rose from the primal sea with a pot of immortal *soma* (see *Amrita*). Through this connection, Sarasvati became the embodiment of culture, linked to sacred language, music, dance, and higher learning. She is known by many titles including *Pratibha* (she who is intelligence); *Kalpanasakti* (the power of formation of ideas); *Jnanasakti* (power of knowledge); and *Sarvasastravasini* (who lives in all books). In her iconography, she is shown with four hands – holding a book, a lute, prayer beads, and a ritual water-pot. Her primary color, white, is reflected in the shining white swan she rides. She is said to be calm, serene, cool as water, white as pure snow, white as the moon, dazzling as the light shining from countless moons.[2] That she should be adorned with white sandalwood paste follows poetically from the word for sandalwood, *chandana*, which is related to *chandra*, "moon." *Chandra*, in fact, refers equally to moon and sandalwood, both of which also share cooling properties (rubbing sandalwood paste on skin cools and refreshes one).

Sandalwood's cooling ability plays a role in the "Churning of the Ocean," in which two teams of deities form an alliance to obtain the *amrita*. Unfortunately, the younger gods deceive the trusting older ones by promising a share in the elixir, a bargain they never intend to keep. Such deception catalyzes a deadly reverse-twin, *Kalakuta*, which moves swiftly, contaminating the waters, spreading like an oil slick of flammable greed and threatening the entire universe. Alarmed, the god Shiva (a non-participant in the alliance) swallows the poison and confines it in his throat. The toxin turns his throat a deep peacock blue, burning fiercely until cooling sandalwood paste is smeared on it. In recognition of Shiva's merciful action, one of his most important titles is *Nilakantha*, Blue-throated One.[3]

Sandalwood's involvement with Sarasvati and Shiva reveals an intrinsic connection with the throat-chakra and linguistic opposites: healing speech/ poisoned speech. The goddess' speech is soothing, healing, graceful – sandalwood is most at home when rubbed on her. Shiva holds the virulence of poisonous words in his throat: Sandalwood, rubbed on him, goes to work and heals. In the first instance, sandalwood affirms the calm, cool, magical, moonlight, musical nature of speech. In the second, sandalwood neutralizes the toxic effect of perverted speech and restores the balance.

The connection with Blue-throated Shiva links sandalwood to the god's own compassion, but the tree is also compassionate in its own right. Indian folklore recognizes this, for sandalwood is said to be the most generous and forgiving of all trees – even when felled by an ax, it remains serene, dignified, and gives the ax the gift of its own haunting fragrance.[4]

Many Buddhists view the godlike body of the sandalwood, with its "divinely sweet odor," as the one tree most capable of expressing the fragrant essence of the living Buddha, when carved into his likeness.[5] The first and most famous of such sandalwood Buddha images belonged to King Udayana, whose castle was at Kosambi in northern India. According to legend, Udayana prayed that one of his artists might be transported to heaven where the artist could then carve a life-sized sandalwood statue of the Buddha. The prayer was answered, but since the Buddha shone with a light too brilliant for the artist's eyes, the Buddha stood by a pool of water, allowing the artist to work from this reflection among the pool's ripples – the wet-appearing, flowing garments of the finished statue paid tribute to the mirroring pool. When it was complete, both artist and statue were transported back to the castle at Kosambi.[6] The statue became so revered that others attempted to steal it, only to discover that no one was strong enough to move it. Many copies were then made from the original, one of which, dating from the 10th century, still exists in Kyoto's temple of Seiryoji.[7]

Sandalwood has an intrinsic connection with yet another Buddha, a Chinese deity known as the Buddha of the South, one of ten gods who guard the directions of earth. His epithet was "Shining with Sandal and Pearl."[8] That conjunction of transcendent light, sandalwood, and the milky, moon-like pearl echoes the far more ancient cluster of meanings associated with the shining goddess of speech, Sarasvati, white as the moon, "besmeared with sandalwood paste."

Finally, although probably unaware of Sarasvati, when the T'ang poet, Chao Luan-luan, used the metaphor "sandal mouth" in her verses, she too was voicing an age-old connection between divine speech and the fragrant sandalwood.[9]

Botany/History

When the sandalwood dies, its dead log is attacked by termites which destroy all its wood but leave the oily, highly aromatic heart of the trunk intact.

~ Ernst and Johanna Lehner[10]

Sandalwood first reached Europe in the 11th century along Arab trade routes. The fragrant wood, preserved by its own oil, was immediately recognized as one of the most precious commodities ever to have arrived from the Far East. *Santalum album*, or white sandalwood, had already been venerated for centuries by Hindus, Buddhists and Moslems. Sandalwood was to the Far East what cedars, used for Egyptian coffins and Solomon's temple, were to the Near East – a metaphor for the immortality of the spirit. In rituals surrounding death, sandalwood oils were ingredients in embalming fluids and its wood was used for funeral pyres. Medicinally, sandalwood was used for intestinal colic and flatulence ("demoniac vapors"); in cases of fever, a thick sandal paste was plastered over the body.[11]

Sandalwood is native to southern India and the Malay Archipelago. The tree prefers a dry climate 2,000-3,000 feet above sea level. It averages 50 feet in height. Its flowers are bell-shaped and start out pale yellow but then turn to brick red; the inedible fruits resemble dark cherries. The trees have evergreen leaves tinged with yellow; the bark is reddish-brown or dark brown (smooth in young trees, but rough and with long deep cracks in old ones). Amazingly, the hard, close-grained, fragrant, oily heartwood is found in branches and roots as small as an inch in diameter. When a mature tree falls in the jungle, its heartwood is not revealed until jungle termites eat away the rotting outer wood.[12]

There are more than 100 species of *Santalum* but all are semi-parasitic and cannot exist without a host. The young sandalwood has branching roots with lateral suckers – when the suckers reach the roots of the host tree, a wart-like attachment occurs. Through enzymes exuded by the "wart," the host root is entered and some of its tissue dissolved until a connection is made to the actual wood of the host root – the sandalwood then draws water through its own water-conducting cells from the outer layer of the host's wood. Some species are excellent hosts; several others (including the *Strychnos nuxvomica*) are "good enough" although they transfer the bitter principle in their own tissues to the sandalwood. Some hosts are indifferent, others bad, and a few are exceedingly dangerous, either killing a young sandalwood outright or within a year or two.[13]

Sandalwood, as Edward H. Schafer points out, "was a wood of luxury as well as a wood of religion." The best scrolls in China's T'ang Dynasty (618-907 C.E.) were mounted on sandalwood rollers with crystal knobs; large pieces of furniture were inlaid or appliquéd with the wood; perhaps most fascinating of all, a great 9th century Buddhist meditation platform in China was entirely covered with sandal paste so that breezes might blow its scent far and near, probably as a reminder of the world of enlightenment continuously surrounding us.[14]

The Reading

After great suffering and a feeling of crumbling into dust and being eaten away by life itself, the aromatic, rich heartwood of this tree stands revealed. This priceless wood is then carved into sacred art, including temple pillars, symbolically holding up the Cosmos. When you draw Sandalwood, you are finally coming into your own.

You may often have reached out to others for help and received only rejection in return. Life has probably not seemed a very generous "host." You may have felt you were given starvation rations, while everyone around you was being fed more abundantly. Yet you kept on going; you made do with what little you received; you learned to live in a dry, arid, emotionally-bleak environment.

Know, however, that what was secretly being nourished through such seeming deprivation was your inner, fragrant, precious heartwood. Now at last this is emerging. The wonderful scent will begin to draw others to your side, others who will welcome your long-hidden richness.

This is a time of transition, a dying to one stage, a grieving, and then a long-awaited creative renaissance, possibly going in an entirely new and unsuspected direction. What you have endured is a "dark night of the soul," made all the more terrible by the rare glimpses of hope you have experienced and then lost along the way. You have been trapped in a black, bitter place where you have felt helpless and hopeless. Not knowing the time of your release has been especially tormenting, because you have so often been fooled into believing it lay just ahead. This process, however, was somehow necessary to clear away hidden impurities and to prepare you for the fragrance of long-lasting creativity lying just at hand. Linda Schierse Leonard writes in her *Witness to the Fire: Creativity & the Veil of Addiction*:

> Resentment is the will's "ill will" against time. If you can will each moment, i.e., if you can say a creative "Yes" to it, then you can take responsibility for your life instead of festering in addictive resentment at the past which says: "if only."....The phoenix emerges from its own ashes....So too can a human being transcend the burning fires of humiliation and resentment to find a life of creativity and transcendence.[15]

The "Yes" of the throat-chakra is strongly aspected here. Let the language rising from your throat come from Sarasvati's realm. Despite the ill treatment you have suffered, take care not to sink into the poisonous realm of resentment, betrayal, and lies. If you do, you risk being further engulfed and victimized. You have paid too high a price to stumble now. Find a way to restore your inner

balance and sense of compassion. Calm your burning resentments. Consider rubbing sandalwood oil on your throat, or bathe with sandal-scented soap, sit among trees, take a walk or perform a ritual near flowing waters, work with wood, seek out a wise person and ask for advice, light a stick of sandalwood incense, put on relaxing music. You are coming into your own.

REVERSED:

You may feel old, cranky, worn out, useless. You think you have nothing to offer, but look more closely: the ugly duckling is turning into a shining white swan – and the goddess herself is pleased to make you her vehicle. Do not be surprised if heightened activity and creativity come unexpectedly rushing upon you like Sarasvati's mighty waters.

Artist's Notes:

The roundel behind Sarasvati is from the dome of a ceiling of Mandapa, Vimala Vasahi (Adinatha Temple), Dilwara, Mt. Abu, South Rajasthan, 12th century. The vina (lute) she is playing is from 20th century India and it is resting on a section from the East gate of the Great Stupa, Sanchi, 1st century B.C.E.

Endnotes

[1] Kinsley, *HG*:62.
[2] Kinsley, *HG*:55-62; also personal communication from Sandra Stanton.
[3] Kramrisch:145-152.
[4] M. Vasant: private communication.
[5] Henderson and Hurvitz:11; Schafer:137.
[6] Henderson & Hurvitz:14; 16, fn.20.
[7] Henderson & Hurvitz:14-15.
[8] Schafer:137.
[9] Schafer:138.
[10] Lehner:47.
[11] Lehner:47; Schafer:136-137.
[12] Bor:238-239; Lehner:47.
[13] Bor:239; also see de Witt, vol.2.
[14] Schafer:137-138; 269.
[15] Leonard:81-82.

31
SEAWEED

Seaweed

> I have never conceived, but whether or not a woman does conceive, she carries the germinative ocean within her, and the essential eggs. We have a spirituality, full from within. Whether we are weaving tissue in the womb or pictures in the imagination, we create out of our bodies.
> ~ Former Benedictine nun, British artist and mystic Meinrad Craighead[1]

The Mythic World

Sea-deities are found worldwide but since human life evolved in Africa, we begin with Yemoja, "Mother of Fish," originally a powerful rain and Ogun River goddess of the Yoruba people in Nigeria. Wherever she walked, fountains sprang forth – even asleep, new waters gushed up whenever she turned over.

When her people were enslaved and shipped to the New World in vessels of horror, she followed in their wake, like the Ogun, which empties into the sea. She flowed into the deepest currents, the darkest depths, merging so completely with that watery vastness that she was transformed into a sea-goddess, no longer limited to smaller bodies of water. Thereafter, seashells, through which priestesses and priests could hear the voice of the universe, were her first gifts to the people.

To her followers, she is a manifestation of the Virgin Mary as *Stella Maris* (Star of the Sea) and the Immaculate Conception. She is petitioned on matters of seafaring, trade, commerce. Like the sea, she is maternal, generous, life-giving, but she is also the source of devastating storms. To placate and honor her, worshippers burn sea-blue candles, wear necklaces strung with blue and crystal beads – and, since her sacred number is seven and her favorite metal is moon-bright silver, they wear seven silver bracelets. She appreciates music, dance, good company, and luxurious surroundings, for these echo her own rich kingdom.

In New Orleans, she is La Balianne. In Haiti, she is Agwe. In Cuba, she is Yemana or Yemaya, appearing in various guises: Yemaya Ataramagwa is "Holy Queen of the Sea," wealthy mistress of the seas' pearls, shells, coral, and all sea creatures; Yemaya Achabba acts as a rigorous, stern parent; Yemaya Oggutte produces violent sea-storms; and Yemaya Olokun is occasionally glimpsed in dreams as a breathtaking, over-powering presence. Further south in Brazil, she is Yemanja or Imanje, sea-goddess of the crescent moon, celebrated on New Year's Eve when thousands of tiny flower-boats are launched on the sea in her honor. Sweet music comes from the goddess' very being – she dances, arms raised, her movements as supple and flowing as seaweed; she carries a comb in one hand and a snail-shell mirror in the other – her silver crown is decorated with pearls, which are considered drops of her purest essence.

As a major goddess of the African Diaspora, Yemoja knows all the secrets of the sea. As Mama Watta, "Mother of Waters," her womb-waters birth oceans as well as her people's deities, the *Orishas*. The "sea" within a woman's womb is also under her special protection, for she is invoked in all issues concerning fertility, pregnancy, and childbirth.[2]

Sea-deities tend to be goddesses – most of them, like Yemaya, intimately connected with the act of birth, both biological and artistic. Their domains include the unconscious, dreams, mysteries, theatre, art, dance, music, and sacred language. In ancient India, for example, the sea-goddess was Vak (*vox, voce, vois,* and "voice" are cognates). Her name relates her to the sounds of water, speech, singing, bee-humming. It was she who rose from the primal ocean with a pot containing the elixir of immortal life (India's sacred theatre originated with this narrative – see *Amrita*). In the *Devyupanisad*, the goddess claims sovereignty over all creative forms, revealing herself as Creative Principle and Origination-point of gods:

> The place of my birth is in the water within the sea: he who knows this, obtains the dwelling of Devi.... It was I who, in the beginning created the father of this world....[3]

Sea-goddesses dwelling in such magically potent waters contrast sharply with later myths in which male Creators come from mountains or sky.

Greece's sea-goddess was graceful Amphitrite, mother of dolphins and wife of sea-god Poseidon, who fell in love the moment he saw her dancing with her sisters. Greece's goddess of love, Aphrodite, although not a sea-goddess, was nevertheless born from the sea, thus making the sea a gateway for Love herself *(see Oak)*. Mature at birth, Aphrodite walked out of the sea and onto a small island as flowers sprang up in her footprints.

Elsewhere, Rome's sea-goddess was Mari – words like "marine" and "maritime" come from her name. Mesopotamia's sea-goddess was she-dragon Tiamat, mother of the gods. Japan's goddess was also a dragoness, Benzai-ten, who generously bestowed gifts of happiness, wisdom, wealth, beauty, music, and art upon humans. In Wales, the "white wave" sea-goddess was Gwenhwyfar, who symbolized both kingdom and throne because no man could rule without her at his side. In her earthly form, she is better known as Guinevere, wife of King Arthur – as goddess, however, according to lore, she sang Arthur back into the sea as he died. Such death songs are called *marswygafen*, "giving-back-to-the-sea-mother."[4]

Worldwide, these and other sea-goddesses rule over kingdoms of immense wealth and abundance, portals into the unconscious, dreams, memory, love, and dazzling creativity. These goddesses guide us into the realm of the Mother – for ocean, even more than earth, is "Mother," the cradle of life.

We learn from these sea-goddesses that the sea is a metaphor for a woman's inner ocean, a complex and wondrous microenvironment.[5] Compared with sperm, which is never more than two months old, a woman's eggs are ancient, their origins lost in time, for a woman's total lifetime supply is produced in her ovaries while she is a fetus in her mother's womb. Throughout childhood, her body will contain a million genetically related but different potential human "universes" – endless strains of mystery held in arrested meiosis, unable to ripen, yet always there, potential geniuses, outlaws, saints, fools, sages, artists, thieves, warriors, healers. What subtle shifts of familiarities, of resonances, are whispering throughout those alternate universes, influencing that child's moods and perspective?

During childhood the eggs remain encircled and sheltered by follicle cells deep within her body, but at puberty hormones will cause those follicles to mature. Thereafter, during each menstrual cycle, a single follicle out of many thousands will rupture and release an egg the size of a grain of sand. "Follicle" comes from the Latin *folliculus*, a small bag, pod, cocoon, husk, sack, cavity, seed-capsule. Since ovarian follicles are filled with fluid holding exactly the same salt-content as the sea, we can think of them as tiny "sea-bags" protecting the elixir of life. Strangely, the image is also found in a late 2nd or early 3rd century Christian Wisdom text, "Teachings of Silvanus":

> ...(It is) he *[God]* who has gathered together such a great sea as in a leather bag and has weighed all the water on his scales....Through it, all has come into being since it became the mother of all.[6]

As most women will agree, the ebbing and surging of hormone-rich fluids are not experienced passively – they generally create a tumult of biochemically-driven emotions. Since these are so unmistakably woven into this process, one has to wonder if, unconsciously, emotions might be essential in altering microenvironments from menses to menses, creating parameters for the selection from among thousands of potentially viable eggs that single egg most likely to respond with perfect pitch. Pinpointing that egg suggests an astonishing complexity – if it were simply a random choice, why involve so much emotion? Somehow, once some guiding factor *has weighed all the water on [its] scales*, a choice is made among alternate universes, as if from the eye of a hurricane, untouched by dense swarmings of energy all around it, and yet empathetic to all possibilities.

Living in such close proximity to "otherness" seems a perfect means of conditioning tolerance for "not-self." Although every embryo's immune system must learn to differentiate between self and not-self, after eight weeks, a female fetus, oscillating between self and vast quantities of not-self in her egg-rich fetal ovaries, never quite develops rigid self-boundaries. This allows her adult immune system to accept a fetus as part of herself instead of an invader to be attacked. Small wonder that women tend to welcome emotion and are more comfortable with "otherness" than most men.

Significant male sea-deities are rare, yet exploring their attributes offers valuable insights. For example, in ancient Egypt there was a netherworld deity, Nun, one of eight primal deities in the Hermopolitan Ogdoad.[7] The priests of

Hermopolis (midway between Giza and Luxor) were obsessed with how *being* could emerge from *non-being*. Their creation narrative – in which there is no creator, only a process – was their solution.

Nun was the personification of the ocean of chaos – a dark, formless, watery mass of negative energies (these are not "evil" – they are akin to a photographer's jumbled piles of negatives, an intense *quantity-x* without reality unless developed). At first, nothing exists except that undifferentiated Nothingness. Then – no one knows how – a mound begins to emerge out of the undulating waters. After more time passes, a blue lotus sprouts from the mound. A long time later, Atum the sun appears from the lotus, opening the way for other life forms to come into being.

The unfolding of creation does not supplant the original ocean of "negatives," however. Instead, Nun's chaotic waters are driven beyond the boundaries of the universe. There they are inhabited by "non-beings" – stillborn fetuses and souls condemned for breaking boundary-taboos on earth. Cold, priestly logic made no space for such "non-beings" except within Nun's dismal waters around the edges of the universe. It is an eerie insight.

Fortunately, not all male sea-deities inhabit such sorrowful realms. The Celtic sea-god, Manannan, rules over a realm filled with magic and wonder. He even has his own "sea-bag" – a leather bag made from the skin of a sacred crane in which he carries his "Treasures of the Sea." One might assume these would be pearls and sunken treasure, but Manannan's treasure is the secret Pelasgian alphabet of the Peoples of the Sea, a matriarchal culture that flourished around the Mediterranean prior to the Bronze Age arrival of the Greeks in the late 4th or early 3rd millennium B.C.E. This secret alphabet is said to have been inspired by crane courtship dances and the sky-patterns made as cranes fly, which is why the sea-bag is made of crane-skin. Thus, *sacred language* is what Manannan keeps safely hidden in his sea-bag.[8] This is very different from follicular bags and hormonal storms buffeting ova, yet analogous to that biochemical turbulence are the creative storms of artists struggling for expression through language and image. From this perspective, the process of bringing forth nurturing, awe-filled knowledge and art is on a par with the creativity of human biology.

Botany/History

Oceans cover more than 70% of the planet's surface. Seaweed, a large form of algae, grows in those marine environments. It evolved in what is known as the Ordovician period (425-500 million years ago), an age when enormous floods swept the planet on a scale never seen before or since:

In seas that inundated the lands, new opportunities for life constantly arose. Seaweeds of every description coated the sea floor with a velvety green cover; the tides streamed through thick forests of slimy fronds; enormous islands of algae grew upon the surface. Organisms that swam or floated near the surface, in the wash of waves and the cycle of sunlight and darkness, developed life styles different from those in the deeper waters of subdued light and even temperatures....[9]

There were as yet no land plants – they would not develop until the Silurian age (405-425 million years ago). The only growing life that existed was held in heaving masses of water. From those early seaweeds came today's descendants, little-changed, still arousing an archaic sense of wonder, still creating dense underwater forests, trailing their long, swaying foliage through the waters and never veering too far from surface light.

Some 400 million years ago, some of those ancestral sea plants first made their way ashore and managed to survive. They were the pioneers from which future land plants evolved. Land plants have to work very hard – they need to anchor themselves with roots, access sufficient water, create creeping vines or towering trunks out of their life-force, find enough light in often overcrowded conditions, cope with changing seasons and extremes of temperatures, and evolve amazingly complex means of reproducing themselves.

In comparison, life is relatively easy for sea plants because water itself tends to all but one of their needs: light. To remain in touch with light, which is necessary for their processes of photosynthesis, they either float near the surface or anchor themselves to coral reefs or rocks, often at great depths as long as the water is clear enough for sunlight to penetrate. Unique sugars and organic compounds allow them to adapt to sudden shifts in temperatures, salinity, and wave-action. For those remaining in the cradle of the sea, there was little need to evolve much further – most of them are as "primitive" today as they must have been when they first appeared.

There are more than 10,000 species of seaweeds, or "sea vegetables," some close to 2,000 feet long, others microscopic; some as delicate as filigree jewelry, others – like kelp – requiring only a year to grow larger than a mature oak. Seaweeds are found from polar seas to the tropics. These forests-of-life are rich in essential nutrients identical to those found in human blood – no food offers a broader range of minerals – but seaweed also includes amino acids, vitamins (especially B vitamins), enzymes, and fatty acids. Where land plants often grow in depleted soils, seaweed luxuriates in nature's richest nutrient soup.

Around the world, seaweed has been harvested for thousands of years by peoples who have made it a significant part of their dietary and medicinal needs.

Many cultures celebrated these harvests with exuberant dancing, singing, and feasting. Archaeological evidence suggests that the Japanese have been celebrating and eating seaweed for 10,000 years – many of our most familiar names for seaweeds come from Japan, including nori, hijiki, kombu, wakame, arame. By 3,000 B.C.E., the Chinese had discovered seaweed's medicinal properties and served it as a royal delicacy; as word spread, slices of seaweed jelly became a daily tonic in many families. In ancient Hawaii, kelp gardens and dozens of rare seaweed varieties were cultivated by the nobility for food, medicine, and rituals. In coastal regions worldwide, seaweed was especially precious during times of famine when little else was available.

The Reading

If you have drawn this card, the seas' treasures of life-force, health, creativity, and time are being offered to you. Use them wisely. Pay attention to health and well-being – make relaxing baths, art, music, and even eating sea vegetables a regular part of your life.

If you are asking about a child, you are being advised to do whatever is necessary to provide a "sea-rich" life for that child.

If you are asking about a creative project, it is being blessed.

If you are a woman asking about getting pregnant, keep your emotions on an even keel. Otherwise, this would probably not be a good time to conceive. If the body's process of selecting one monthly ovum depended upon random chance, why would emotional swings, corresponding to hormonal swings, be programmed into the biological process? Your response to emotional storms might, along with other factors, determine which follicle releases its egg. If you are depressed, for example, might not your emotions evoke ovulation in an egg that happens to resonate to such a troubled state? This is not to suggest that there are "sad" eggs and "happy" eggs and that if a mother gives birth to a depressed child, it is her fault. In actuality, the unique combinations possible between ovum and sperm can never lend themselves to such over-simplification. What is being suggested, however, is that you remain trusting and centered in the midst of emotional upheavals. Stay emotionally vibrant, yet serene.

If you are a male having difficulty engendering a child, you might feel as if you have been relegated to a quasi-existence in Nun's dark waters along the margins of the universe. Yet, *pre*-creation (and each day is another *pre*-creation), that infertile realm was the chaotic gateway from which a mound emerges (which suggests an ovum), and an elegant blue lotus (implying phallic activity), and finally the sun's birth, from which all other lives are nourished. Thus, Nun's undifferentiated waters are what safeguard the dimension from which life emerges. What seems to be a bleak existence on the far-edges of the universe nevertheless continues to be the doorway through which being arises out of non-being. Trust that seemingly chaotic male realm of nothingness, emptiness, for it is the other side of female fecundity, and neither gender can sustain life or creativity without both.

REVERSED:

Regardless of gender, you might be invited to explore a new definition of "self." You are not your emotional wars and turmoil. To split yourself into positive and negative, happy and sad, hopeful and despairing, is to lose sight of the central core out of which those emotional energies are constellated. That core remains a compassionate, creative, playful awareness lying within you.

If you feel you might be blurring too many self/not-self boundaries and getting lost, the solution might be to anchor yourself, as seaweed anchors itself to coral reefs or rocks, to an aspect of creativity that leaves you feeling bathed in ocean-light. If you have children, no matter how beloved they are, *they* are not your creativity. Go into your depths, discover what your creativity really is, and take it seriously.

If you feel your boundaries might already be so rigid and well-anchored that you are trapped, consider role-playing, exploring new creative forms that interest you, listening more to others, and practicing empathy and Buddhist techniques of "lovingkindness."

For either gender, if you identify "self" with exhaustion or hopelessness, you are leaving your miraculous body behind, letting it fend for itself, making it feel sluggish and joyless. Your body deserves better.

If you remain clear and focused, you will come into alignment with regions of immense creative energy, enabling you to give birth either to "tissue in the womb or pictures in the imagination." In either event, as Meinrad Craighead emphasizes, you create out of your body. Your *body* is your generative ocean. Allow your body to be like seaweed, swaying in deep waters, at peace in the light from above. Then create out of your body.

Artist's Notes:

Yemanja is wearing an 18th century Ijebu armlet with a fish-legged figure. Behind her on the left is a fan from Cuba, first half of the 20th century, decorated with beads and cowrie shells which symbolize the richness of the ocean.

Endnotes

[1] Cited in Gadon:241.
[2] Yemoja data has been woven from many sources, including personal communications from artist Sandra Stanton; also Monaghan:320-321.
[3] Eliade, YIF:350.
[4] Walker:WEMS:61.
[5] Biology data here and following is taken from: Jenks, 1992, Part I, ch. 5, "Sea-Bags."
[6] From "The Teachings of Silvanus" (Tractate VII,4), trs., Malcolm L. Peel and Jan Zandee, in Robinson, ed.:360.
[7] Shaw:206-7, "Nun" entry; also my Pacifica Graduate Institute lectures on Egypt.
[8] Graves, WG:248.
[9] T/L: LBM:30. Other sources used for this section include Attenborough:232; *Life Nature Library: The Sea*:40; Vickery:58; and the publisher's web review for David Thomas, *The World of Seaweed – From Arctic Underwater Forests to Ice Cream*. London: Natural History Museum, 2002.

32
SYCAMORE FIG

Sycamore Fig

Names differed, but everywhere the Milky Way was regarded as the Goddess's star-milk, which formed curds to create worlds and creatures.

~ Barbara Walker[1]

The Mythic World

The sycamore (wild fig, *Ficus sycamorus*) was Egypt's Tree of Life. In both Egypt and India, the fig represented the goddess' procreative organs, but whereas India's pipal-fig highlights the goddess' erotic, playful dimension (see *Pipal*), Egypt's sycamore-fig focuses on her restful, calming, reassuring dimension.

Egypt's sycamore-goddess is Hat-hor, an ancient World Mother. In tomb murals, she is shown standing in a sycamore, nourishing the dead from a container of celestial milk from the Milky Way. Life and death are not separate to her – she nurtures souls regardless of where she finds them. She is also depicted as a cosmic cow, spangled with the Milky Way, feeding creation from her inexhaustible udders. Whether depicted as a cow or a goddess in the sycamore, she is a manifestation of the joy-sustaining power winding through the universe.

Hat-hor means "Womb-of-Horus," the sun-god, but she is not Egypt's only sun-mother. There is also cobra-goddess Wadjet, whose mythology is set in the papyrus swamps of Lower Egypt's northern delta (see *Papyrus*), not the sycamore's sandy deserts or residential locales. Vulture goddess Nekhbet births the sun in steep, rocky regions of the south's Upper Egypt. Thus, each sun-mother births Horus in her personal environment.

Hat-hor was said to live in a grove of sycamores at the far end of the world,[2] from where Horus rose like a great bird from her swaying cosmic branches.[3] A sun-creation myth briefly describes the setting from Horus' perspective:

> I [the Sun] built a house...there on the hillside
> where my mother resides beneath her sycamores.[4]

The Book of the Dead also speaks of the sun-birthing tree:

> ...I know the tree of emerald green
> from whose midst
> Ra [an alternate sun-name] rises to the height of the clouds.[5]

Hat-hor, this tree of emerald green, is goddess of fertile abundance, dance, joy, and music. She invented the *sistrum*, a rattle whose tinkling represented sounds made by the four elements as they came together to create the universe.[6] When Hat-hor's priestesses danced with *sistra*, they were deliberately replicating the origins of life and infusing their own world with those sacred energies.

Botany/History

Egypt's sturdy, broad *nehet*, or sycamore (*Ficus sycamorus*), like India's pipal, is one of the approximately 800 varieties of fig trees. All secrete a milky lac, or juice, from the bark. "Sycamore" comes from Greek *sycos*, "wild fig" and *moros*, "mulberry" (their leaves are similar and the *ficus* genus belongs to the Mulberry family). The tree is native to Egypt and Asia Minor.[7]

Egypt was poor in wood-giving trees. For important projects like ships, temple doors, or royal sarcophagi, she had to send abroad for Lebanese cedar. Local trees like sycamore, acacia, willow, palm, and large thorn-trees served for everything else. Sycamore was used for coffins, the inner lid often painted with the goddess arching through the stars in token of her eternal care of the deceased. Sycamore was also carved into many beautiful statues as well as simple household goods. Wood was too precious to be used as fuel so most people fed their fires with dried dung.[8]

Sycamore figs were found everywhere in villages and at crossroads. Wealthy Egyptians planted walled gardens with pools and many trees – the two most favored trees were sycamores for their dense shade and palms for their grace.[9] The wild fig also thrives in Egypt's sandy soil and often stands in solitary magnificence at some distance from the Nile's waters. In the midst of a desolate wasteland, the tree's lush, densely leafy foliage provides a miraculous shade for travelers. The tree's roots are able to tap into rills of water from underground streamlets flowing from the Nile – this "long-distance" ability is what keeps it green. Each tree was regarded as Hat-hor's altar and place of residence. Egyptians placed offerings of milk, fruits, vegetables, flowers, and pitchers of water at the base of sycamore trees. Travelers were then free to partake of the sacred food.[10]

In the earliest dynasties, not only were coffins made of hallowed fig wood, but dried figs were placed inside to represent the goddess' womb. The newly dead expected one day to travel through her birth-canal yet again and emerge reborn.[11]

The Reading

Let the bird sing without deciphering the song.

~ Ralph Waldo Emerson

The sycamore addresses patterns of self-doubt, especially in intellectual, scientific, or creative work. These and other patterns lie at deep levels where you have lost something you valued. It might be a loved one, a whole phase of your life, confidence, health, ambition, life-style, even a special project you have just completed. You may feel postpartum depression, lost, aimless, and unclear about where to go next. Into this unlikely Wasteland comes the gentle goddess of the Milky Way, Hat-Hor. Perched in a sycamore tree, she feeds the newly dead, whom she does not distinguish from the newly born, from a pail of sweet, rich milk. She tilts her pail and streams of star-milk pour down through the branches to the opened mouths of her children.

Let whatever in you feels "newly dead" be open to nourishment from the mother-soul. Deep rest is needed. This is no time for major decisions. Let yourself be a passive child waiting expectantly to be fed. The world-mother has not forgotten you. She created you from star-milk – now she feeds you with it.

The need for rest is a recurring theme but each tree handles it differently. Hawthorn, for example, imposes it while Holly gives you a choice. Sycamore neither imposes nor asks for choice. You are already numb when she finds you, probably past choice and all thought. Something has ended for you – not something dreadful that you somehow survived, as with Myrrh. This is someone or something you loved, valued, enjoyed – and will miss very much. When Hat-hor finds you, you may still be grieving. She approaches discreetly – some milk, a tinkling rattle, and she sings you to sleep. Rest for as long as it takes – a few days, weeks, months. When your juices begin to run again and you feel restless, even eager to get on with your life, that is your signal that it is time to leave.

REVERSED:

You are being pushed out of the nest. A child who is nurtured learns to nurture, just as a child who is abused learns to abuse. You have been nurtured and mothered by the goddess of music, joy, and dance. Her arts and rich milk are in your blood and bones, gifting you for journeys ahead. Now it is time to leave. Find your own food, sing your own song, soar into the light.

Go easy at first. Test your wings, knowing that your celestial mother watches with a loving eye. She is not abandoning you – but she has prepared you well. She releases you to claim strength and power in your own right. Other cycles in your life may draw you back to Hat-hor and her sycamore – but for now, stretch your wings and get going. Do not forget that, like Egypt's sun-mothers, each of us births the sun in our own environment.

Artist's Notes:

Hathor is depicted in her Cow Goddess form in the sculpture on the tree trunk, 1390-1353 B.C.E.; under it she is depicted as a human goddess with cow ears in the Hathor column, 380-342 B.C.E. In her right hand, she is holding a container with a wall painting depicting herself in this role from the Tomb of Sennedjem in Deir of Medineh, New Kingdom, 13th century B.C.E.; in her left hand she pours out starry milk from a vase with a Hathor portrait on it from Tutankhamun's Tomb, 14th century B.C.E. She wears a Hathor bracelet from Jebel Barkal, Nubia, 1st century B.C.E. and a collar with beads representing lotus petals, dates and cornflowers, 1350 B.C.E.

Endnotes

[1] Walker, *WEMS*:658.
[2] Buffie Johnson:274-277.
[3] Walker, *D*:402.
[4] Cited in Johnson:276.
[5] Jung, *S of T*:246.
[6] Walker, *D*:105.
[7] Montet:33; Lehner:49; Walker, *D*:470.
[8] *DEC*:303a&b.
[9] Montet:33; *DEC*:130c.
[10] Frazer:ii.15; Lehner:49.
[11] *DEC*:303a; Walker, *D*:470.

33
WILLOW

Willow

> Like Artemis, Helice the Willow-maid was associated with both the moon and Ursa Major, eternally circling the pole, known as Helice's Axle. Witches thought a willow wand a microcosmic *axis mundi*.
>
> ~ Barbara Walker[1]

The Mythic World

East and west, the willow came to represent the quintessence of an invisible energy underlying the ever-changing universe. The ash, also a tree of cosmic order, catches the "weave" of creation in a freeze-frame: it is energy-as-*particle*, defined, measurable. The willow, however, is energy-as-*wave*, impossible to measure, fluid as water, filling what is empty and continually flowing on.

In China, the willow is associated with spring and an awakening into the Buddha-mind. There is a Chinese belief that water sprinkled with a willow branch will bring purifying energy. Thus, Kuan Yin, serene goddess of compassion, is often depicted holding a willow branch. Sometimes she holds it while seated near flowing water, sometimes while riding Lung, the benevolent, celestial dragon who brings spring rain. Goddess, willow, dragon are equals – fluid, serene, supple, powerful, for within each, under each form, there flows an identical energy.

Among the Ainu on the northernmost islands of Japan, it is believed that the Creator used willow wood to craft the invisible structure of the first human's backbone. Since the Ainu believe the soul lives in the spine, the backbone is the most important part of the body. Further, the willow is the Creator's own tree – in giving part of it to humankind, he was also giving himself.[2]

In Tibet the world-tree is known as "far-spreading willow." It grows atop a Himalayan mountain, its roots deep in the earth and its branches in the clouds with the sky-deities. This tree has six great limbs and on each limb is a nest with a bird sitting on her egg; from these six eggs come all life on earth.[3]

In Greece, the willow was the tree of Helice ("willow"), the new-moon form of the goddess Hekate. Helice's sacred bird, the hissing dragon-like wryneck, nests only in willows.[4] The Willow-Maid guarded the willows' sanctuary on Mount Helicon ("willow-stream"), home of the nine Muses and their waters of inspiration (see *Apple*).[5] Willow wands were used in oracular rituals – their power lay in their being a representation of the cosmic axis around which wove the stars of Helice's Axle, more familiar to us as Ursa Major, the bear-form of Artemis who, like Helice, was the new-moon aspect of Hekate and closely associated with willows.[6]

In the New World, the Navajo "Home of the Plants," built in late summer to invoke rain, was made of two stalks of blue-bark willow, one in the east, the other in the west, braced against two stalks of red-bark willow, one in the south, the other in the north. Cattail flag was woven between the willow stalks; flowers collected from the four directions were laid over the cattails, tips pointing downward, inviting the rain to stream downward as well. Willow branches thus provided the invisible structure, other plants the walls. Flowing waters came from the sky as guests to this ritual "Home of the Plants."[7]

This overall concept of a continually life-renewing universe, aligned along an invisible axis, presents us with a vision of cosmic harmony. For the Greeks, the earthly willow-weave is held together on Mount Helicon; in the heavens, in the constellation of Helice's Axle. The Chinese embraced a kindred awareness in their images of Kuan Yin, willow branch in hand, seated either on earth or gracefully riding through the skies on the back of her rain-bringing dragon.

Botany/History

In pre-historic times, the willow (*salix*) grew from the tropics to the arctic treeline. Three proto-Indo-European word-roots exist for willow *(*wyt-, *wrb-, *s/wVlyk-)* – all three are related to cognates for weaving, twisting, turning, wickering, winding, bending. The same word in many cases refers both to the willow as well as to the process of braiding and twisting willow's supple withies into useful objects.[8] Although there are several hundred species, two basic categories exist: the tree or bush form and the osier (e.g., pussy willows).[9] The trees, which are the focus of this oracle, grow thirty to eighty feet high, although Siberian varieties soar more than a hundred feet.[10]

Shortly after the glaciers withdrew 11,000 years ago, willows began spreading west into Europe. Willows are moisture-loving pioneers, produce vast amounts of pollen, seed quickly, and can withstand severe cold and poor soils. Like many pioneer trees, however, they require a great deal of light and do not live long (about fifty to a hundred years). Thus, willows face either being crowded out by two other pioneer species, birch and pine, or else surviving as a minority, especially along the many waterways of Russia and Europe.[11]

Willows are same-gendered. Since their twigs and branches, whether male or female, can fall into a river and root themselves further downstream, an entire colony spread along a stretch of riverbank from a single upstream parent will all be same-gendered.[12]

Contrary to popular belief, the trees of Babylon where the Hebrews wept were poplars, not willows – no species of willow was ever native to the lower Euphrates River. The graceful "weeping willow" is native to China but long after the Hebrews' Babylon exile it did reach the Middle East and Europe along the Silk Road. It is now found throughout the world. In addition to Eurasian varieties, more than forty species of willow trees and twice that many shrubs are native to North America. Native Americans knew its medicinal uses and also valued its wood for tipi poles.[13]

In more recent times, because its strong network of roots can secure riverbanks, the tree is often planted along streams where erosion from flooding is a danger. Willows prefer having their roots in flowing water rather than in lakes or ponds, although they will thrive in either place.[14] When planted near a home, willows may develop an unusual sensitivity to humans – cases exist where they weaken and die after their human friends die or move away.[15]

Since the willow is primarily wind-pollinated, its flowers are fuzzy catkins without petals. Male flowers produce little nectar but female catkins do and are loved by bees in early spring. Goats love to munch willow leaves.[16] The bark is too bitter for people to eat, even during times of famine, yet when brewed as a tea, the bark provides salicylic acid (aspirin), an ancient painkiller used to treat colds, fevers, headaches, and rheumatoid arthritis.[17]

The Reading

Willow is beauty, grace, an intimate connection with deep wellsprings of Mother-wisdom, and secret knowledge welling up from dimensions not ordinarily accessible to you. She may even give you glimpses of your life's destiny and path, of shimmering thread being spun, humming, around you. This tree has an active synergy with Mother-wisdom, a moving flow, to and fro, drawing forth insights, letting them spring up like fountains around you.

The arts are highly favored, especially music, chant, dance, poetry or anything to do with cloth, weaving, and basketry. The willow-goddess loves all artistic forms, from the simplest to the grandest, as long as they emerge from your depths. Do not be afraid to *feel* and to express what you feel through your work. Cold logic is of no interest to her. She herself feels, intuits, senses, and spins her art from within. She offers you the gift of doing the same. She is supportive as you risk going more deeply, stretching farther. Ask and she may send the Muses to inspire you.

The willow-goddess is also the moon-goddess, capable of infusing your work with inner whorls of magic. Do not go soft or sentimental in your dealings with her, however. From the moon comes deep, lucid insight – but for the careless or unwary, she is Luna, from which comes our word, lunacy.

In terms of relationships, of all the trees, the willow is the least interested in gender and labels. She points you towards what makes you feel beautiful, handsome, graceful, simple, loving, shining. Bodily forms are constantly changing and reversing polarities from lifetime to lifetime. It is the integrity of the invisible structure that speaks from one soul to another, not the temporary physical form.

If your life is currently in one of the outer, slow-moving planetary spheres, drawing the water-loving willow invites you to relax into the on-going stream of your life. Be languid and dreamy for a time – or dance, at least in spirit, through the trailing willow leaves. If health is a concern, anything involved with water should be helpful: swimming, walking along the shore, relaxing baths. Do not overlook the simple cleansing practice of drinking six to eight glasses of water a day.

If your life has swung you into the inner reaches of the planetary spheres where everything transits rapidly, you may find yourself in a period of intense activity. Things may move swiftly around you, changing continually. You may be too busy to see the larger picture so just stay with the flow. Be like water which approaches an abyss – it does not pause in fright nor take a timeout to measure the depth of the plunge. It is water's nature to flow unhesitatingly. Stay with that clarity of awareness and know that these are matters of destiny for you. During such times, you meet the creative force within your own body. You "rupture" out of your solitary isolation to dissolve and re-structure whole new genetic patterns around you, organizing them, re-combining them, separating, fusing, sending up new life in delighted processes of busy, efficient alchemy. Then you metamorphosize, resting, like the moon, quiet, dark, getting ready to begin all over again.

REVERSED:

That about which you are asking may not be part of the natural flow of your life – at least not at this time. No matter how right it feels, how altruistic your motives, how noble your intentions, what you seek might block the flow of energy urgently required in other areas of your life right now. You cannot ride two horses at once nor should you change mounts midstream. Continue along your original trajectory and avoid all temptation to alter your course – at least for now. Do not erode your strength by adding the last-minute baggage of longing, doubt, indecision or ego-inflation. Wait at least a week or two before asking the trees about this issue again.

If you are not asking about a specific issue and are simply making a general inquiry of the trees, reversed willow may be telling you that you are a willow-twig that has been floating too long on life's current. It is time to focus more clearly, make choices and put down roots. Your energies are strong and unique. They have a purpose. Plant them where your heart draws you – and watch them grow. You may plant them in a relationship, an art, idea, vision, belief – there are many possibilities along the riverbanks, each offering new vistas but subject to the same cycles of moon and sun overhead. You cannot make a mistake as long as your choice is based upon your deepest, most heartfelt values.

Artist's Notes:

Kuan-Yin is holding a Kuang (ritual wine vessel) from China, Shang Dynasty (Anyang Period), c. 13th-11th century B.C.E. The statue of Kuan-Yin on the branch is from early 8th century China, T'ang Dynasty. The dragon design on her necklace is from a Chinese disk, E. Zhou Dynasty, 4th-3rd century B.C.E.

Endnotes

[1] Walker, *E*:383; also see Allen:433.
[2] Helfman:45.
[3] Helfman:35.
[4] Graves, *WG*:178 + n.
[5] Walker, *D*:475.
[6] Walker, *D*:475; Jung, *S.ofT.*:244, w/n.
[7] Haile:10-11.
[8] Friedrich:57;56.
[9] Friedrich:56-57.
[10] Friedrich:57; Brockman:76-82.
[11] Friedrich:19.
[12] Mitchell:8.
[13] Mitchell:10; Brockman:76.
[14] Mitchell:8.
[15] Baker:129.
[16] Sargeaunt:119.
[17] Rodale:503-504.

CONCLUSION

I did not plan to add any closing thoughts, but tonight one of my "Life Journey" university students, Andrjka, stayed after class to ask if she could do an extra credit blog on daily Tarot readings. Since I had told the class that oracles were often an important guide along one's journey, I was pleased that she wanted to do this. We spoke at some length and I was very touched by her approach to oracles.

First, like many of us who work with oracles, she sees all the cards as a community of friends who are glad to help her. She takes it further, however, when she does a reading for another person. She begins by shuffling the deck until she gets a sense that it is time to stop. Then she places the deck facedown and draws the top card, which will represent the person for whom she is doing the reading. She explains the meanings in the card and the two take time to dialogue about the implications.

Once both are clear on how the card represents the other, Andrjka returns the card to the middle of the deck and begins shuffling again. While doing this, she senses that the "surrogate" card is introducing the new person to the other cards so that the entire community has a sense of that person. That immediately caught my attention—what a wonderful insight! Only then does Andrjka ask the person for his/her question. After more shuffling, she then does a layout and begins the reading.

It had never occurred to me to physically introduce someone to the cards themselves. I just assumed the cards would pick up on my own connection with that person. What Andrjka brings to the process, however, is a new sensitivity, a new awareness of the inter-relational aspects of cards in their "field" of unexpectedly dynamic energies. I love this approach and, with Andrjka's permission, am now sharing it with those using the *Green World Oracle* in doing readings for others.

Warm wishes on all your Green World journeys,
Kathleen

BIBLIOGRAPHY

ABBREVIATIONS

APS: American Peony Society
DEC: Dictionary of Egyptian Civilization
EEC: [See DEC]
F&TB: Forestry and Timber Bureau, *Forest Trees of Australia*
Gimbutas, G&G: *The Goddesses and Gods of Old Europe*
F&W: Funk & Wagnalls' *Standard Dictionary of Folklore, Mythology, and Legend*
Graves:WG: *The White Goddess*
Graves:GM: *The Greek Myths*
Hooker, BF: *The British Flora*
Hooker, SF: *The Student's Flora of the British Islands*
Kinsley, GM: *The Goddesses' Mirror*
Kinsley, HG: *Hindu Goddesses*
Jung, A&CU: *Archetypes and the Collective Unconscious*
Jung, P&A: *Psychology and Alchemy*
Jung, S of T: *Symbols of Transformation*
Luckert, NRCSV: See Luckert, Karl W.
NG: National Geographic
OED: Oxford English Dictionary
PP: *Psychological Perspective Jungian Journal*
RV: *Rig Veda*
TBO: *The British Oak*
T/L: LBM: TIME-LIFE, The Emergence of Man Series: "Life Before Man"
T/L:TF3000: TIME-LIFE, TimeFrame: " 3000-1500 BC: The Age of God-Kings"
T/L:TFC: TIME-LIFE, The Emergence of Man Series: "The First Cities"
Walker:D: *The Woman's Dictionary of Symbols & Sacred Objects*.
Walker:WEMS: *The Woman's Encyclopedia of Myths and Secrets*.
YIF: Eliade, *Yoga: Immortality and Freedom*

REFERENCES

Adrian, Ann and Judith Dennis. *Herbal Tea Book*. San Francisco: Health Publishing Co., 1959.
Allen, Richard Hinckley. *Star Names: Their Lore and Meaning*. New York: Dover Publications, Inc., 1899/1963.
Altman, Nathaniel. *Sacred Trees*. San Francisco: Sierra Club Books, 1994.
American Peony Society. *Handbook of the Peony*. Hopkins, MN: American Peony Society, 1983, 4th edition.
Ames, Delano, tr. *Egyptian Mythology*. London: Paul Hamlyn Limited, 1965; based on *Mythologie Generale Larousse*; original author unnamed.
Anderson, William. *Green Man*. London & San Francisco: Harper Collins, 1990.
Apuleius. *Metamorphoses*, XI, 23; Robert Graves, tr.; cited in Hans Leisegang, "The Mystery of the Serpent," in *The Mysteries: Papers from the Eranos Yearbooks*, ed. Joseph Campbell. Princeton UP, Bollingen Series XXX.2, 1978.
Armstrong, Edward A. *The Folklore of Birds*. New York: Dover Publications, 1958/1970.
Attenborough, David. *The Living Planet*. Boston, Toronto: Little, Brown and Company, 1984.
Audas, James Wales. *Native Trees of Australia*. Melbourne: Whitcombe and Tombs Ltd., 1936.
Bailey, Henry Turner. *The Tree Folk*. Cambridge: Washburn & Thomas, 1929.
Baker, Margaret. *Gardener's Magic and Folklore*. New York: Universe Books, 1978.
Baring, Anne and Jules Cashford. *The Myth of the Goddess: Evolution of an Image*. New York, London, Toronto, et al.: Arkana/Penguin Books, 1993.
Batchelor, Martine. "Even the Stones Smile," in *Buddhism and Ecology*. London & New York: Cassell Publishers Ltd, 1992.
Beau, Georges. *Chinese Medicine*, tr., Lowell Bair. New York: Avon, 1972.
Berndt, Ronald M. *Australian Aboriginal Religion*, in 4 Fascicles. Leiden: E. J. Brill, 1974.
Bibby, Geoffrey. "Looking for Dilmun," pp.54-59 in *Horizon*. New York: American Heritage Publishing Co., Inc., Autumn, 1969, volume XI, number 4.
Bishop, Peter. *The Greening of Psychology*. Dallas: Spring Publications, 1990.
Blofeld, John. *Bodhisattva of Compassion: The Mystical Tradition of Kuan Yin*. Boston: Shambhala, 1978.
Blyth, R. H. *Haiku*, Vol. 3, "Summer-Autumn." Tokyo: Hokuseido Press, 1952/1968.
Bonnefoy, Yves, compiler (tr., under direction of Wendy Doniger). *Greek and Egyptian Mythologies*. Chicago and London: The University of Chicago Press, 1992.
Bor, N. L. *Manual of Indian Forest Botany*. London: Oxford UP, 1953.
Borgeaud, Philippe. *The Cult of Pan in Ancient Greece*. Chicago and London: The University of Chicago Press, 1988.
Boyer, Regis. "Elements of the Sacred among the Germanic and Norse Peoples," in *American, African, and Old European Mythologies*, compiled by Yves Bonnefoy; tr. John Leavitt. Chicago and London: University of Chicago Press, 1993.
Brockman, C. Frank. *Trees of North America*. New York: Golden Press, 1968.
Burghardt, Gordon M. "On the origins of play," pp.5-41, in *Play in Animals and Humans*, Peter K. Smith, ed. Oxford, England: Basil Blackwell Publisher Limited, 1984.
Butcher, Roger W. *A New Illustrated British Flora*. London: Leonard Hill Ltd., 1961.
Butler, W. E. *How to Read the Aura*. New York: Samuel Weiser Inc., 1971.
Caldwell, Richard S. *Hesiod's Theogony: Translated, with Introduction, Commentary, and Interpretive Essay*, tr. Richard S. Caldwell. Cambridge, MA: Focus Information Group, Inc., 1987.

Campbell, Joseph. *The Masks of God: Occidental Mythology.* New York: Viking Penguin Inc., 1964.

Campbell, Joseph. *The Way of Animal Powers.* San Francisco: Harper & Row, Alfred Van Der Marck Editions, 1983.

Carper, Jean. *The Food Pharmacy.* New York: Bantam Books, 1988.

Cook, Roger. *The Tree of Life.* London: Thames and Hudson, 1974/1992.

Coomaraswamy, Ananda K. *Elements of Buddhist Iconography.* Cambridge: Harvard UP, 1935.

Cowles Encyclopedia of Animals and Plants, from Cowles Volume Library. New York: Cowles Education Corporation, 1968.

Darrah, John. *The Real Camelot: Paganism and the Arthurian Romances.* London: Dorset Press, 1981.

Davidson, H. R. Ellis. *Gods and Myths of Northern Europe.* New York: Penguin Books, 1964.

Davis, Wade. *Shadows in the Sun: Travels to Landscapes of Spirit and Desire.* Published in the U.S. by Island Press and in Canada as *The Clouded Leopard* by Douglas & McIntyre; no date or page provided. *Shadows in the Sun* edition also published by Broadway Books, NY, 1998; passages cited: 55-57.

de Bary, William Theodore, ed. *The Buddhist Tradition.* New York: Vintage Books, 1969/1972.

de Castillejo, Irene Claremont. *Knowing Woman: A Feminine Psychology.* New York: Harper & Row, Publishers, Perennial Library edition, 1974; reprint of 1973 G.P. Putnam's Sons edition.

de Silva, Lily. "The Hills Wherein My Soul Delights," pp.18-30, in *Buddhism and Ecology,* eds., Martine Batchelor and Kerry Brown. London and New York: Cassell Publishers Ltd., 1992.

de Witt, H. C. D. *Plants of the World, The Higher Plants,* vol. 2. New York: E. P. Dutton & Co., 1967.

Dictionary of Egyptian Civilization. Georges Posener, Serge Sauneron, and Jean Yoyotte, contributors. New York: Tudor Publishing Company, undated; translated from the French, copyright 1959.

Downing, Christine. *The Goddess: Mythological Images of the Feminine.* New York: Crossroad, 1984.

Dragomanov, M. P. *Notes on the Slavic Religio-Ethical Legends: The Dualistic Creation of the World.* Bloomington: Indiana University, 1961.

Drury, Susan M. "The Use of Wild Plants as Famine Foods in Eighteenth Century Scotland & Ireland," pp.43-60, in *Plant-Lore Studies,* ed., Roy Vickery. London: The Folklore Society, Mistletoe Series, vol. 18, 1984.

Durdin-Robertson, Lawrence. *The Goddesses of Chaldaea, Syria and Egypt.* Enniscorthy, Eire: Cesara Publications, 1976.

Eliade, Mircea. *Shamanism: Archaic Techniques of Ecstasy,* tr., Willard R. Trask. Princeton: Princeton UP, Bollingen Series LXXVI, Second Princeton/Bollingen Paperback Printing, 1974; originally published in French, 1951.

Eliade, Mircea. *Yoga: Immortality and Freedom,* tr., Willard R. Trask. Princeton: Princeton UP, Bollingen Series LVI, Third Princeton/Bollingen Paperback Printing, 1973; originally published in French, 1954.

Ethnologic Dictionary of the Navaho Language. The Franciscan Fathers. Saint Michaels, Arizona, 1910; reprinted in Germany, 1929.

Euripides. "The Bacchae" in Vol. 2 of *The Complete Greek Drama,* eds., Whitney J. Oates and Eugene O'Neill, Jr.; tr., Gilbert Murray. New York: Random House, 1938.

Fellman, Bruce. "An engineer's eye helps biologists understand nature." *Smithsonian,* July 1989.

Fontenrose, Joseph. *Python: A Study of Delphic Myth and Its Origins.* Berkeley, Los Angeles, London: University of California Press, 1959/1980.

Forestry and Timber Bureau. *Forest Trees of Australia* (no further data listed).

Foster, Steven. "Ginkgo Leaves of Life," in *Better Nutrition,* August 1995.

Frazer, Sir James George. *The Golden Bough* in 12 volumes. New York: The Macmillan Company, 1935.

Frazer, Sir James George. Dr. Theodor H. Gaster, ed. *The New Golden Bough* in a one volume abridgment. New York: Mentor, 1959/1964.

Friar, Kimon. "The Stone Eyes of Medusa" in *Greek Heritage: The American Quarterly of Greek Culture,* Volume Two, Number Six, 1965; pp.27-39. Chicago: The Athenian Corporation.

Friedrich, Paul. *Proto-Indo-European Trees: The Arboreal System of a Prehistoric People.* Chicago and London: University of Chicago Press, 1970.

Fry, Christopher. *The Lady's Not for Burning.* New York: Dramatists Play Service, Inc., 1953 Revised Acting Edition.

Funk & Wagnalls' Standard Dictionary of Folklore, Mythology, and Legend. HarperSanFrancisco:1949/1984.

Gadon, Elinor W. *The Once & Future Goddess: A Symbol for Our Time.* San Francisco, et al.: Harper & Row, 1989.

Gardiner, Sir Alan. *Egypt of the Pharaohs.* London, Oxford, New York: Oxford UP, 1961/1969).

Gavin, F. *The Jewish Antecedents of the Christian Sacraments.* New York: KTAV Publishing House, Inc., 1928/1969.

Gimbutas, Marija. *The Goddesses and Gods of Old Europe: Myths and Cult Images.* Berkeley and Los Angeles: University of California Press, 1982: new and updated edition based on 1974 edition.

Ginzberg, Louis. *The Legends of the Jews* in 7 volumes. Philadelphia: Jewish Publication Society of America, 1909/1968.

Goelitz, Jeffrey. *Secrets from the Lives of Trees.* Boulder Creek, CA: Planetary Publications, 1991.

Goff, Beatrice Laura. *Symbols of Prehistoric Mesopotamia.* New Haven and London: Yale UP, 1963.

Graves, Robert. *The Greek Myths* in 2 volumes. Baltimore: Penguin Books, 1955/1964.

Graves, Robert. *The White Goddess.* New York: Vintage Books, 1948/1960.

Grigson, Geoffrey. *The Englishman's Flora.* London: Hart-Davis, MacGibbon, 1958.

Haddon, Genia Pauli. *Body Metaphors.* NY: Crossroad, 1988.

Hadfield, Miles. "The Oak and Its Legends," pp.123-129, in *The British Oak.* The Botanical Society of the British Isles, 1974.

Haile, Fr. Berard, O.F.M. *Waterway.* Flagstaff: Museum of Northern Arizona Press, 1979.

Hausman, Patricia & Judith Benn Hurley. *The Healing Foods.* Emmaus, Pennsylvania: Rodale Press, 1989.

Helfman, Elizabeth S. *Maypoles and Wood Demons.* New York: Seabury Press, 1972.

Henderson, Gregory and Leon Hurvitz. "The Buddha of Seiryoji," pp. 5-55, in Vol. XIX of *Artibus Asiae.* New York University, Institute of Fine Arts, 1956.

Höeg, Ove Arbo. "Country People in Norway and Their Knowledge of Plants," pp. 111-119, in *Plant-Lore Studies,* ed., Roy Vickery. London: The Folklore Society, Mistletoe Series, vol. 18, 1984.

Homer. *The Iliad,* tr., Richmond Lattimore. Chicago, London: University of Chicago Press, 1951/1965.

Homer. *The Odyssey,* tr. Robert Fitzgerald. Garden City: Doubleday and Co., Anchor Books, 1963.

Hooker, Sir J. D. *The Student's Flora of the British Islands.* London: Macmillan & Co., 1994.